D0966649

REVISED EDITION

The *New* Options Advantage

Gaining a Trading Edge Over the Markets

David L. Caplan

McGraw-Hill
New York San Francisco Washington, D.C. Auckland Bogotá
Caracas Lisbon London Madrid Mexico City Milan
Montreal New Delhi San Juan Singapore
Sydney Tokyo Toronto

Library of Congress Cataloging in Publication Data Available.

ISBN 1-55738-863-6

Printed in the United States of America

7 8 9 0 BRB/BRB 9 0 2 1 0 9 8

Credits
The author wishes to acknowledge the following corporations for granting permission to use the materials listed on the following pages.

FutureSource 955 Parkview Blvd., Lombard, IL 60148 (800-621-2628):
pages 4, 5, 22, 45, 46, 47, 54, 64, 65, 76, 77, 96, 97, 100, 103, 107, 111, 112, 113, 117, 124, 126, 127, 132, 135, 137, 138, 158, 159, 173, 174, 191, 192, 194, 195, 223, 224.
CQG P.O. Box 758, Glenwood Springs, CO 81602 (800-525-7082):
pages 16, 36, 37, 42, 95, 123, 124.
Com-Tech Software: 141 W. Jackson, Suite 1531-A, Chicago, IL: pages 105, 106, 186.
Chronometrics: page 56.
Los Angeles Times: page 6.
Dow Jones and Company: pages 19, 57, 197.
Optionomics: pages 222, 223.
OptionVue 175 East Hawthorne Parkway, Vernon Hills, IL 60061 (708-816-6610): 45, 46, 47, 48, 49, 50, 51, 61, 62, 63, 90, 91, 92, 93, 214–221, 226–233.

Table of Contents

Preface

Since finishing my first option trading book, *The Professional Options Trader's Manual* in 1987, I have been continually asked when a new and "updated" version would be available. As I explain in the Introduction, even though the original *Manual is* only eight years old, and all of the concepts and theories are current and accurate, the changes in the options market and results of continuous research and trading require important additions.

This book presents the most up-to-date information that can be used as a "fine tuning" mechanism to my original work to improve our chances for success. It is a culmination of the last eight years' research and actual "hands-on" trading.

If I had to summarize the two most important things that I have learned these past several years, they would be flexibility and patience. I use flexibility in two ways: (1) Flexibility in not being married to a particular view of the market, but being able to flow with the trend of the market. Listen to what the market is telling you by its actual price action. (Others' interpretations may be right or wrong, and your own views of last month may now be incorrect.) and (2) Flexibility in your choice of options strategies by not just using one or two strategies that you like just because they were successful in the past. These strategies may be inappropriate for today's market.

For example, in 1984 and 1985, ratio option spreads were my favorite. Options were just being introduced, and quite often there were pricing inefficiencies in out-of-the-money options. This, coupled with a previous bull market in gold, silver, and sugar, provided for very high option premiums in out-of-the-money calls, perfect for ratio spreads. At that time, I wanted to do nothing else but these positions. However, in 1986 they began to disappear as the bull markets subsided and more traders began recognizing the inefficiencies.

In the quieter, trading range markets of 1986 and 1987 neutral option positions became my favorite. These ended in late 1988 when volatility continued to drop steadily. In 1989, option volatility was substantially trailing the futures market volatility, making it inappropriate to sell options. In 1994, with low option volatility and large moves in underlying markets, "free trades" were favored.

What we are doing, therefore, is using *flexibility* in working with what the markets give us, not "forcing" a trade that we may like, but does not fit the current technical pattern in the futures or option pricing levels.

Patience can be summarized by not overtrading, and waiting for the best opportunities. Overtrading tends to put too much pressure on us both emotionally and financially, forcing us into difficult situations if a market temporarily moves against us. Waiting for the best opportunities means that we will not buy a call option just because the market is moving up. As I will show, purchasing an option can lose money even if the market continues to move as expected. I require that the market not only be in a trending mode, but also that option volatility be at favorable levels. This allows us the benefits of options (limited risk, lower cash outlay, etc.,) while not being severely hampered by their negative factors (overvaluation, time decay, etc.).

Again readers will note these articles and reports continue to be the product of my actual, hands-on option trading, which has been my primary profession since futures' options were reintroduced in 1982. There is a lot of "mileage" in this book. Take advantage of it. I have experienced the victories and the defeats, and hopefully will save you the dollars that I had to spend in learning what "not to do."

(If you would like a current copy of the *Opportunities In Options* newsletter containing our most up-to-date research, contact our office C/O O.I.O., P.O. Box 2126, Malibu, CA 90265 or call (800) or (310) 456-9699.)

David L. Caplan
Malibu, California

Introduction

This is not just another options book! Since I immersed myself in options thirteen years ago, I have purchased and read every book on the subject I could find. In the beginning, there were few others available than the free booklets provided by the various futures exchanges. These books uniformly provided a definition of what an option was, a glossary of option terminology, and a description of basic option strategies. In fact, my "Bible" at the time was *Options As a Strategic Investment* by McMillan, a book that was about ten years old. When I wrote my first book on options several years later, *The Professional Option Trader's Manual*, I could still count the number of books on options on both hands. Even more distressing, these books were still very similar to each other. They were technically correct, clinical discussions of options, providing the necessary definitions, Greek letters, mathematics, and probability distribution graphs. The problem was that after reading and studying these books, and feeling I understood them, I still had no idea how options would help me in my trading. Being no different from most other traders, I was searching for the system, method, or black box that would provide me with some type of lead over others, and the markets. Knowing that most traders lost, made me determined to work harder to succeed. Options appealed to me because there seemed to be very few people that understood them. The typical comment from traders was: "Sure I know options. You buy a call if you want the market to go up, and you buy a put if it's going to go down." However, my investigation of options showed that by combining options of different expiration periods or strike prices, and having the ability to buy or sell options, that there were literally billions of combinations of potential strategies. Because of the few individuals or books that had any information on options, I felt that this was an overlooked and underutilized trading strategy and, more importantly I felt that with hard work and research I could find the "trading edge" I was searching for. Also, having an aptitude in mathematics and probability, I decided that this was the best way to put my talents to use. After all of my work, study, and research into options, simply buying calls or puts did not appeal to me as having a trading edge. (In fact, as I will discuss in detail, I have found that the odds of buying options are heavily against you, except in three specific instances.) Discussions with other traders still provided me with no hint of how to use options. In fact, it was not until a discussion I had with my former broker, who I had chosen because he was more knowledgeable than any other on option trading, that I began to formulate my strategies. He recommended a ratio spread involving gold options. At first, this trade seemed unappealing, since it involved several positions which would cost me three times as much commission, slippage, etc. Further, it seemed that the main benefit of the trade was that there would be little loss if gold went lower. There was something about the strategy that interested me though. Fortunately, this position was recommended to me on a Friday, and I was able to spend the weekend studying this trade and the gold market in detail. I found that by using the ratio spread that he suggested, but changing the parameters (strike prices and expiration periods) I could formulate a position that would be profitable if gold dropped over $400, if it didn't move at all, or even if it rose over $100 per ounce! Gold was trading at about $425 an ounce at that time, and I determined that my range of profitability was from zero to $530. However, even more importantly, if gold did not rise over $75 in the next month (which it had only done once in history), I would not lose, if I took the precaution of closing out the spread if gold rose above $500 after that first month.

Although quite concerned that I had made a mistake in my calculations, I decided to jump in the water and initiated the position. After all, I was bullish on the gold market and these positions had profit potential of up to $10,000 per position with margins of about 10% of that figure, and best of all, a large range of profitability. Well, there was good news and bad news. First, the bad news, the gold market collapsed. I was wrong on the market's direction. But, the good news was even better. The option strategy had totally protected me from loss. In fact, as I expected from my calculations, I was profiting from these positions even though my prediction of market direction was wrong! I then knew that options was what I was looking for. Although they cannot help you to predict market direction, I found that options still could provide an unbelievable advantage of:

1. Magnifying your gains when you are correct on the market;
2. Providing strategies that can be profitable over a wide range of prices; and
3. Strategies that can sometimes make money when your prediction of market direction is wrong.

In 1987 I presented my findings in *The Professional Option Traders Manual.* On the cover it was described as "The first hands-on trading manual detailing the most effective option strategies that can be used to any trader's advantage." I also avoided mathematics, Greek letters, and theoretical discussions of probability, and instead discussed how to use options in trading to get a "trading edge," what type of markets to look for, my favorite strategies, etc.

Although the manual was well received by both the public and the industry, there were two factors that I had failed to consider in my original work. The first was the changing nature of the options markets. As option volatility ranged from extremely low levels to extremely high (sometimes without regard to the volatility in the underlying markets), the use of different strategies was required.

The second factor I failed to take into consideration was insights from the daily use of options over the years—that can only be gained by savoring the victories and stomaching the defeats. Although I was able to relate many of these in my *Opportunities in Options* newsletter, I felt frustrated because I knew that no one read everything, and many times because of lack of time or space limitations, I was not able to relate some important new concepts or ideas. This is the reason for the revised *Options Advantage* book.

There are two final notes I would like to mention to my readers. First, even though my book uses mostly examples from options on futures, these strategies can also be applied to equity options. The main differences between future options and equity or stock options is use of margin and exercise as discussed at the end of Chapter 1.

Second, I am including a chapter on basic option trading, because my publisher thought that it could benefit new traders that happen to pick up the book as one of their first. If you're an experienced option trader, skim it quickly as a refresher, or skip it entirely. However, I did not include mathematical formulas, or complicated hypothetical discussions. Computers can do all the math you'll ever need, and there are many good texts that cover these subjects already. However, there are few, if any, books that show how to use all this great theory. Just understanding the mathematics of options without knowing how to use them is like knowing how to build a car, but not being able to drive—you just can't get anywhere!

My past subscribers and readers will recognize some of the material in this book from my previous manual, newsletters, and articles. This is necessary both for maintaining continuity, and due to the fact that there is just so much that is worthwhile that can be said about options. Use this material as a refresher to review these important principles, which are the cornerstones of our option trading techniques.

CHAPTER 1

The "Trading Edge" Philosophy

BEYOND "LIMITED RISK," "CHEAP," AND "LEVERAGE"

In numerous seminars I've given on options trading, I have often asked participants the main reason that they have used options in the past. Invariably, more than 90% cite limited risk, cheap, and/or leverage as their primary reasons. While options provide these advantages, the use of options for only these reasons can almost guarantee that you will eventually lose your money.

Limited Risk

There is no question that when purchasing options your risk is absolutely limited to the amount of premium that you paid for the option. You know in advance how much you can lose. However, just knowing how much money you're probably going to lose is not very comforting when your chances of making money are very slim. Buying far out-of-the-money options, purchasing overvalued options, and purchasing options in trading range markets are usually "dead ducks." You have almost no chance of making money.

Cheap

Cheap options are always available. For example, you can purchase an option for $25 on an S&P contract that has a value of close to $200,000. However, when was the last time you bought something just because it was cheap? How many of us have bought a "cheap" old car, piece of equipment, clothes, etc., only to find it costing a lot more money later on when it needed repair. This is exactly the same with options. Buying an option just because it is "cheap" is never a good reason.

Leverage

In the example of the S&P option above, you are obtaining leverage of over 99%. However, if leverage is the only factor that impresses you, lotteries provide an abundance of this. For a $l investment in a lottery you can win tens of millions of dollars, and your chances are probably just as good at making money as with that $25 option in the S&P contract.

Yes, options are cheap and do provide limited risk, and leverage. However, you should not consider only these reasons for buying them: options should only be bought when premiums are reasonable, and your trading plan indicates the market is likely to make a large move with the potential for big profits.

POPULAR MISCONCEPTIONS ABOUT OPTIONS

Learning how to obtain a "trading edge" over the market with options is similar to improving your golf game. You can't go very far unless you unlearn your old bad habits. With options, popular misconceptions that have been advanced by many books and brokers are responsible for significant losses by many traders. Let's examine five of these misunderstood ideas.

1. *"If you buy an option and the market goes in your favor you will always profit."*

Wrong. When you purchase an option you pay not only for its intrinsic (actual) value, but for its time value. Each day you hold an option, the time value must drop somewhat. The market must move in your favor enough to offset this decay of time value premium. Even if the market has made a large enough move to make your option profitable, unless you cash the option out at an opportune time it must continue to a move in your favor. Buying options is like swimming upstream against a heavy current; unless you move very fast you'll be swept away.

As shown in Exhibit 1.1, the S&P 500 had moved over 3,000 points higher in four months (a gain of $15,000 per futures contract). However, some call options would have provided no profit to the trader during this period. Even more distressing, a not so well-priced call option, that could have been purchased by many investors because of its reasonable price, actually lost value, even while the market made new all-time highs. There are many examples of this in recent trading as shown in Exhibits 1.2, 1.3, and 1.4.

2. *"There is big money to be made in selling overvalued options."*

This is another good news-bad news situation. The good news is that over 80% of the time this statement is correct. You will make money selling overvalued options. The bad news is that the other 20% of the time can cost you far in excess of all the profits you've made. This is because when selling options your profits are strictly limited to the premium you receive. However, your risk is not. And over time, all markets make giant, unexpected moves. Over the last several years I've seen moves in silver equal to $20,000 in a futures contract in one hour; 5,000 ($25,000) point moves in the S&P in one day; moves in bonds of 10 ($10,000) points overnight, etc. Getting caught in one of these moves without a trading plan can wipe out years of profits.

3. *"It is easy to find arbitrage spreads to guarantee profits."*

The truism here is that discrepancy in prices sometimes allows trades to be done with little or no risk, and when done in large quantities, substantial profits can be locked in by these traders. However, for those interested in arbitrage, you will be competing with firms with capital bases of $100,000,000 or more, employing many full-time analysts, computer technicians, mathematicians, etc., who use both round-the-clock and full-time computer analysis of markets in the United States and around the world at costs of tens to hundreds of thousands of dollars per month. Additionally, because of the volumes in which they deal, their trading costs are much lower than the average traders. They are able to obtain the fills without the slippage (loss occurring in executing an order) that others would experience. You have the same chance of competing against these firms and profiting at arbitrage as you would in beating Jack Nicklaus in golf or John McEnroe in tennis.

Finally, if you're still not convinced, ask the "derivative" trader of 1994, if arbitrage spreads are an easy way to profits!

4. *"Computer programs can tell you how to trade options, which ones to buy and sell, and which strategy to use."*

Exhibit 1.1

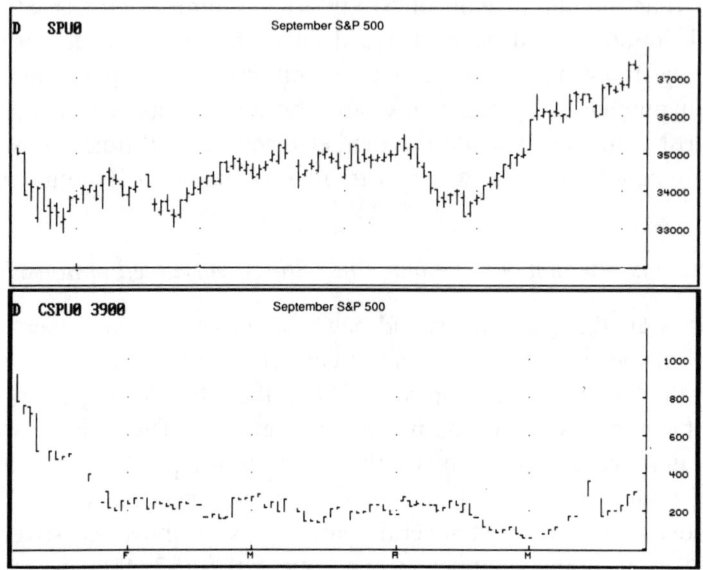

Note: Although the S&P 500 moved to new highs, many calls lost value.

Exhibit 1.2
August Gold 360 Put

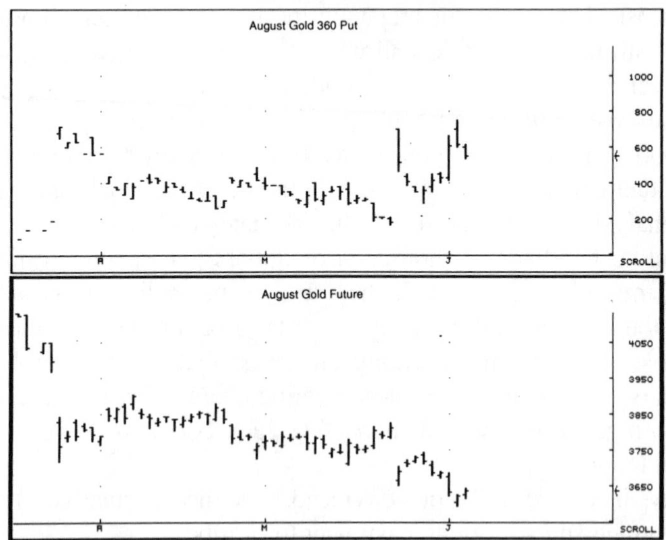

Note: The August gold 360 put lost premium value, even though gold dropped almost $50 ($5,000) per contract.

Exhibit 1.3
September Bond 90 Put

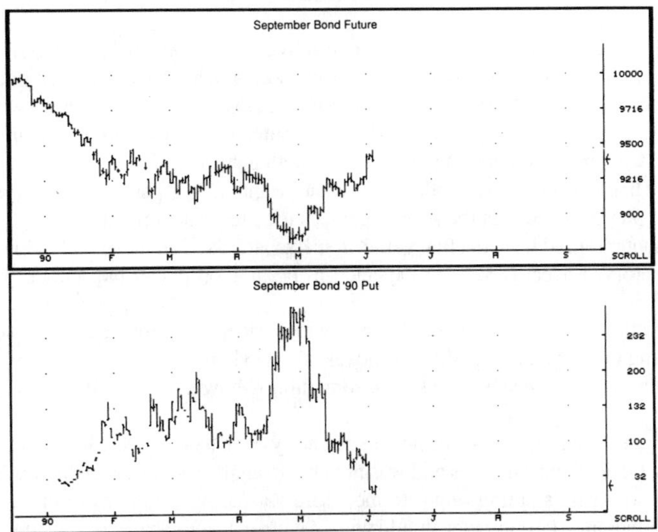

Note: Although bonds were 5 points ($5,000 per contract) lower in June than at the beginning of the year, the September 1990 put lost value.

Exhibit 1.4
June Live Cattle 76 Call

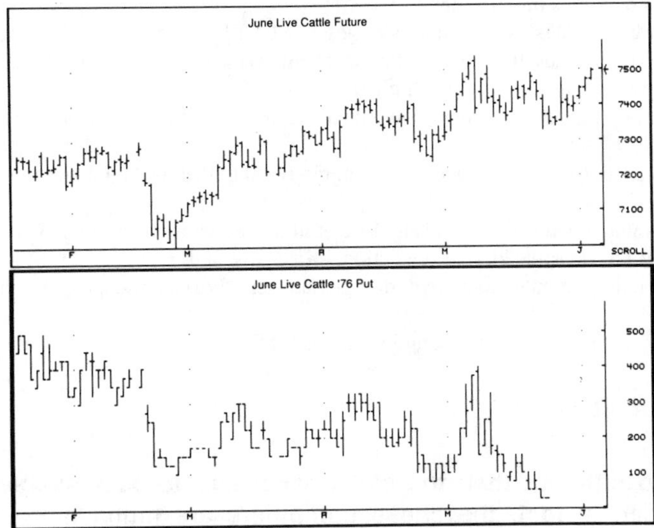

Note: In a rising cattle market, the June 76 call still lost value.

Exhibit 1.5

Chess King Kasparov Beats Computer—Twice

It was a battle of two chess champions—one active and outspoken, known to sip tonic water during matches, the other sitting quietly on a desk, taking in a different kind of juice.

World chess champion Gary Kasparov, who has not lost a tournament since 1981, met Deep Thought, the winner of this year's World Computer Chess Championship in Edmonton, Canada, for two games Sunday. The human won both games.

"I'm very happy I could do in both games what I wanted," Kasparov said. "In the first game, with black, I played quietly. In the second game, I tried to crush it in the opening."

The computer retired from the first game after Kasparov's 52nd move and 2½ hours of play. After that victory, Kasparov said: "I expected it. It's a good player but without position and experience."

Playing white in the second game, Kasparov took Deep Thought's queen in move 18. The computer hung on, surrendering after 37 moves and two hours.

"I think the computer needs to be taught something—how to resign," the 26-year old Soviet said.

Kasparov said after the first game he realized early on that he would win when the computer missed some tactical opportunities and was not able to analyze all of the champion's decisions.

"I don't mind who's sitting opposite me," said Kasparov, who lives in the Soviet city of Baku, in Azerbaijan. "If a computer should win, of course, I would have to challenge it to protect the human race."

Murray Campbell, who helped create the computer program at Carnegie Mellon University in Pittsburgh, Pa., said it appeared there was a bug in the computer.

"It wasn't looking at the right moves," he said. "It wasn't given a chance to show its best style of play."

Deep Thought, created by five graduate students at Carnegie Mellon, can analyze 700,000 possible positions on the chessboard per second and 5 to 20 moves ahead by each side, as well as discern each move's implications.

Deep Thought evaluates the millions of possible board positions created by each sequence of five moves it imagines. It assigns a numerical value to the positions created by each sequence and moves toward positions with the highest values.

The computer remained in Pittsburgh with a telephone line to relay its moves to a computer terminal in New York.

Kasparov said the computer was "fully aggressive" but that its "mind was too straight and too primitive."

"Chess is much wider than just calculations. It's even wider than logic. You have to use fantasy, intuition and some kind of prediction," Kasparov said.

But he said the computer does have some advantages: "We can lose hope. A computer can't lose hope."

Kasparov captured the world championship in 1985.

Source: *Los Angeles Times*

This is no different than the skills necessary to be a successful options trader. In fact, the chess computers are much more sophisticated than option computer programs.

There are uses for computers in trading options (See Chapter 7); however, the state of the art in computers is not developed well enough to analyze all of the various factors that go into option trading. The computer should be used as a helpful assistant to the trader by evaluating different types of strategies, crunching numbers, producing what-if scenarios, etc., not as the trader.

5. *"Trading is a zero sum game."*

This often maligned statement is quoted over and over again telling you for every loser there is a winner. The truth of the matter is that there are many more losers than winners. This is because all of the costs for trading must be borne by the trader. The brokers, exchanges, all of their employees, regulatory agencies, and are all paid for by you. Add to this the cost of a computer, publications, and software, and what finally happens is that for each trading dollar available at the end of the year an average of 15 to 20 cents is gone for expenses. This means that every year you must profit by this amount before you break even. This is not an easy task, and is another reason you should look for only the best positions that can give you a "trading edge" over the markets.

MY PHILOSOPHY OF TRADING OPTIONS

My objective is to initiate trades that have either favorable risk/reward ratios or high probabilities of profit. I avoid initiating trades just because it is my opinion that the market is going up or down; I try to initiate positions that give some kind of "edge over" the markets through the characteristics available in options. This means that in buying options I prefer positions that have the potential for large rewards, while still keeping risk at manageable levels. When selling options, I seek options that have high volatility ("overvalued" premium).

I will discuss the methods I use for seeking out the markets with the best opportunities, how to buy the most favorably priced option that has the greatest potential of profit, and how to use to protect profits, while still being able to build a large position that has a potential for big rewards by using principles of money management.

In using these techniques, the alert, knowledgeable option trader should be able to find many opportunities throughout the year that allow him to obtain a "trading edge" over the markets. It may require a little additional work and research; however, this time is very well spent in improving your trading skills.

WHAT IS A "TRADING EDGE"?

A "trading edge" is using options only when you can obtain some "advantage" from them. These advantages can take the form of positions that improve probability of profit, risk/reward, or loss control. This also includes strategies that allow for better money management, lessen the need to constantly predict the market or have precise market timing, and allow you to be wrong in your predictions of market direction and sometimes still profit.

This "trading edge" through the use of options has the same objective as other systems or methods that have been designed to give a trader an advantage such as trendline, stochastic, %R, Gann, etc. All are designed to improve your trading and give you a "lead" over others. This is the same way I recommend using options only when they can provide us with a "trading edge" over the markets.

THE ART AND SCIENCE OF TRADING OPTIONS

Trading options is both an art and a science. The "science" is becoming familiar with how an option works, time decay, expiration period, and volatility. The "art" is having an insight on trading options that can only be gained by experience. This includes how to get the best prices for options orders in the different markets, how to best use disparity in option pricing, and which option strategies work the best under various market conditions.

It is my goal to give you as many rules and concepts as possible to improve your knowledge in the area of "science." Unfortunately you must gain your "art" experience on your own in your actual trading. For this reason, it will always be best to trade as small as possible, for as long as possible. There will always be new opportunities in the market to take advantage of . . . unless you've lost your trading capital.

"TRADING EDGE" STRATEGIES CAN BE USED WITH FUTURES, OEX, AND STOCK OPTIONS

Although the examples of options strategies in this book are of futures options, the same concepts apply for using these strategies with OEX or stock options. The major differences are in the areas of option exercise and use of margin. Before trading you should obtain a complete updated list of all of the margin and exercise requirements for the options you are considering.

There are several reasons why I prefer trading futures options. First, I like the variety of having over 30 different markets from which to choose. These markets are always in a variety of chart patterns and volatility, allowing me to scan all of the various markets for the most effective option strategies. When it comes to using price disparity between options, I have no bias, whether the market is treasury bonds or soybeans.

Another reason that I favor futures options is the more favorable margin requirements for short options and the ability to receive interest on both investment capital and premium received.

For example, suppose you set up a $10,000 account to be used to obtain premium through selling neutral option positions in the Treasury Bond contract. Let's assume that position was initiated and $5,000 in premium was collected from the sale of these options. Even though this $5,000 in premium value is not yet profits, it can be invested in Treasury Bills to obtain interest along with the initial $10,000 investment. This would allow you to obtain Treasury Bill interest on $15,000, although your original investment was only $10,000. At the end of the year, even if all of your trading broke even, you still would have received Treasury Bill interest on 150% of your initial capital, in addition to your profit opportunities in the markets.

There are also more advantageous rules, recently introduced, in the use of options on futures contracts. A new margining system, the Standard Portfolio Analysis of Risk (SPAN), commenced in 1990 and has provided for a more flexible margining system. SPAN evaluates the overall risk in an entire futures and options portfolio and matches the margin to this risk, applying principles that usually allow for lower margins than in the OEX or stocks.

The OEX options do have more liquidity than the S&P 500. This increased liquidity with Index options provides for more trading opportunities with less slippage (loss due to the difference in the bid/ask spreads). However, I find that often there is more *disparity* in out-of-the-money option premium on the S&P 500. Often, these options are trading at a much higher volatility rate, particularly in overly trendy markets. This can provide a great advantage to the options trader.

Since the objective of this book is to learn how to use the characteristics of options to get a "trading edge," knowledge of these differences is important. Traders should also become familiar with the underlying securities, index, or future before initiating positions including the potential volatility of the option or underlying market. However, other than differences inherent in the market underlying the option, and the above differences in the margin and exercise, these option strategies and trading principles can be effectively applied to any market.

CHAPTER 2

Basic Option Trading Concepts

WHAT IS AN OPTION?

Many chapters, books, volumes, seminars, and tapes have been devoted to complicated discussions of options, trading concepts, formulas, positions, and theories. Unfortunately these materials provide very little in the way of a *concrete plan* on how to use this information for profit.

Too much knowledge can be confusing. A successful real estate investor may not be able to build a house or even draw a plan. However, he may know other more important attributes of the property such as favorable location and marketing techniques. He is only required to use his own innovative talents, which may consist of less than 10% of the entire project. However, the creative aspect may be the most important part. Expensive house plans and landscaping ideas may beautify the property; however, if it is in the wrong location or an improper marketing technique is used, it may lose money.

The new investor in options has a similar problem. While there are many books providing accurate descriptions of options, their benefits, varying strategies, and mathematical formulas, none have provided a "road map" or plan on how to use this information. Limited risk, price disparity, over- and undervaluation may sound great, but without a plan on how to use it to profit, where is the opportunity? The following chapters reveal how you can recognize these opportunities and put them to use.

First you need some idea of what an option is, and how it works. Suppose that your next door neighbor has a one-acre parcel of land that he is considering selling for $10,000. You feel the property is appreciating and that if you could get the proper permits it would be a great place to build a home and make a profit. However, you want to make sure that you can get the necessary permits and appraise the market in the area before you make the purchase.

In this case you could go to your neighbor and offer him $500 for an "option" or right to buy the property. His answer would probably be: "Well, okay, but I will only let you have this right for one year, and then the property will cost you $12,000."

In this transaction you are granted a "call" (right to purchase) option to buy the property for a "premium" (or value) of $500 for a period of one year, "the expiration period," at a price of $12,000—"the strike price." You are the buyer of that option and your neighbor the seller. You can only lose $500, the price you pay for the option; however, you have a potential for unlimited gain. If the property goes up in value to $25,000 you would gain $13,000 on your $500 investment when you sold it.

Your neighbor, the option grantor or seller, only has $500 to gain, which is the premium he receives; however, if the property goes up in value, he has an unlimited loss potential (even though in this case it would be only of prospective profits).

This is similar to how options work in the futures and stock markets. For example, if silver is currently priced at $4 an ounce, you may decide silver is going up and buy a futures contract. A silver contract consists of 5,000 ounces. Although the contract value is $20,000 (5,000 ounces × $4 an ounce) you must place a deposit of margin (usually 5–10% of the contract value) with your brokerage firm which is proof that you can pay your losses if silver goes down. You then make (or lose) $50 for each one-cent movement and have unlimited losses or gains.

You can then decide, similar to the option on the land, to instead purchase a silver "call" option. There are several advantages to this. First, no margin is necessary; second, losses are strictly limited to the premium paid for the option; and third, your profit potential is still unlimited.

For example, if you purchase a $4 silver call for $500, if silver goes up during the term of the option to above $4, you can exercise or sell the option to profit. However, if silver fails to move above your option "strike price," or drops in value, similar to the land option, your risk is never more than $500 (Exhibit 2.1).

An option differs from a futures contract or stock in that when you purchase an option, it confers a *right*, but not an *obligation*, to purchase (call) or sell (put) the commodity.

There are thousands of stocks that have options; approximately 100 index options ranging from the OEX 100 to Philadelphia currency options; and over 30 options on futures. The following futures have options that can be traded:

Gold
Silver
Copper
Swiss Franc
Japanese Yen
British Pound
German Mark
Canadian Dollar
Nikkei
Platinum
Gas
Corn
Cotton
Wheat
Soybeans
Cocoa
Orange Juice
Hogs
Cattle
TOPIX
U.S. Dollar
Coffee
Treasury Bonds
Treasury Bills
Treasury Notes
Eurodollars
S&P 500
NYFE
Sugar
Crude Oil
Japanese Bonds
Heating Oil
Pork Bellies

Puts and Calls

There are two types of options: a *call* and a *put* option. The purchaser of a call option has the right to buy the underlying contract at a specified price (the strike price) within a certain time (prior to the option expiration). The seller of a call option has an obligation to sell the underlying contract at the strike price prior to the expiration. A put option gives the option buyer the right to sell the underlying contract at a certain price (the strike price) prior to the expiration time, and conversely obligates the seller to take delivery at this price on or before the expiration date, if the option is exercised.

The option buyer must pay the option seller a certain amount, which is called "option premium." The size of this premium is determined by several factors: the strike price of the option (whether it is "in" or "out" of the money); the time remaining before the option expires; the volatility of the option or the underlying contract; current interest rates and, is some cases, supply and demand. (These factors are discussed in more detail later in this chapter.)

The buyer of an option has the opportunity for unlimited profits, with his risk limited to the premium paid for the option. An option seller conversely has unlimited risk, with his profit potential limited to the premium received from the option sale.

All option transactions are opened by either the purchase or sale of a put or call. However, over 98% of option transactions are either closed out with an offsetting sale or purchase of the same option, or by letting the

Exhibit 2.1

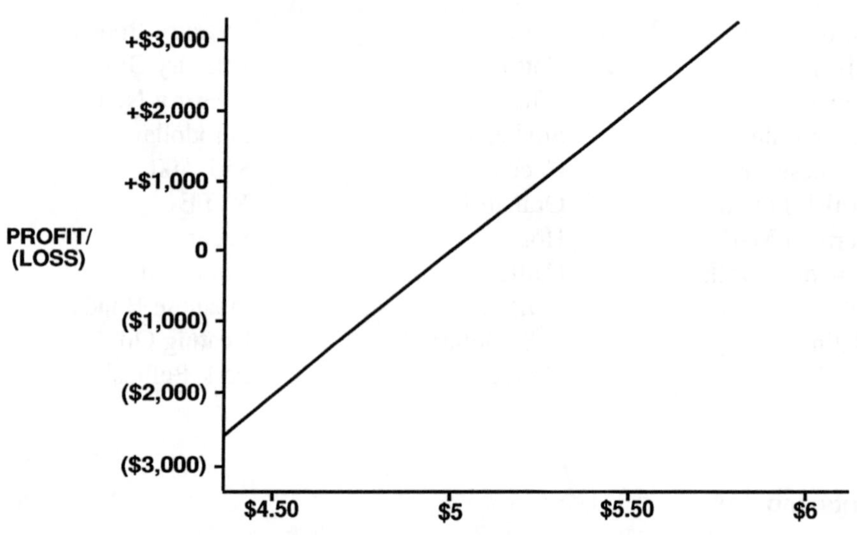

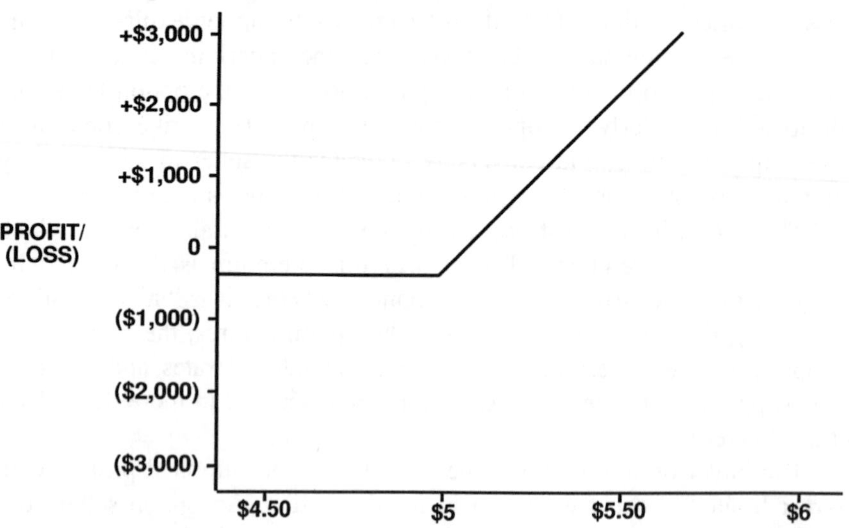

Where futures contract has potential for unlimited loss, option risk is strictly limited to $500.

option expire worthless, without exercise of the right to take or tender delivery.

For example: gold for delivery in December is priced at $400 an ounce. A gold contract consists of 100 ounces. You decide gold is going up and buy a futures contract. Although the contract value is $35,000, you must place a deposit with your brokerage firm of $1,500 margin to pay losses if gold goes down. You then make (or lose) $100 for each $1 movement and have unlimited losses or gains. Instead, you can decide to purchase a gold call option at $700. There are several advantages to this. First, no margin is necessary; and second, losses are limited to the $700 premium paid for the option (plus commission and fees). (However, your profit potential is still unlimited.)

HOW AN OPTION WORKS

As shown in Exhibit 2.2, I entered the market at point "A" with *futures contracts*, and was stopped out at "B" with loss of approximately $750 per contract (not counting potential profit loss of $10,000+). In this instance, I was right on the market, but the need for *precise timing* and *stop loss* was my undoing. Contrast this example with Exhibit 2.3, where I wrongly predicted the market direction, and still made money with a *good option spread.*

At "A," the bullish option spread of long the December 195 call short the 175 put was initiated at $300 credit. In this position, $300 would be collected on a $1,000 margin (30 percent return in 3 months—120 percent annualized) if the market stays in trading range, or moves either slightly lower or higher (below 175 = losses, above 195 = profits of $500 per 100 points). We predicted a trading range market of between 185–192.

We were completely wrong. First, the market dropped to 182, and then took off straight up. We probably would have been stopped out of a futures position (which would have been at $2,500 loss per position), but our option spread was never at more than a $150 loss. Even though our market prediction was wrong, we were profitable!

Somewhat different from the example of purchasing your next door neighbor's property where you set the strike price (the price at which you would ultimately have the right to purchase the property) and expiration period (the length of time for which you would have this right) by negotiation, the purchaser of a future, stock, or OEX option has many different choices. You can purchase options that may expire anywhere from one day to one year. The further away the expiration period (giving more time for your option to become valuable), the more expensive it will be.

Exhibit 2.2

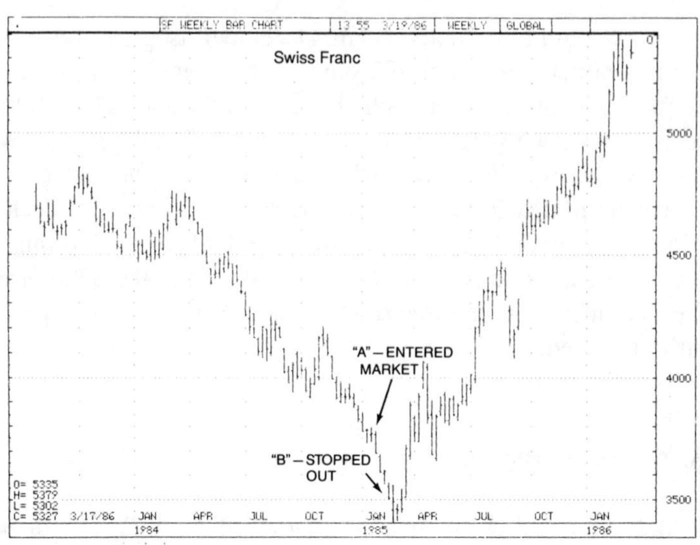

Exhibit 2.3

You must also decide on the strike price of the option being purchased. If silver is at $6 today, you can purchase silver options, which give you the right to purchase silver at different strike prices of $5, $5.50, $6 . . . all the way up to $9.00. If the market price of silver (the price at which you could sell your silver) is $6, the $5 option is very valuable (and costly) since it would allow you to purchase silver at $1 per ounce under current prices. The $7.50 option will cost much less since it has no actual value currently, but only has what is called "time value." This means that people who purchase the option today know it is currently worthless (who would want to pay $7.50 for silver, when it could be bought anywhere else for $6), but are paying the price because of the chance that silver will go up past the strike price they select sometime in the future.

For example, in May with silver at $6 an ounce, you could purchase a December (the expiration date) at $7.50 (the strike price) silver call for $100 (option premium). This would give you the right to purchase 5,000 ounces of silver (the contract size) at $7.50 any time during the next six months (before the option expires).

If silver stays under $7.50, no one would want to exercise (use) this right, because they could purchase silver elsewhere at under $7.50. However, if silver were to shoot up to say $10 per ounce, this option would become very valuable. In fact it would be worth $50 an ounce to the holder of the option ($10 current price less $7.50 strike price = $2.50 profit). Since their option was for 5,000 ounces of silver their option would be worth at least 5,000 x $2.50 = $12,500! Not bad for a $100 investment in six months.

Also important is that the $100 (premium) paid for the option was your entire risk. If someone discovered how to make silver from dirt, and the price of silver fell to $1 or less, your loss could never be more than $100.

Although it would be nice to always buy a cheap $100 option and have the opportunity to make $10,000 or more, buying the cheapest option is not always best. A slightly more expensive option that is "closer-to-the-money" (actual price) provides the best chance to profit. You may have to pay more for this option initially, but it would be more profitable if the market moves as expected. An option with a strike price closer to the actual price of the underlying market is always more expensive. This is because there is a better chance that this option will have value if the market makes a small move, and will be even more profitable in the event of a large move.

For example, with silver trading at $6 an ounce, you may consider purchasing silver call options ranging from $6 to $7.50. Let's assume that the $6.50 call is trading at $500 and the $7.50 call is trading at $100. If silver makes a large move to $10, both option purchasers will be very pleased. The purchaser of the $6.50 silver call will make $3.50 per ounce times the 5,000 ounce contract, or $17,500. The purchaser of the $7.50 call will make $2.50 per ounce times 5,000 ounces, or $12,500. Although the purchaser of the $7.50 call makes less of a dollar return, his percentage return is more than twice as great! In this case, the trader would have been better off purchasing five $7.50 calls at $100 each (the same cost as one $6.50 silver call) because his total profit would be $62,500 ($45,000 more than the purchaser of one $6.50 call).

Since this once-in-a-lifetime move is unlikely, a more common occurrence would be a move to the $7.00 level. In this case the $7.50 call will be worthless because silver remains under the strike price of the option you own. (Who would want to pay $7.00 for something that could be bought anywhere else for $6.50?) However, the more expensive option, the $6.50 call (which allows you to buy under its current price) is worth $2,500.

The expiration period, or how long you can hold the option before you lose your right to exercise it is also important. It would be great if you could get an option to purchase silver for $7.50 at any time in the future. But, who would want to sell this kind of option? For every buyer of an option, there must be a seller; therefore, all options have a definite expiration date.

Exhibit 2.4 shows the previous day closing prices for the soybean option contract. It also lists all the strike prices and trading months, along with the open interest and weekly volume, for all the individual strike prices. In the case of options on commodities, there are different contract months and expiration dates for all options. For example, in the case of silver, the most active expiration months are March, May, July, September, and December. Unfortunately, many options have different expiration months as shown in Exhibit 2.5. In addition to this confusion, most options expire the month before their stated expiration.

For example, the December 1994 silver option expires on November 14, 1994. Since it is natural to think that a December option should be valid until the end of December, these actual expiration periods can come as an unhappy surprise. For this reason, you should always refer to the chart before purchasing an option.

The more time an option has before expiration, the more costly it will be. Just as close-to-the-money (actual price) strike price's of options are more expensive, so is an option with a longer expiration period because there is a greater chance that it will eventually be valuable.

For example, in May with silver at $6, a one-month (July) option with a $7 strike price will cost about $100. A December silver option with the same $7 strike price having six months before expiration would cost

Exhibit 2.4
Barron's/Market Week—Futures Options Closing Prices Soybeans

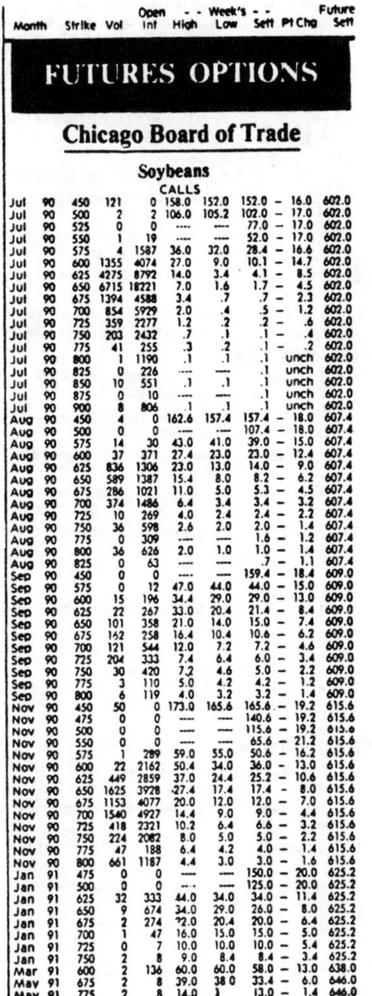

FUTURES OPTIONS

Chicago Board of Trade

Soybeans

CALLS

Month		Strike	Vol	Open Int	- - Week's High	Low	- - Sett	Pt Chg	Future Sett
Jul	90	450	121	0	158.0	152.0	152.0	- 16.0	602.0
Jul	90	500	2	2	106.0	105.2	102.0	- 17.0	602.0
Jul	90	525	0	0	----	----	77.0	- 17.0	602.0
Jul	90	550	1	19	----	----	52.0	- 17.0	602.0
Jul	90	575	4	1587	36.0	32.0	28.4	- 16.6	602.0
Jul	90	600	1355	4074	27.0	9.0	10.1	- 14.7	602.0
Jul	90	625	4275	8792	14.0	3.4	4.1	- 8.5	602.0
Jul	90	650	6715	18221	7.0	1.6	1.7	- 4.5	602.0
Jul	90	675	1394	4588	3.4	.7	.7	- 2.3	602.0
Jul	90	700	854	5929	2.0	.4	.5	- 1.2	602.0
Jul	90	725	359	2277	1.2	.2	.2	- .6	602.0
Jul	90	750	203	2432	.7	.1	.1	- .4	602.0
Jul	90	775	41	255	.3	.2	.1	- .2	602.0
Jul	90	800	1	1190	.1	.1	.1	unch	602.0
Jul	90	825	0	226	----	----	.1	unch	602.0
Jul	90	850	10	551	.1	.1	.1	unch	602.0
Jul	90	875	0	10	----	----	.1	unch	602.0
Jul	90	900	8	806	.1	.1	.1	unch	602.0
Aug	90	450	4	0	162.6	157.4	157.4	- 18.0	607.4
Aug	90	500	0	0	----	----	107.4	- 18.0	607.4
Aug	90	575	14	30	43.0	41.0	39.0	- 15.0	607.4
Aug	90	600	37	371	27.4	23.0	23.0	- 12.4	607.4
Aug	90	625	836	1306	23.0	13.0	14.0	- 9.0	607.4
Aug	90	650	589	1387	15.4	8.0	8.2	- 6.2	607.4
Aug	90	675	286	1021	11.0	5.0	5.3	- 4.5	607.4
Aug	90	700	374	1486	6.4	3.4	3.4	- 3.2	607.4
Aug	90	725	10	269	4.0	2.4	2.4	- 2.2	607.4
Aug	90	750	36	598	2.6	2.0	2.0	- 1.4	607.4
Aug	90	775	0	309	----	----	1.6	- 1.2	607.4
Aug	90	800	36	626	2.0	1.0	1.0	- 1.4	607.4
Aug	90	825	0	63	----	----	.7	- 1.1	607.4
Sep	90	450	0	0	----	----	159.4	- 18.4	609.0
Sep	90	575	0	12	47.0	44.0	44.0	- 15.0	609.0
Sep	90	600	15	196	34.4	29.0	29.0	- 13.0	609.0
Sep	90	625	22	267	33.0	20.4	21.4	- 8.4	609.0
Sep	90	650	101	358	21.0	14.0	15.0	- 7.4	609.0
Sep	90	675	162	258	16.4	10.4	10.6	- 6.2	609.0
Sep	90	700	121	544	12.0	7.2	7.2	- 4.6	609.0
Sep	90	725	204	333	7.4	6.4	6.0	- 3.4	609.0
Sep	90	750	30	420	7.2	4.6	5.0	- 2.2	609.0
Sep	90	775	3	110	5.0	4.2	4.2	- 1.2	609.0
Sep	90	800	6	119	4.0	3.2	3.2	- 1.4	609.0
Nov	90	450	50	0	173.0	165.6	165.6	- 19.2	615.6
Nov	90	475	0	0	----	----	140.6	- 19.2	615.6
Nov	90	500	0	0	----	----	115.6	- 19.2	615.6
Nov	90	550	0	0	----	----	65.6	- 21.2	615.6
Nov	90	575	1	289	59.0	55.0	50.6	- 16.2	615.6
Nov	90	600	22	2162	50.4	34.0	36.0	- 13.0	615.6
Nov	90	625	449	2859	37.0	24.4	25.2	- 10.6	615.6
Nov	90	650	1625	3928	27.4	17.4	17.4	- 8.0	615.6
Nov	90	675	1153	4077	20.0	12.0	12.0	- 7.0	615.6
Nov	90	700	1540	4927	14.4	9.0	9.0	- 4.4	615.6
Nov	90	725	418	2321	10.2	6.4	6.6	- 3.2	615.6
Nov	90	750	224	2082	8.0	5.0	5.0	- 2.2	615.6
Nov	90	775	47	188	6.4	4.2	4.0	- 1.4	615.6
Nov	90	800	661	1187	4.4	3.0	3.0	- 1.6	615.6
Jan	91	475	0	0	----	----	150.0	- 20.0	625.2
Jan	91	500	0	0	----	----	125.0	- 20.0	625.2
Jan	91	625	32	333	44.0	34.0	34.0	- 11.4	625.2
Jan	91	650	9	674	34.0	29.0	26.0	- 8.0	625.2
Jan	91	675	2	274	?2.0	20.4	20.0	- 6.4	625.2
Jan	91	700	1	47	16.0	15.0	15.0	- 5.0	625.2
Jan	91	725	0	7	10.0	10.0	10.0	- 5.4	625.2
Jan	91	750	2	8	9.0	8.4	8.4	- 3.4	625.2
Mar	91	600	2	136	60.0	60.0	58.0	- 13.0	638.0
May	91	675	2	8	39.0	38.0	33.4	- 6.0	646.0
May	91	775	2	8	14.0	[illegible]	13.0	- 1.4	646.0

PUTS

Month		Strike	Vol	Open Int	- - Week's High	Low	- - Sett	Pt Chg	Future Sett
Jul	90	500	0	126	----	----	.1	unch	602.0
Jul	90	525	0	865	----	----	.1	unch	602.0
Jul	90	550	175	3792	.3	.2	.2	- .1	602.0
Jul	90	575	857	4170	2.0	1.2	1.4	unch	602.0
Jul	90	600	2751	5940	10.0	5.0	8.2	+ 2.0	602.0
Jul	90	625	898	5051	28.0	17.0	27.0	+ 8.0	602.0
Jul	90	650	489	2245	49.4	34.0	49.4	+ 12.6	602.0
Jul	90	675	50	532	73.5	68.0	73.5	+ 14.5	602.0
Jul	90	700	0	40	----	----	98.2	+ 15.6	602.0
Jul	90	800	0	0	----	----	198.0	+ 17.0	602.0
Jul	90	825	0	0	----	----	223.0	+ 17.0	602.0
Jul	90	875	127	0	----	----	273.0	+ 17.0	602.0
Jul	90	900	231	3	298.0	282.4	298.0	- 17.0	602.0
Aug	90	500	0	10	----	----	.2	unch	607.4
Aug	90	525	0	149	----	----	.5	+ .1	607.4
Aug	90	550	1	218	2.0	1.6	1.6	- .1	607.4
Aug	90	575	95	481	5.4	3.4	5.0	+ 1.4	607.4
Aug	90	600	348	1296	16.0	9.0	14.2	+ 4.2	607.4
Aug	90	625	95	474	31.0	22.0	30.0	+ 8.4	607.4
Aug	90	650	13	76	49.0	44.2	49.0	+ 11.0	607.4
Aug	90	675	0	3	----	----	71.0	+ 13.4	607.4
Sep	90	525	0	12	----	----	2.0	+ .6	609.0
Sep	90	550	1	49	4.6	4.2	4.6	+ 1.6	609.0
Sep	90	575	5	49	10.0	9.0	10.0	+ 3.0	609.0
Sep	90	600	63	153	20.4	15.0	20.4	+ 6.0	609.0
Sep	90	625	4	147	36.0	31.4	36.0	+ 9.0	609.0
Sep	90	650	1	31	55.0	50.0	55.0	+ 11.0	609.0
Sep	90	675	0	2	----	----	74.0	+ 11.4	609.0
Sep	90	700	0	1	----	----	96.0	+ 13.0	609.0
Nov	90	500	5	128	----	----	1.0	+ .2	615.6
Nov	90	525	1	840	2.1	2.0	2.2	+ .4	615.6
Nov	90	550	382	2157	5.0	3.2	5.0	+ 1.4	615.6
Nov	90	575	528	2516	10.6	7.4	10.4	+ 2.2	615.6
Nov	90	600	406	4124	21.0	14.0	20.4	+ 5.2	615.6
Nov	90	625	520	2796	35.0	24.0	34.4	+ 8.0	615.6
Nov	90	650	107	1525	52.0	38.4	50.0	+ 9.4	615.6
Nov	90	675	515	1352	70.0	64.0	70.0	+ 11.4	615.6
Nov	90	750	0	0	----	----	134.6	+ 14.6	615.6
Jan	91	575	0	11	----	----	12.0	+ 3.2	625.2
Jan	91	600	0	19	----	----	20.0	+ 4.0	625.2
Jan	91	625	2	284	29.0	29.0	33.0	+ 7.0	625.2
Jan	91	650	552	941	48.0	35.0	48.0	+ 9.2	625.2
Jan	91	675	0	600	----	----	66.0	+ 11.0	625.2
Mar	91	650	0	2	----	----	44.0	+ 8.0	638.0

Call Volume 24,471 Open Int 86,557
Put Volume 9,722 Open Int 43,210
Volume prev Fri. thru Thu.

Exhibit 2.5
Options Trading Fact Sheet

OPTION	EX-CHANGE	TICK VALUE	TRADING MONTHS	TRADING HOURS (CST)	LAST TRADING DAY (Subject to Change)
FINANCIAL					
TREASURY BONDS	CBT	01 = $15.63	ALL	7:20–2:00 5:00–8:30	Friday (12:00 CST) which precedes contract month by at least 6 business days
TREASURY NOTES	CBT	01 = $15.63	ALL	7:20–2:00 5:00–8:30	Friday (12:00 CST) which precedes contract month by at least 6 business days
EURODOLLAR	IMM	01 = $25.00	ALL	7:20–2:00	First Monday preceding third Wednesday of contract month
S&P 500	CME	05 = $25.00	ALL	8:30–3:15	Third Thursday of contract month (Quarterly) Third Friday of contract month (Serial)
NYFE	NYFE	05 = $25.00	ALL	8:30–3:15	Third Thursday of contract month (Quarterly) Third Friday of contract month (Serial)
NIKKEI	CME	05 = $25.00	ALL	8:00–3:15	Second Friday of contract month (Quarterly) Friday preceding third Saturday of contract month (Serial)
TOPIX	CBT	1/100 = ¥2,000	H, M, U, Z	7:00–2:00 5:40–8:15	Second Thursday of month
JAPANESE GOVTBONDS	CBT	1/2pt = ¥2,500	H, M, U, Z	7:00–2:00 5:40–8:15	Friday (12:00 CST) of month preceding contract month by at least 6 business days
METALS, CURRENCIES, AND OILS					
COPPER	CMX	05 = $12.00	ALL	8:25–1:00	Second Friday of month preceding contract month
GOLD	CMX	01 = $10.00	ALL	7:20–1:30	Second Friday of month preceding contract month
SILVER	CMX	01 = $5.00	ALL	7:25–1:25	Second Friday of month preceding contract month
PLATINUM	NYMEX	05 = $5.00	ALL	7:00–1:30	Friday preceding first Saturday of contract month
SWISS FRANC DEUTSCHE MARK BRITISH POUND JAPANESE YEN	IMM	01 = $12.50	ALL	7:20–2:00 5:00–8:30	Second Friday preceding third Thursday of contract month
CANADIAN DOLLAR	IMM	01 = $10.00	ALL	7:20–2:00	Second Friday preceding third Thursday of contract month
U.S. DOLLAR INDEX	NYCE	01 = $25.00	ALL	7:20–2:00	Second Friday preceding third Wednesday of contract month
CRUDE OIL HEATING OIL UNLEADED GAS	NYMEX	01 = $10.00	ALL	8:45–2:10	Second Friday of month preceding contract month
AGRICULTURE AND LIVESTOCK					
SUGAR	CSC	01 = $1.20	ALL	9:00–12:43	Second Friday of month preceding contract month
ORANGE JUICE	NYCE	01 = $1.50	ALL	9:15–1:45	First Friday of month preceding contract month
COTTON	NYCE	01 = $5.00	H, K, N, V, Z	8:30–2:00	First Friday of month preceding contract month
COCOA	CSC	01 = $10.00	H, K, N, U, Z	8:30–1:15	First Friday of month preceding contract month
COFFEE	CSC	01 = $3.75	H, K, N, U, Z	8:15–12:50	First Friday of month preceding contract month
WHEAT (HARD, RED,WINTER)	KC	1/8 = $6.25	H, K, N, U, Z	8:30–1:15	Friday which precedes contract month by at least 10 business days
CORN	CBT	1/8 = $6.25	H, K, N, U, Z	8:30–1:15	Friday (12:00 CST) preceding contract month by 6 business days
SOYBEANS	CBT	1/8 = $6.25	F, H, K, N, Q, U, X	8:30–1:15	Friday (12:00 CST) preceding contract month by 6 business days
LIVE CATTLE	CME	2.5 = $10.00	ALL	8:45–1:00	First Friday of contract month
FEEDER CATTLE	CME	2.5 = $10.00	F, H, J, K, Q, U, V, X	8:45–1:00	First Friday of contract month
LIVE HOGS	CME	2.5 = $7.50	ALL	9:10–1:00	First Friday of contract month
PORK BELLIES	CME	01 = $2.50	G, H, K, N, Q	9:10–1:00	Friday which precedes contract month by at least 3 business days

about $600. However, in many cases paying more for additional time can make the difference between profit and loss.

Several years ago, I recommended purchasing May and July 10 cocoa options to my *Opportunities in Options* newsletter subscribers. Several of them complained that the March cocoa calls were much less expensive, and, if the market was going to make a large move that they could buy more of them and make more profit. They were correct in their analysis, but sometimes the market just does not want to cooperate immediately. In this case, having extra time was very important. As shown in Exhibit 2.6, the March cocoa option purchasers would have been very disappointed as the contracts expired in early February under 10 with no profits for them, while the May contract continued to rise providing profits of over $2,000 per option. July cocoa option purchasers paid slightly more for their options (about $150), but were able to hold while the market exploded, with a profit of almost $5,000 per option (Exhibit 2.7).

Therefore, it seems best to buy very-long term options that are very close to the actual price of the commodity. Or is it? Unfortunately these options are much more expensive, requiring a large cash outlay as well as more risk. And, from a money management standpoint, you lose one of the main benefits of options—leverage—if you have to expend large amounts of money in purchasing options.

I have devised a method that combines these sometimes conflicting goals in purchasing options and allows me to purchase what I consider to be the best-priced option—the one having the best chance for success, while still providing enough leverage to produce huge returns if the trade is successful. This method is discussed in detail in Chapter 4.

DETERMINING AN OPTION'S VALUE

The following items determine an options's value: (1) strike price; (2) expiration period; (3) volatility; (4) interest rate; (5) supply and demand.

(1) Strike Price and (2) Expiration Period

As discussed above, the strike price of an option is very important in determining an option's value. An option can be "in-the-money" (when the strike price of the option for a call is lower, or for a put, higher than the market price of the underlying future); "at-the-money" (when the strike price of the option is the same as the underlying future); or "out-of-the-money" (when the strike price of the option is higher (call) or lower (put) than the underlying future contract.

Exhibit 2.6
July Cocoa Futures

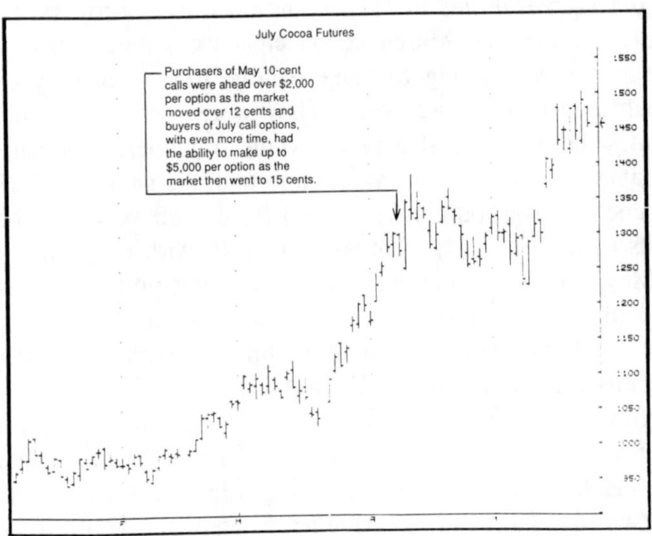
July Cocoa Futures
Purchasers of May 10-cent calls were ahead over $2,000 per option as the market moved over 12 cents and buyers of July call options, with even more time, had the ability to make up to $5,000 per option as the market then went to 15 cents.
1550
1500
1450
1400
1350
1300
1250
1200
1150
1100
1050
1000
950

Exhibit 2.7
July Cocoa Futures

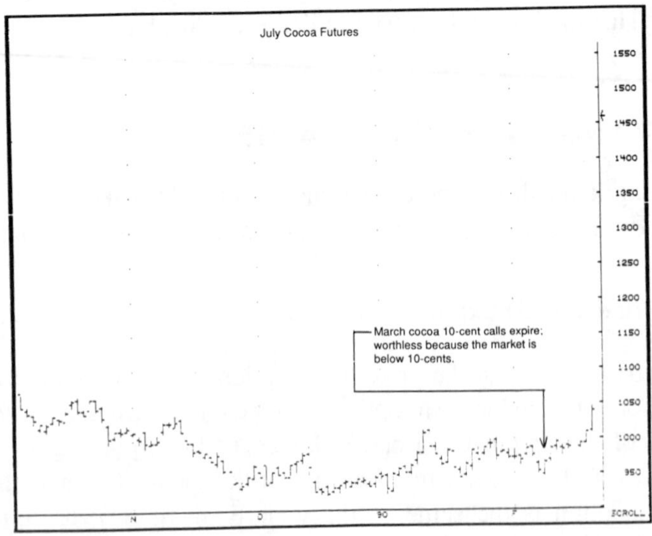
July Cocoa Futures
March cocoa 10-cent calls expire; worthless because the market is below 10-cents.
1550
1500
1450
1400
1350
1300
1250
1200
1150
1100
1050
1000
950
90

An in-the-money option is always the most expensive option, and an out-of-the-money option is always the least expensive. This is because the further out-of-the-money the option is, the less likely it is to have any value at expiration; and the further in-the-money the option is, the more intrinsic value the option has. Intrinsic value is the actual value the option would have if it were to expire today.

For example, an S&P 460 call (allowing you to buy at 46000) would have 500 points of intrinsic value if the S&P was at 46500 at expiration. Only in-the-money options contain intrinsic value. At-the-money and out-of-the-money options contain only time value. This is because if the option expired today, those options would be worthless. Therefore the only value they contain is the potential for a profit in the future. This potential is called "time value." Even in-the-money options contain some time value until close to expiration; however, the closer to the money or the deeper in-the-money an option is, the less time value it contains.

Exhibit 2.8 shows an example of the time decay of an option. Note that the curve begins to accelerate between 30 and 90 days prior to the expiration of the option. This is very important to know when determining whether to buy or sell an option, or which expiration period to use. Also, the time value of in-the-money, at-the-money, and out-of-the-money op-

Exhibit 2.8
Time Decay of an Option

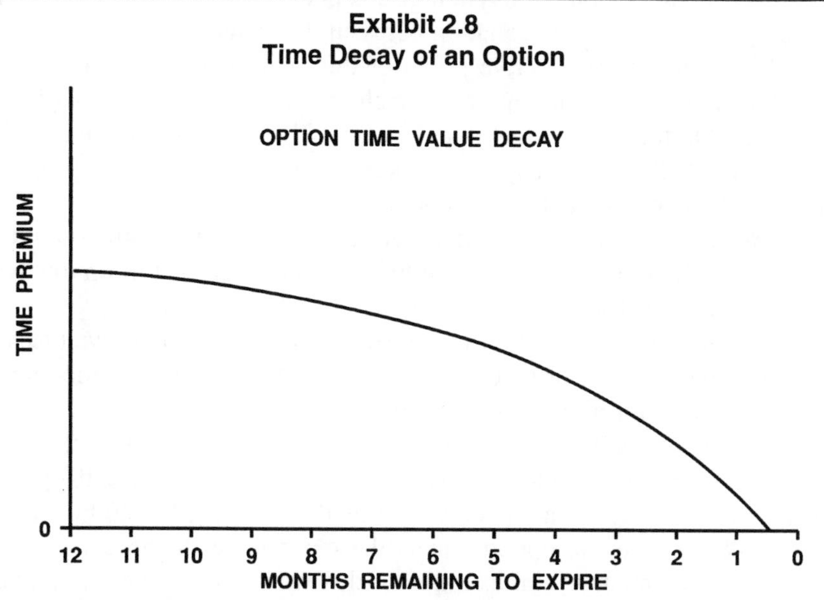

If an option moves closer to expiration, the "time value" decays (drops) at an increasing rate. Decay is especially prevalent in the last months before expiration.

tions decays at different rates, with out-of-the-money options decaying at a greater rate near expiration.

As previously noted, the longer the option has until its expiration, the more time value it has. Therefore, a December option to purchase gold at $400 will always have more time premium and value than an October option to purchase gold at $400 (unless we have an inverted market). This is because the additional time gives the option purchaser more of a chance to receive a profit on his transaction.

Although it seems complicated, this is no different than the negotiations entered into when obtaining an option to purchase the house discussed in the preceding chapter. If, for example, the house is worth $100,000 today, there is a good chance that the house could be worth $110,000 in one year. Therefore, a seller would be reluctant to grant you an option to purchase the house at $100,000 in one year.

The negotiations may go something like this:

Seller (option grantor): I'll give you an option to purchase the house in one year at $110,000 (the strike price) if you pay me $5,000 in option money now (premium).

Buyer (option buyer): I prefer to have an option to purchase the house at $100,000 in one year; and am willing to pay you $10,000 for that option.

This type of negotiation (see Exhibit 2.9) occurs before purchasing an option. When an "option" to buy a house is purchased, the "premium" paid for the option is fixed by negotiation between the buyer and seller.

The lower the price (strike price) of this "call option," the more premium the seller will want; and, conversely, the higher the price that is set (e.g., $125,000 for a house that is only worth $100,000 today), the less the option buyer will want to pay, since there is less chance that the property will be worth that price before the option expires.

Similarly, the longer the option period (time before "expiration"), the more the seller will want, since there is a better chance the option will become valuable before it expires.

The longer time the option is granted for (allowing you to wait to see where the house market or gold market is at that time), the more the option grantor will want for giving you that privilege.

If an option (call) is below the actual price of the market, that option is deemed to be "in-the-money." With gold trading at $375, call options below that figure are in-the-money, such as the 370 call, the 360 call, etc. If the strike price of an option equals the exact price of the commodity, then it is "at-the-money." An example of this would be if gold had moved up to $380 an ounce, the 380 gold call or put would be at-the-money.

In the case of a put, it is just the opposite. If the strike price of the put option is above the actual price of the commodity it is in-the-money. That

Exhibit 2.9
Option Negotiation

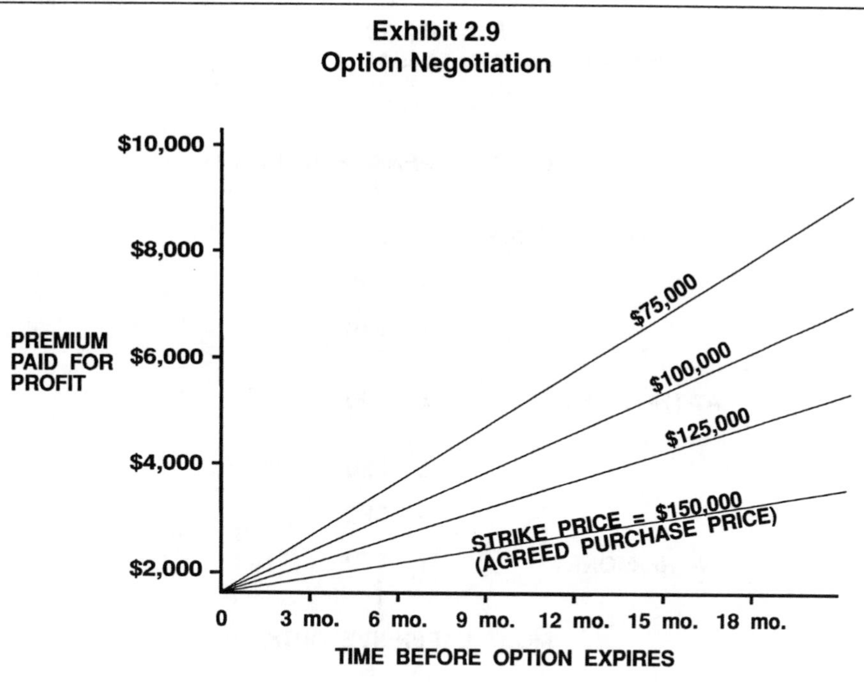

is because when you are the owner of a put option you have the right to sell the commodity to someone else, so you want that strike price to be as high as possible. With gold trading at $375 per ounce, the 380, 390, and all puts above that are in-the-money.

An option is "out-of-the-money" when, in the case of the call, the strike price is higher than that of the actual price of the commodity, or in the case of the put, the strike price is lower. In Exhibit 2.10, with gold at $400, all the calls from 410 and above are out-of-the-money and all the puts from 390 and below are out-of-the-money.

When an option is out-of-the-money it contains only time value. That is because you would not want to exercise that option currently, since you could buy the commodity cheaper on the open market. For example, if you were granted an option to purchase the house that is currently worth $100,000 today for $110,000 (the strike price), in one year, the only value that option would have is time value. It has no real value today, and its only actual value relies on the fact that at some time in the future it may become more valuable if the price of the house goes up.

This is exactly the same with commodity or stock options. An out-of-the-money option has no real value, only "time value." That continues until the price of the underlying market, in the case of the call, exceeds the

Exhibit 2.10
If the Value of Gold Is $400 Today . . .

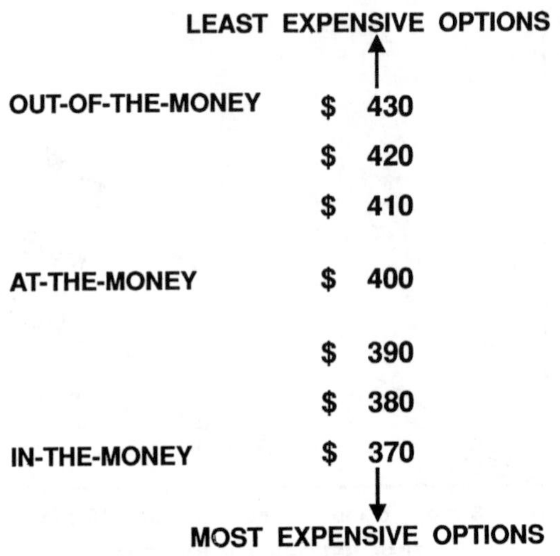

strike price of your option, or in the case of a put where the price declines below the strike price of the put you hold. Once this occurs, the option then has real value, "intrinsic value." It has a value of its own, in addition to the time value.

All options contain time value up until the day they expire. However, this time is constantly eroding, causing the time value of the option to decline. This is referred to as "wasting away of the time value." Exhibit 2.11 shows how the time value of the option decays. The time decay wastes away slowly until the option gets about 30 days from expiration. At that time the time value decay accelerates, causing the option to quickly lose value, as purchasers then think it is unlikely the commodity will gain value.

In the case of the option to buy the house in one year for $110,000, if you paid $10,000 for the option on June 1st and a friend of yours wanted to buy the option from you in two months, if conditions had not changed substantially, you probably could sell it to him for about $9,000 since there are still 10 months left.

Contrast that with the situation where the price of the house had not changed and there were only two weeks before the $10,000 option expired. In that case, few people would be willing to pay anything for the option as

Exhibit 2.11
Decay of Time Value

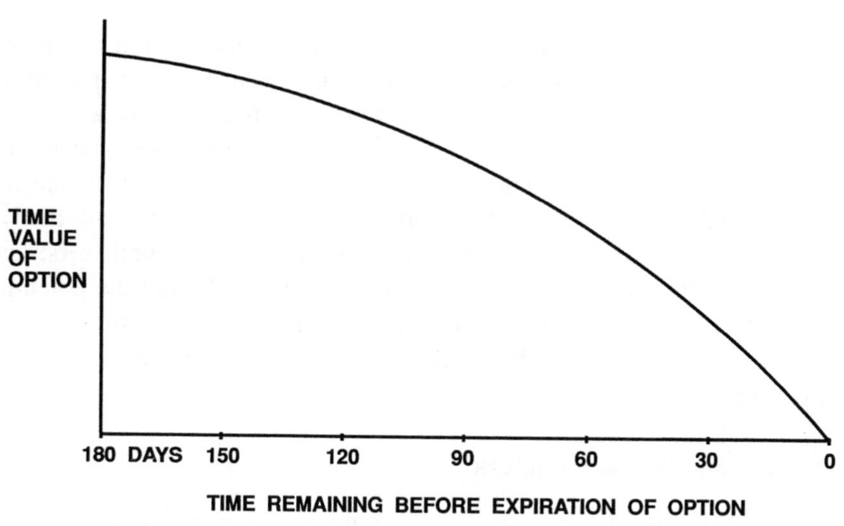

it is unlikely that the price would move fast enough to make the option valuable.

It is important to be aware of the time decay of an option. I recommend buying options of at least three months duration, allowing you to hold them so the time value does not decay too quickly; and selling options at least three weeks before expiration if it has not reached your profit objective, so that you do not end up losing all of the premium paid for the option.

These concepts of option strike prices and time value decay are very important in determining the premium of an option that you purchase.

(3) Option Volatility

Volatility is the measure of price changes in an option's premium. If a market were to stay in a tight trading range for a long period of time, the option would have low volatility, and therefore little premium, as the market participants see this option as not likely to make a large move. Conversely, if a market were subject to violent price fluctuations, the option would have high volatility and correspondingly high premiums.

Volatility is the most important component in option pricing and is discussed in more detail in Chapter 3.

(4) Interest Rates

Interest rates are also a factor in pricing options. As interest rates increase, option premium decreases; and as interest rates decline, option premiums increase. This is because, from the option buyer's point of view, as interest rates rise an option investment must yield a larger return to keep pace with alternate investments. As rates rise, the option premiums fall to make the investment attractive to prospective purchasers. Therefore, when alternative investments become more attractive to prospective option purchasers, less money is bid for an option premium; premiums will fall, and the potential rate of return on the option rises to reflect the increased opportunity costs. However, of all the factors discussed here, interest rates have the least effect on option pricing.

(5) Supply and Demand Factors

Supply and demand factors can help determine option prices to some extent, but are not normally a major factor in a liquid option market. However, in a rapidly trending market (such as crude oil options during the Gulf War), the supply of options to be sold could be lessened since grantors would be reluctant to sell an option with a limited reward if a market is trending strongly. Similarly, in a market that is stable, there could be an oversupply of grantors, thereby lowering the price of an option.

BUYING AND SELLING OPTIONS

On a typical day, buy and sell orders are entered by individuals, brokerage firms, institutions, and floor traders on the floor of the exchange. Let's say that the $6 silver call option closed at $500 the preceding day. The next day when trading opens, prices will be tugged in both directions as investors who think silver is heading higher and would like to buy, pressure the market upward. And investors who are afraid silver's going lower and would like to sell, pressure the market downward.

I may have an order to buy a $6 silver call at a cheaper price than the day's before, for example, at $400. Trader "A," however, may only be willing to pay $350 and Trader "B," $450.

On the other side of the market is Trader "X" who is willing to sell his silver option if he can get $550, Trader "Y" who will sell at $600, and Trader "Z" who wants $650 before she'll sell.

It seems that this silver option cannot be bought or sold, as the highest buy order is $450 and the lowest sell order is $550. This is the normal market scenario, however. If you were to call your broker for a quote on the silver market, he or she would tell you the price of silver is $500 an ounce last price, currently $450 bid, at $550 ask.

So how is this "standoff" broken? There are two ways: (1) new traders' orders entering the market, and (2) negotiations.

As new traders enter the market, they are likely to have different price levels at which they are willing to buy or sell. If a new trader enters the market, for example, to buy at $550, his or her order would be matched with Trader "X" who wants to sell his silver at $500, thereby completing the transaction. Other new traders may come in with "market orders" to buy and sell also. These orders must be filled immediately with the best then-available price. Therefore, new traders constantly entering the market can affect price levels as they place orders to buy and sell.

Here's an example of the second way standoffs are broken—through negotiation: if an option is trading at $450 bid (the highest price at which someone will buy it), at $550 ask (the lowest price at which someone is willing to sell it), what often occurs is that the person with the $450 bid, after not being able to complete his purchase, will eventually move his price up. He is, in effect, stating, "I was trying to get a good deal, but I really want to purchase silver. Is there someone who will meet me halfway and sell?" Similarly, the $550 seller may say, "I would really like to sell my silver today; I think I will lower my price." So they often "meet" in the middle at $500 an ounce.

As in the negotiations to buy and sell most items, such as cars, houses, and antiques, the process between a buyer and seller continues until a mutually acceptable price has been reached. Most of the time, prices are at an equilibrium or balanced level. This provides both parties a potentially equal chance to profit from a transaction. However, these are not the types of situations for which you are looking. You are only interested in situations where you can have a significant, advantageous "edge."

There are many reasons why these out-of-balance situations might occur. One would be seeing value where others don't. Have you ever purchased an antique, an old car, or a piece of furniture no one else wanted, but after some work or ingenuity, you were able to fix it up and resell it for much more than you paid? Have you ever purchased an item a seller had, in your mind, "underpriced" and were able to turn around and quickly sell it for more?

Yes, these are rare cases; prices are usually at equilibrium (balanced) levels. Experience in the markets, however, proves there are many occasions when prices are out-of-line, when there are real price disparities, when there are great opportunities to profit.

OBTAINING FILLS ON OPTION ORDERS AND SPREADS

As mentioned in Chapter 1, trading options is part art and part science. The science in trading options is in knowing how to use volatility, delta, and mathematical probability. However, there is also much that has to be learned in options through actual trading and experience (the "art").

One of the areas that can be learned by only experience is obtaining fills on option orders. The problem with options as compared with futures is that they are much less liquid. Only the most active option contracts, such as crude oil and treasury bonds, have near the volume of a futures contract. Other option contracts, such as heating oil, have about 10% of the daily volume of the underlying contract. This may sound like bad news, but it actually just gets worse. This is because this smaller trading volume and open interest in the options is spread between up to 100 different strike prices. The at-the-money options contain about 10% of the open interest, down to several strike prices away which may have only a few percent.

This makes "fishing" for better prices much more difficult in options than in futures. For example, because of the illiquidity in options, you may see the price of the underlying futures contract change and little or no movement in the price of options, making it difficult or impossible to be filled even at the previous closing price. Further, use of market orders and stops are ill-advised, because of the illiquidity and the substantial slippage that will occur in an active trader's account.

One question that frequently confronts an option spread trader is whether it is advisable to attempt to get filled on a spread individually, or put the entire spread in as one order. For example, if you intend to buy a December 5.50 silver call and sell a 6.00 call, you may find that the spread quote (there are separate brokers that work almost exclusively on filling spread orders alone) is 8 cents bid at 9 cents asked. You would feel reasonably certain of being filled at 8½ cents.

However, if you would like to obtain a better fill, you could put an order in to buy the December silver 550 call at 12 cents and sell the December 600 call at 6 cents (called "legging in"). If the market did have its usual daily swings, you would have a good chance of being filled on at least one side more favorably, if not both. However, there is also the chance of being filled on one side, and watching the other fly away. This type of risk must be assessed, like any other in trading, to determine which method is best for you. I do not recommend that anyone without on-line quote equipment attempt to “leg-in” to option spreads.

The most common spread quotes are for bull and bear spreads and similar common two-sided positions. Anything having more than two positions such as ratio spreads or butterflies are almost impossible to get filled as spreads at reasonable prices. Even conservative traders will have to “leg-in” to these positions at some risk.

I would rate options with a daily volume of under 1,000 as illiquid, from 1,000 to 3,000 as tradable with some difficulty, from 3,000 to 10,000 as liquid and freely tradable, and 10,000 and above as active trading option contracts. Treasury bond options stand in a class of their own with an average daily volume exceeding 50,000 contracts.

The bottom line is that only through experience (the art form of trading) can you determine the best methods of obtaining fills on your option positions or spreads. My years of trading experience in the various option markets are summarized in the tables below. Remember these are the usual bid/ask spread that I have found could be greatly affected by increased or decreased volatility.

Illiquid

Orange Juice
Canadian Dollar
Australian Dollar
Muni-Bond
Soybean Meal
Soybean Oil
Feeder Cattle
Live Hogs
Pork Bellies
Lumber
NYSE Index
U.S. Dollar Index

Barely Tradable

Cotton
Cocoa
Live Cattle
Copper

Liquid and Freely Tradable

Silver
Corn
Soybeans
Swiss Franc
Sugar
Gold
British Pound
Wheat
Coffee
Gasoline
T-Notes

Active Trading Options

T-Bonds
Eurodollars
German Mark
Crude Oil
OEX
S&P 500
Heating Oil
Natural Gas
Japanese Yen

Exhibit 2.12
Obtaining Fills on Option Spreads

CONTRACT	USUAL BID-ASK (TICKS)- - - - - - - - - -				
	SINGLE OPTION: FRONT MONTH	SINGLE OPTION: BACK MONTH	TWO-OPTION SPREAD: FRONT MONTH	TWO-OPTION SPREAD: BACK MONTH	COMMENTS
BRITISH POUND	2-3	3-4	3-4	6-12	With the British pound, buyers can usually get filled a little better than market. Back months are difficult to trade, and participants must be prepared to pay on a hasty exit.
CATTLE	5	10	10	20	On spreads, doing legs individually is usually better.
COPPER	2-5	3-10	3-10	4-20	Most of the action occurs in front month.
CORN	2	3-4	2-4	4-6	Getting filled is usually 2–8 ticks better than the market.
CRUDE OIL	1-3	2-5	2-5	3-9	Buyers can usually get 1 tick better than market. Do spreads as spreads. Prices do not move far out of line because of good volume.
EURO-$	1-2	2-3	4-6	4-6	Do spreads as spreads. If quotes are 2–3 wide, buyers can usually get 1 better than market; with 5-6 wide, it might be possible to get 2 ticks better than market.
GERMAN MARK	2-3	2-5	3-5	4-8	Front months are liquid. Back months are not.
GOLD (COMEX)	2-3	2-5	3-5	4-8	Unlike silver, it is almost always possible to do better than market. Place single-option orders a tick off round numbers to facilitate fills.
HOGS	4-6	6-10	6-10	8-12	Similar to cattle, but harder to trade.
J-YEN	2-3	4-10	3-5	6-20	Similar to Deutsche Mark, volume has increased, making options easier to trade than in the past.

Figure continues

Exhibit 2.12 (Continued)

CONTRACT	USUAL BID-ASK (TICKS)- - - - - - - - -				
	SINGLE OPTION: FRONT MONTH	SINGLE OPTION: BACK MONTH	TWO-OPTION SPREAD: FRONT MONTH	TWO-OPTION SPREAD: BACK MONTH	COMMENTS
SILVER (COMEX)	2-4	3-6	3-6	4-8	Difficult to get filled better than market. Back months very difficult to trade; spreads can often be done better individually.
SOYBEANS	4	4-8	6-10	6-12	Similar to corn, we recommend doing spreads as spreads. Orders can usually be done 2-6 ticks better than market.
S&P 500	2-3	4-5	2-4	4-8	Expect 1-2 tick-slippage in and out.
SUGAR	3-6	4-8	5-10	10-15	Similar to Deutsche Mark, volume has increased, making options easier to trade than in the past.
SWISS FRANC	2-4	4-10	4-7	6-20	Back months are difficult. Few market-makers. Less liquid than D-Mark, but front months not a problem, sometimes can get better than market.
TREASURY BOND	1-2	2-4	2-5	3-10	The best option trading market. Fills can be had up to half way across bid-ask.
TREASURY NOTES	2-4	3-6	4-8	5-15	Front month is OK, but back months do not trade much. Tough to get filled better than market. Bond options are superior for short option strategies.

CHAPTER 3

Volatility

WAYS TO USE OPTION VOLATILITY

The most overlooked and underutilized factor by most option traders is the significance of volatility. This includes both the effect of volatility on the premium cost of the option when purchased and of future changes in volatility on the position.

Volatility is simply a mathematical computation of the magnitude of movement in an option. This is based on the activity in the underlying market. If the market is making a rapid move up or down, volatility will rise; in a quiet market, volatility will be low (Exhibit 3.1).

It is volatility that decides whether options are high or low priced. (Most books and analysts commonly refer to these as "overvalued" and "undervalued" options.) This can be a dangerous misnomer and the cause of unnecessary losses for traders. For example, during the explosion in lumber prices in 1993, which carried lumber from 10000 to over 40000 in several months, lumber call options could have been said to have been "overvalued" (when lumber reached 20000). These options were trading at the highest volatility in their history, up to 10 times above levels of "normal" markets. However, what do think happened to the trader who sold these grossly "overvalued" call options? Or to the trader who sold "overvalued" puts during the October S&P drop in 1987 and 1989 and during the plunge in crude oil during the Gulf War? Similarly, the purchase of "undervalued" call options in gold and silver in 1991–1992 (trading at their lowest volatility levels in their history) were also losers, as those markets failed to move, and 100% of out-of-the-money calls expired worthless.

Exhibit 3.1
Market Volatility

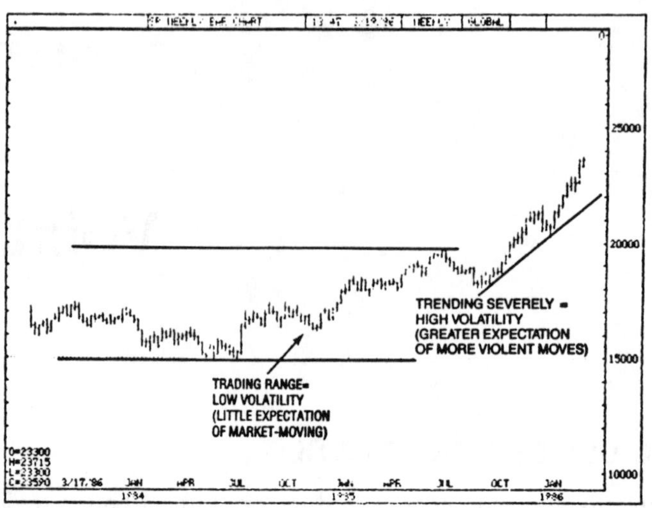

When volatility is relatively low, you should look for option buying strategies as the market is quite likely to make a strong move (Exhibit 3.2); and, when option premium is high, option selling strategies should be considered to take advantage of the relatively overvalued premiums.

Volatility is an important factor in determining the price of an option because all option models depend heavily on the calculation of volatility in determining the fair market value of an option. What we are actually saying when we calculate volatility is that the odds are 67% or better that the market will hold within the calculated range over a period of one year.

For example, if gold is trading $500 per ounce and had a volatility of 20%, the probability is that gold will hold a range of $400 to $600 (20% on either side of $500) for a one-year period. Based on this, option sellers can calculate the premium they would want to receive for selling various gold puts and calls based on the probability that the strike price would be reached prior to the expiration of the option. If the volatility is high, option sellers would determine that it is more likely that the option price could be reached and ask a higher premium; if volatility is low, the option seller would determine that it is unlikely that the option would be exercised and therefore ask less for selling that option.

Exhibit 3.2
Option Buying Strategies in Low Volatility

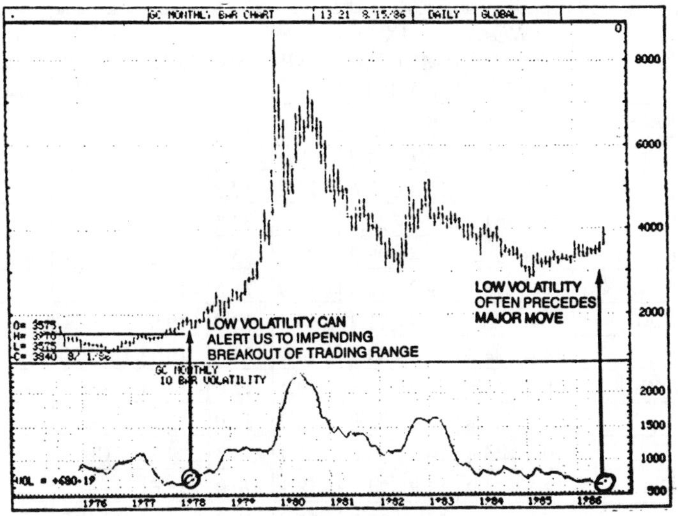

There are two types of volatility—*historical* and *implied.* Historical volatility is calculated by averaging a past series of prices of options. For example, a trader could use a 90-day price history, a 30-day price history, a 10-day price history, etc. . . . to determine the option's historical volatility. Obviously, each set of calculations result in a different figure for volatility and produce different theoretical (fair value) for the options.

Implied volatility is calculated by using the most current option prices, commodity price level, time to expiration, and interest rate. This method provides a more accurate picture of the current volatility of an option, compared to the historical volatility which is a smoothing of past price action. I use "implied volatility" in my option pricing calculations, and then compare the current numbers to past records of implied volatility (Exhibit 3.3) to determine whether volatility is relatively high or low.

Another overlooked area is the differences in volatility between different months and strike prices of options. When I calculate volatility, I always use strike prices that are nearest to the money, as I feel that this is the most accurate representation of the actual volatility of the option contract. Many times, premiums of out-of-the-money options can be distorted greatly.

Exhibit 3.3
Volatility Composite Index

	TWO-YEAR RANGE	SIX-MONTH RANGE	MAR	JAN	FEB	VOLA-TILITY TREND	RANKING *1=LOW 10=HIGH*
BRITISH POUND	9.6 - 16.7	9.6 - 12.8	12.8	11.1	9.8	UP	8
CATTLE	9.0 - 17.6	9.1 - 14.2	9.1	10.5	9.7	DOWN	1
CORN	14.5 - 28.6	15.4 - 28.6	21.2	17.3	19.8	—	5
COPPER	22.1 - 41.8	22.7 - 34.2	24.5	33.5	27.5	DOWN	3
CRUDE OIL	24.6 - 98.2	29.4 - 98.2	32.4	93.2	63.7	DOWN	2
DEUTSCHE MARK	9.2 - 16.7	9.2 - 12.9	12.9	11.5	10.6	UP	8
EURODOLLAR	10.4 - 28.8	10.4 - 21.2	14.7	13.0	19.9	—	3
GOLD	14.9 - 34.3	14.9 - 34.3	14.9	23.5	18.1	DOWN	1
JAPANESE YEN	8.2 - 17.5	8.2 - 13.6	12.1	12.9	11.3	—	6
S&P 500	15.7 - 33.8	15.7 - 31.8	16.7	22.9	18.2	DOWN	2
SILVER	19.5 - 46.4	19.5 - 34.6	30.1	24.4	34.6	UP	8
SOYBEANS	13.2 - 24.2	13.2 - 24.2	18.3	20.9	18.6	—	5
SUGAR	22.7 - 36.4	25.0 - 35.8	25.0	23.7	22.7	DOWN	2
SWISS FRANC	10.0 - 18.8	10.0 - 13.8	13.2	11.3	10.8	UP	7
TREASURY BOND	8.5 - 16.3	8.5 - 14.2	9.2	14.2	10.1	DOWN	2

For example, in June 1987 silver ratio spreads provided a high probability of profit, because the volatility for the out-of-the-money silver calls were double the volatility of the at-the-money calls. This can lead to significant opportunities. When options approach expiration, volatility for all of the strike prices will tend to equalize. In this instance I purchased the most fairly priced call (near-the-money), and sold the most overvalued calls (out-of-the-money). I could expect the options sold to lose premium faster as the market moved in either direction. Even if the market were to move higher (unless making a straight up vertical move) this spread would have also worked as the nearer-to-the-money option would have gained value faster than the already overpriced out-of-the-money options.

Another overlooked characteristic of volatility is that option volatility tends to drop gradually, then level off. However, volatility increases, at times, can be characterized by very sharp changes in volatility driving option premium to extremely high levels. These events occur rarely, but when they do they can be very damaging to those holding short option positions. One example was the volatility increase in many markets at the beginning of the Gulf War. Oil volatility doubled, while other markets such as gold, bonds, and currencies increased 20% or more. Even seemingly unrelated markets such as cattle increased dramatically.

There are also intraday fluctuations in volatility and premium. Since implied volatility is based on the closing price of the option, many times intraday fluctuations in prices will create option volatility that is much higher than the volatility based on the closing price. (These types of fluctuations seem to always be of the higher nature. Rarely does option volatility drop any significant degree during a trading day.) Taking advantage of these intraday price swings and distortions in option valuation can provide a trader with significant trading opportunities.

Changes in volatility affect the premium levels in options you are going to purchase, as well as those you have already purchased or sold. A good example of this is in the crude oil and the S&P 500 option market where volatility has ranged between 20% to over 100%. With high volatility, if one were to purchase an out-of-the-money option, you would need a substantial price rise before that option would be profitable at expiration. Both the expense of the purchase price of the option and time value would be working severely against you. However, with volatility at lower levels, this option would not only cost much less but would require a smaller move for the position to be profitable. This is because many times as prices begin to rise volatility also increases, thereby increasing the premium of the option purchased.

The first thing that most option floor traders (who are generally the most successful of all option traders) do before initiating any position is to check their volatility charts or daily sheets that are available at most of the Exchanges. They look for any overpricing or underpricing, or disparity in value. After determining whether any potential opportunity exists, they then review the trend of the market. They do this to make certain that they are not "fighting" against the trend even in a position that may contain a high degree of option disparity. For example, at the end of July 1994, the out-of-the money S&P puts were trading at a volatility level of almost 100% higher than the out-of-the-money calls. Therefore, one could make a case for buying these calls and selling puts whose option valuation was twice as high. However, all this would lead to losses if the trend in the S&P were lower, causing the calls to lose value and the puts to even gain more. In fact, this trader could experience greater difficulties if he was unaware of the fact that although out-of-the money puts are trading in a range of around 13–15%, historically option volatility in bearish markets has been many times higher. This is another factor that the experienced floor trader takes into account before initiating a trade.

For example, in July 1994 we took profits on our short S&P 500 puts both because the implied volatility for the puts had fallen over 20% to unusually low levels, and the premium for the out-of-the money calls was too low to recommend selling options to hedge our short puts. Further, the action in the currency and bond markets presented the potential of causing a large move in the S&P 500. Our evaluation was based on these factors, the risk/reward was inadequate to maintain the positions, *even though the market had not yet moved against our position.* However, these are aspects that the experienced option trader must use in his trading to provide the best risk control and money management. It is our view that in both options and futures trading, that the winners seem to be able to take care of themselves; however, it is the losers that can really "reach out" and grab you.

The actions of the floor trader in evaluating volatility are different than those of most off-floor traders. Most traders first look for a market that they are bullish, bearish, or neutral on, and then initiate some type of option position or strategy to reflect their views. However, what traders fail to consider in these situations is whether this strategy in some way can give them a "trading edge" by using options—if, in fact, there is advantage involved in the position, such as limited risk, time decay, or premium disparity. If these advantages do not exist, or the trader ends up buying an option that is too highly priced, and too far out of the money, or selling undervalued options in a severely trending market, they could put themselves in worse shape than if they had just used futures! Further disadvantages include that options are less liquid than futures, making higher slippage likely, as well as the extra commissions that may accrue from doing option strategies instead of a single futures position.

There is no question that option trading is more complicated, takes more time and more knowledge than trading futures alone. That is because in addition to having knowledge of the futures markets similar to that of any experienced successful futures trader, you must be an astute option trader as well. Harder, and much more work? . . . Absolutely! However, this is one of the reasons that option trading provides such a large advantage to the experienced trader. Too many other people want to do it the easy way—and just buy or sell options indiscriminately. It is this type of trader that "fuels" the advantages available in the option market. Not only do we want to make sure that we are not one of those traders, but we must be knowledgeable and alert to take advantage of the opportunities that may occur in any market.

Similar to floor traders, in our own trading we first review the volatility levels of all of the futures options markets to determine whether any market has particularly high or low option volatility. For example, this review alerted us to option selling opportunities in cattle in 1994, which was at its highest volatility levels in over seven years, and also option selling opportunities in bonds over the last several months, which was also trading at its highest volatility levels since 1988.

However, we also must review the charts of the futures markets to determine whether there is a market trend or technical pattern that we may want to consider taking advantage of, IF *we can find an appropriate option position or strategy that will present us with a trading edge over the markets.*

The concepts of option volatility, along with the time decay characteristic of options, are the two most important and most overlooked factors in option trading. These concepts can be difficult to learn and use, but the proper use of these option characteristics can result in a trading edge over the markets.

HOW OPTION VOLATILITY CAN ALERT YOU IN ADVANCE TO SIGNIFICANT MARKET MOVES

As discussed above, when option volatility is at low levels, there is a high probability that a large move is about to occur. It seems that when a contract is very quiet, traders seemingly fall asleep and don't expect anything to happen. Of course, this is exactly when everything explodes! On the other hand, many times when the market has been very active (volatile) for a period of time, since most traders are already in the market, it is likely to maintain a trading range. However, understanding this concept of volatility is much easier than using it in trading.

The beginning option trader disregards volatility. He determines only that a market is moving in a certain direction, and purchases an option that best fits his view of the market and risk exposure. This trader will lose 100% of the time when the market moves against his desired direction or remains neutral. The trader will also often lose, even when the market moves in his direction, because of the time decay of the value of the option premium.

The professional option trader will examine the volatility of the option contract and determine whether it's in the high, low, or middle of its historical range. He will then examine a computer evaluation of what the different strike price and months of options will do under various market conditions, and not only choose the option that is the most likely to be profitable, but also determine whether this is an appropriate time to be purchasing options.

For example, call option purchases provided positions with an excellent risk/reward ratio in silver and in the grains in 1993. The options had low volatility combined with reliable technical chart patterns, which suggested that there was a strong probability of a breakout to the upside (Exhibit 3.4).

The opposite picture was evident in bond options in 1993. A trader who would have purchased any out-of-the-money options in the December bonds would have lost money, since the market had very high option volatility (premium) and a short time to expiration. All of the out-of-the-money options, both puts and calls, lost value during this period. Therefore, it didn't matter in this market whether you were bullish or bearish. All buyers of options were wrong, all sellers were right.

Changes in volatility can also occur over short or long periods of time. Treasury bonds had decreased in volatility almost 50% in the beginning of 1987, reflecting a change in traders' views on the market from volatility to stability. On the other hand, Swiss Franc options decreased 30% in volatility in one day after a meeting of the European countries to reevaluate currency rates at which no segment changes were made. Volatility on both puts and calls had increased dramatically during the previous

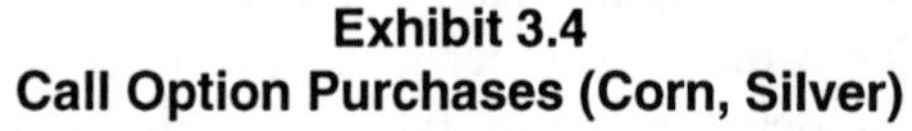

Exhibit 3.4
Call Option Purchases (Corn, Silver)

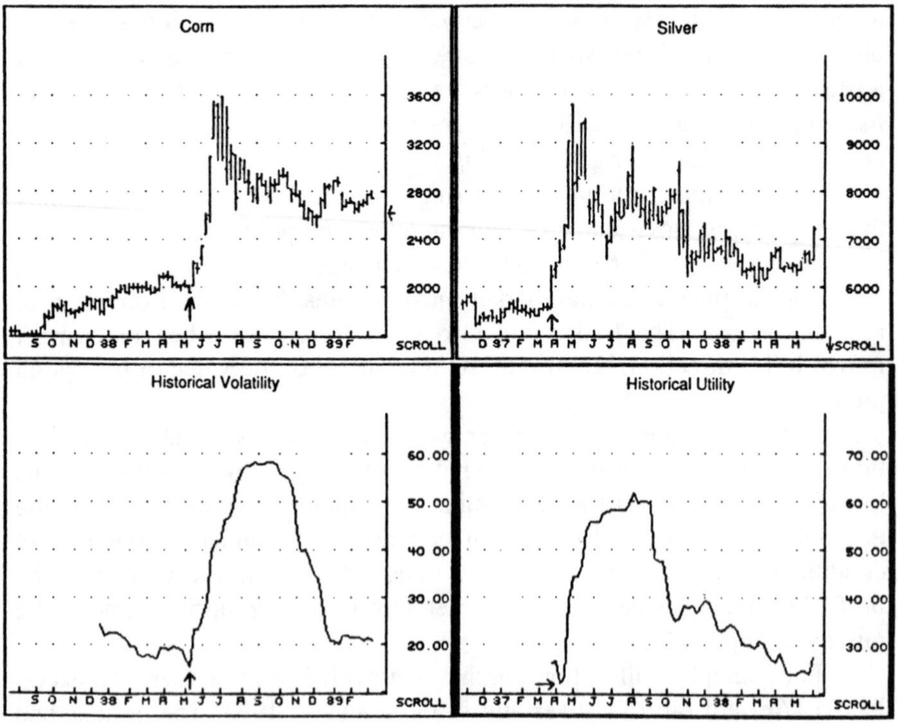

week, and when it was determined that no significant changes were going to occur, in one day, put and call options lost over one-fourth of their value.

Recognizing these principles are not only important in determining the best option strategy to use, but also can alert you to potential changes in the direction of the underlying market.

OPTION VOLATILITY HIGHLIGHTS

Option Volatility: The Most Accurate, but Overlooked Indicator in Trading

Traders have used various option indicators as an attempt to predict the direction of the underlying market. The most popular of these are the "put-call ratios" and volume of options traded. The theory is that these traders may be "insiders" or know more than other traders, and the ratio and number of options purchased or sold could be very important. Although these indicators may be sometimes accurate in trading particular stocks, we have found no correlation exists by use of these indicators for futures options. There are several logical reasons for this.

First, the increase in volume of option contracts often occurs because options are still in their infancy for use by institutional traders, and their many uses are now being discovered by these large traders. Often the increase in volume in option contracts is tied solely to the fact that more traders are beginning to use options.

Similarly, the put-call ratio is inaccurate because options can be used for many purposes. A large trader who is bullish on the bond market may purchase 1,000 bond calls to profit from this expected move. However, another trader who also bullish on bonds, may sell 1,000 bond call options to hedge a long futures or cash bond position and lock in a rate of return he is comfortable with.

Therefore, with the many types of trading objectives by those in the marketplace, there is no mathematical significance in the increase in volume or changes in put or call ratios that would help determine the direction of the underlying market.

However, there is one extremely accurate indicator that can provide an accurate signal of a large move in the underlying market. This indicator is the *implied volatility* of the option contract. (Implied volatility is calculated by averaging the most current option prices of the at-the-money, close to expiration options.) Implied volatility provides a more accurate picture of the current volatility of an option compared to the historical volatility which is a smoothing of past price action. We use implied volatility in determining whether an option is relatively "under- or overvalued" by comparing the current numbers to our past records of implied volatility in our *Volatility Composite Index.* This tells us whether implied volatility is relatively high or low and this helps us determine whether we should initiate option buying or selling strategies.

While researching the correlation of option volatility to futures prices, we have found one reliable occurrence: WHEN OPTION VOLATILITY MOVES TO HISTORICALLY LOW LEVELS, THE UNDERLYING MARKET IS LIKELY TO HAVE A SIGNIFICANT MOVE. **This indicator has been extremely accurate in the past, the only variable being when this move is going to occur.**

Perhaps the most dramatic of these moves occurred in 1994 in coffee. Between December 1993 and April 1994, coffee had moved to new historical lows in option volatility (Exhibit 3.5). At that time the coffee market was trading in an extremely narrow trading range, making very little movement at all. However, with our warning signal in place, we would then move to the chart of coffee and await the breakout of this technical pattern which occurred in May 1994 (Exhibit 3.6). Coffee subsequently moved almost 300% higher in the next three months. Several other cases of similar indications of impending moves occurred in 1994. In the S&P 500, option volatility moved to new historical lows in February of 1994 as the market maintained a trading range (*warning sign*) (Exhibit 3.7); subsequently, in late March, the market quickly broke out of this trading range with a gap and plunged almost 4,000 points in just over one week (Exhibit 3.8). Other markets showing similar signals in 1994 include live cattle, which made new lows in option volatility in April 1994 before breaking out of its trading range and rapidly plunging 600 points (Exhibit 3.9), and in the Swiss Franc in June, which made new implied volatility lows, near 7% before its breakout and summer rally of over 10%.

The metals market is another market that is providing an excellent example of this rule. In early 1993, gold moved to new historical lows in option volatility *(warning sign);* then subsequently broke out of its long-term downtrend and quickly moved over 20% higher. In late 1994 we had another example of this with gold moving to historical volatility lows near 10% and the chart pattern beginning to break out of a one-year triangle pattern (Exhibit 3.10).

In using this rule it is important to remember that this is a two-step process. Use the first sign of a potential large move (historical volatility lows) as your *warning sign* to be aware of a change in the chart pattern (Exhibits 3.11–3.20). Do not initiate any trades on this signal yet. The next step is to review the chart pattern of the underlying market. In the cases we have reviewed above, we have used either a breakout from a long-term

Exhibit 3.5

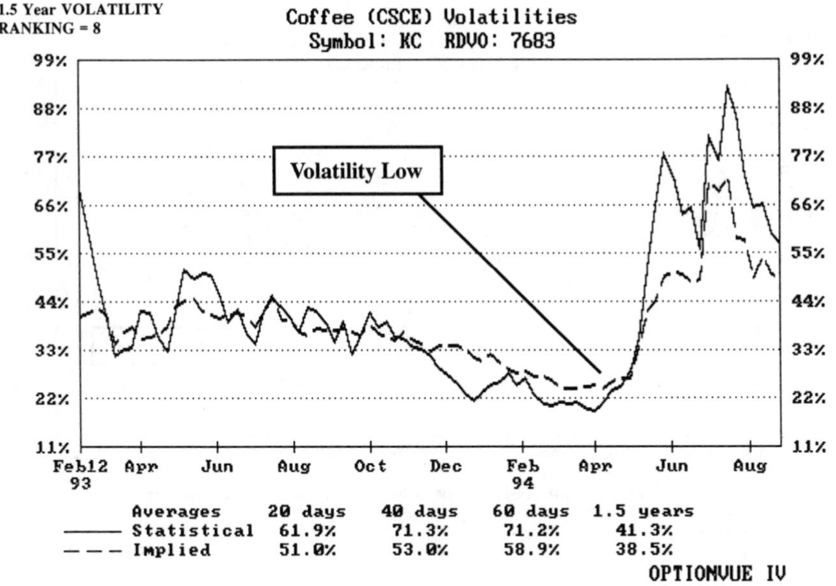
1.5 Year VOLATILITY
RANKING = 8
Coffee (CSCE) Volatilities
Symbol: KC RDVO: 7683
99%
88%
77%
66%
55%
44%
33%
22%
11%
Volatility Low
Feb12 93
Apr
Jun
Aug
Oct
Dec
Feb 94
Apr
Jun
Aug
Averages 20 days 40 days 60 days 1.5 years
Statistical 61.9% 71.3% 71.2% 41.3%
Implied 51.0% 53.0% 58.9% 38.5%
OPTIONVUE IV

Exhibit 3.6

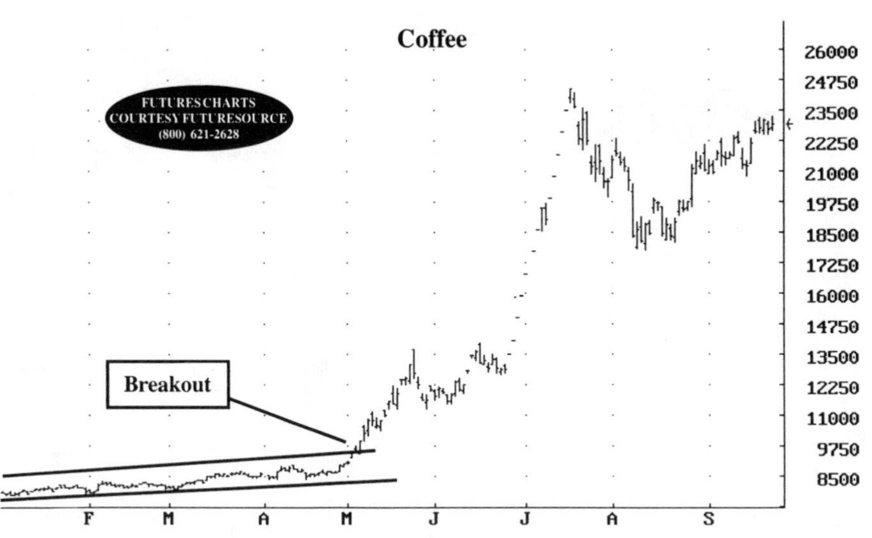
Coffee
FUTURESCHARTS
COURTESY FUTURESOURCE
(800) 621-2628
Breakout
26000
24750
23500
22250
21000
19750
18500
17250
16000
14750
13500
12250
11000
9750
8500
F
M
A
M
J
J
A
S

Exhibit 3.7

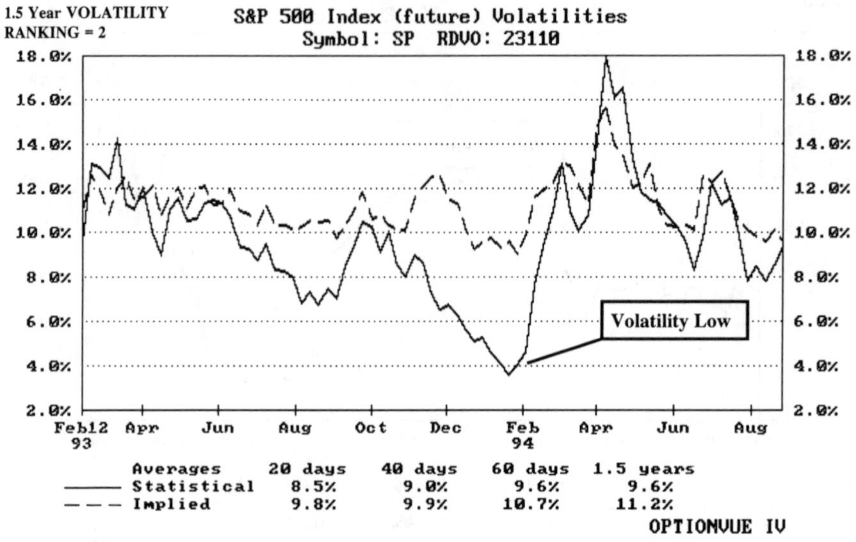

Exhibit 3.8

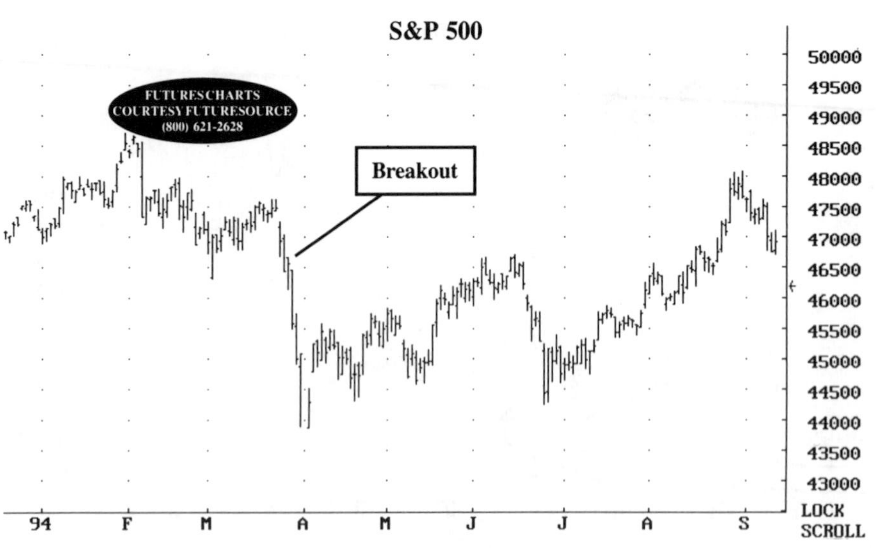

Exhibit 3.9

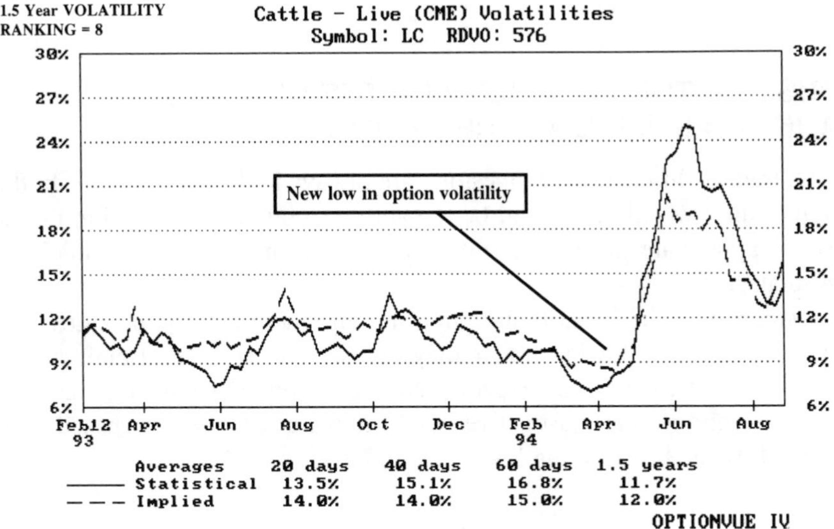
1.5 Year VOLATILITY
RANKING = 8
Cattle - Live (CME) Volatilities
Symbol: LC RDVO: 576
New low in option volatility
30% 27% 24% 21% 18% 15% 12% 9% 6%
Feb12 93 Apr Jun Aug Oct Dec Feb 94 Apr Jun Aug
Averages 20 days 40 days 60 days 1.5 years
Statistical 13.5% 15.1% 16.8% 11.7%
Implied 14.0% 14.0% 15.0% 12.0%
OPTIONVUE IV

Exhibit 3.10

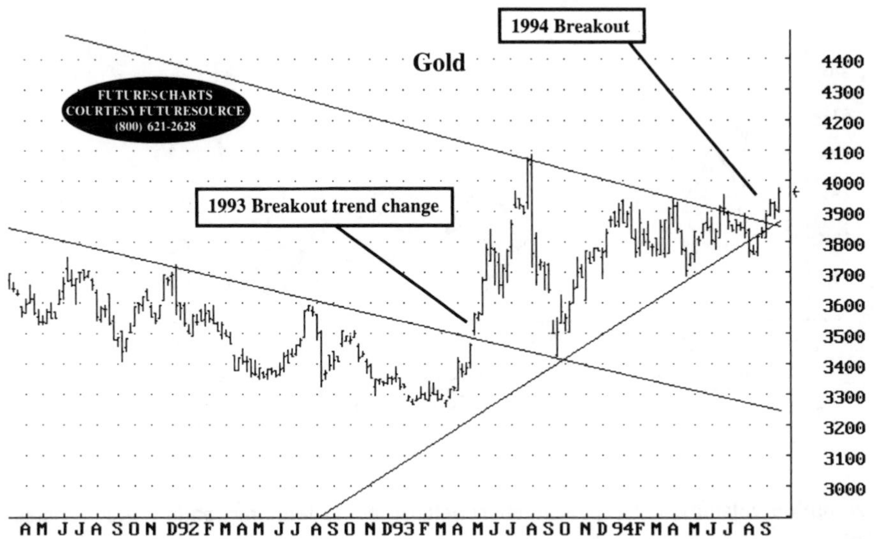
1994 Breakout
Gold
FUTURESCHARTS
COURTESY FUTURESOURCE
(800) 621-2628
1993 Breakout trend change
4400 4300 4200 4100 4000 3900 3800 3700 3600 3500 3400 3300 3200 3100 3000
A M J J A S O N D92 F M A M J J A S O N D93 F M A M J J A S O N D94 F M A M J J A S

consolidation, a trading "triangle," or a change of trend indicated by the breaking of a long-term trendline as a signal to initiate a trade. Using these two confirming signals together presents a high likelihood of a successful trade once the breakout has occurred.

CONSIDER THE VOLATILITY OF THE UNDERLYING MARKET, AS WELL AS THE OPTIONS

Option traders, like all other investors, are always looking for a deal. In the option trading world this would be the ability to buy a cheap option that is likely to appreciate greatly, or sell an expensive option which is likely to deteriorate.

Along with the benefits in option trading, there are complexities. For example, a trend-following trader may decide that Treasury Bonds are in an uptrend; the market has experienced a 30% retracement of its current rally, and therefore the most active bond futures contract is purchased with a stop below the last reaction low.

Exhibit 3.11

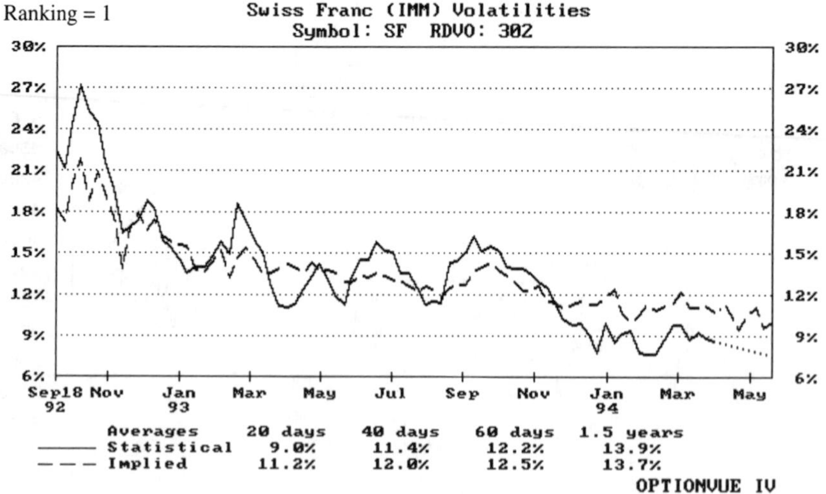

Low option volatility and explosive chart pattern makes large moves in the currencies likely.

Exhibit 3.12

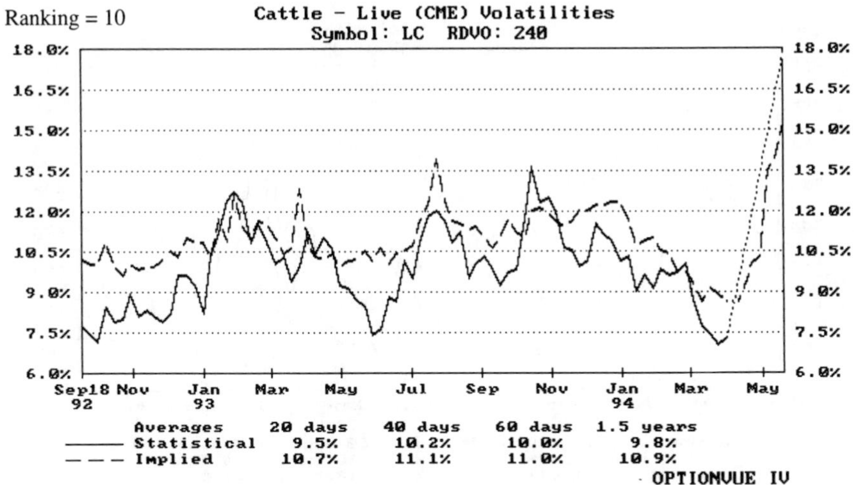

Cattle option volatility makes an unprecedented move from historical lows to new highs in one month!

Exhibit 3.13

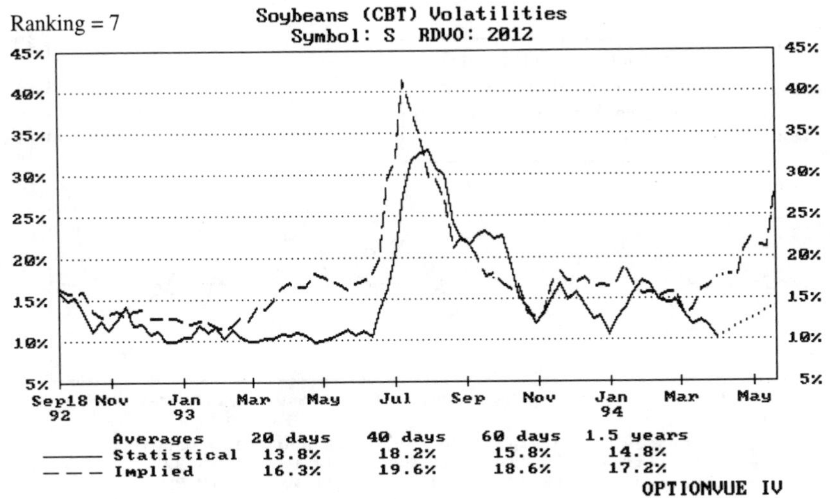

Volatility has begun to increase; particularly for the out-ot-the-money options.

Exhibit 3.14

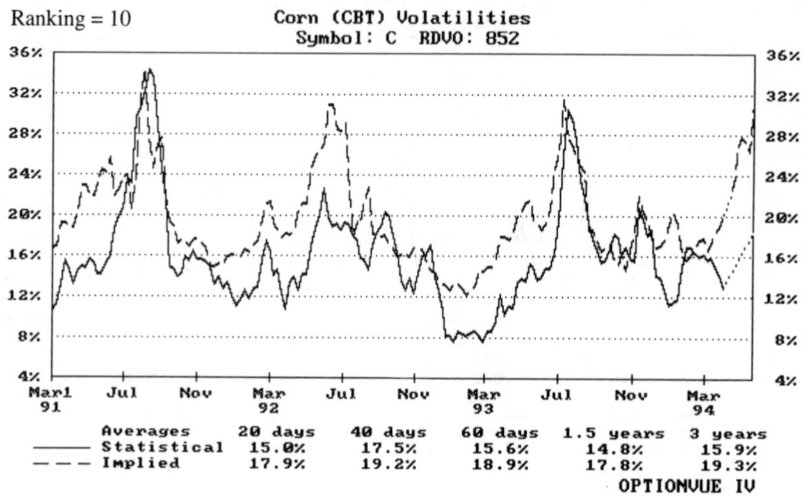

Summary volatility spike in the grains begins early this year.

Exhibit 3.15

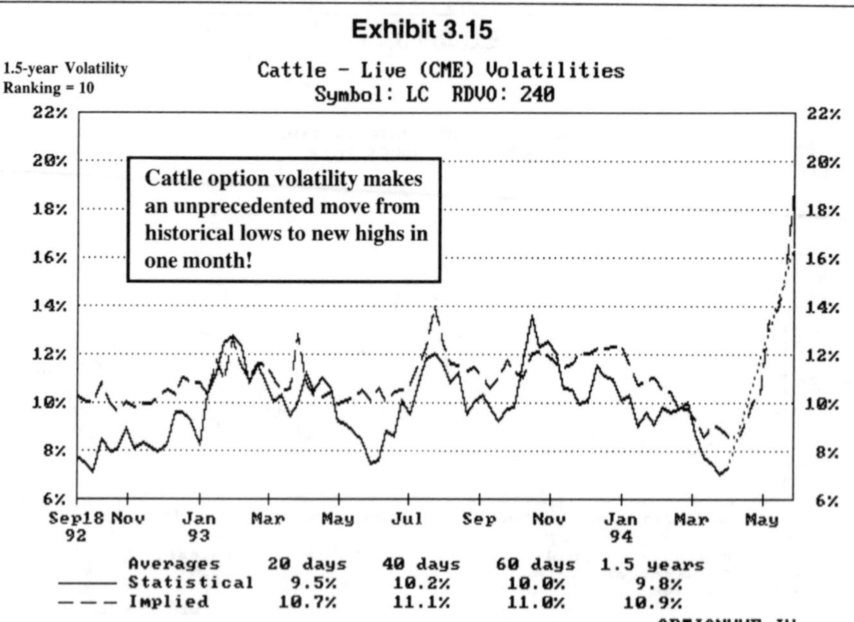

Cattle option volatility makes an unprecedented move from historical lows to new highs in one month!

Exhibit 3.16

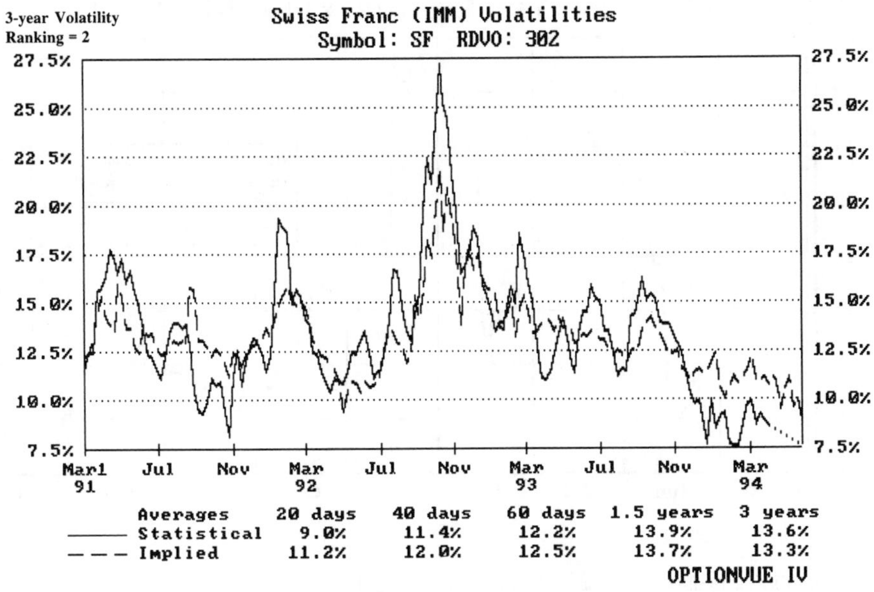

Exhibit 3.17

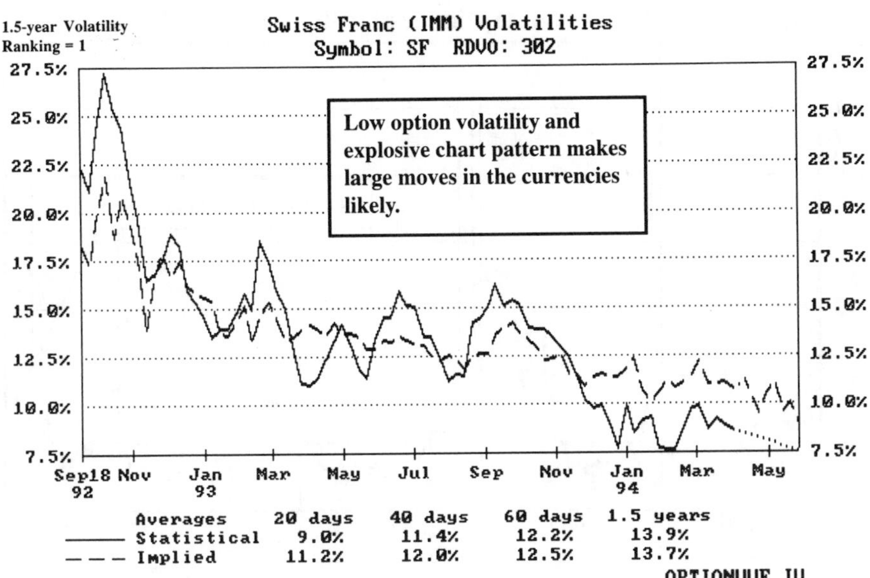

Exhibit 3.18

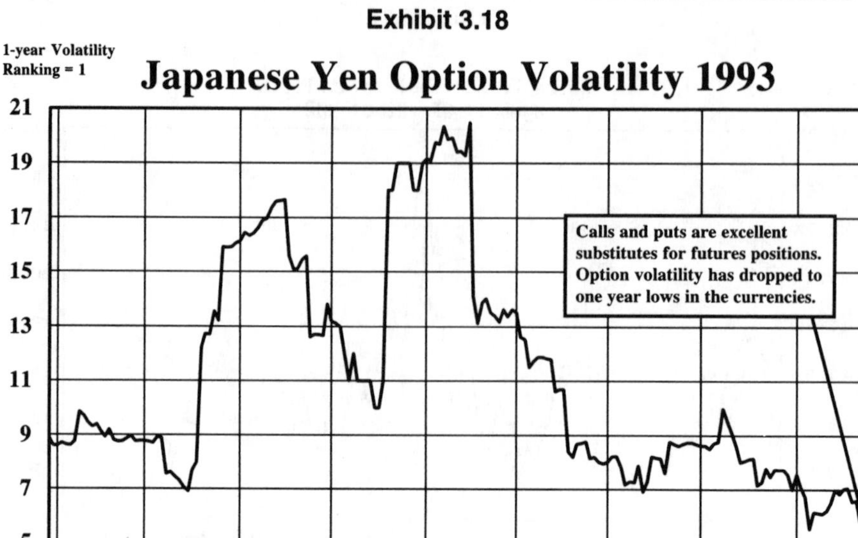
1-year Volatility
Ranking = 1
Japanese Yen Option Volatility 1993
21
19
17
15
13
11
9
7
5
Apr May Jun Jul Aug Sep Oct Nov Dec Jan
Calls and puts are excellent substitutes for futures positions. Option volatility has dropped to one year lows in the currencies.

Exhibit 3.19

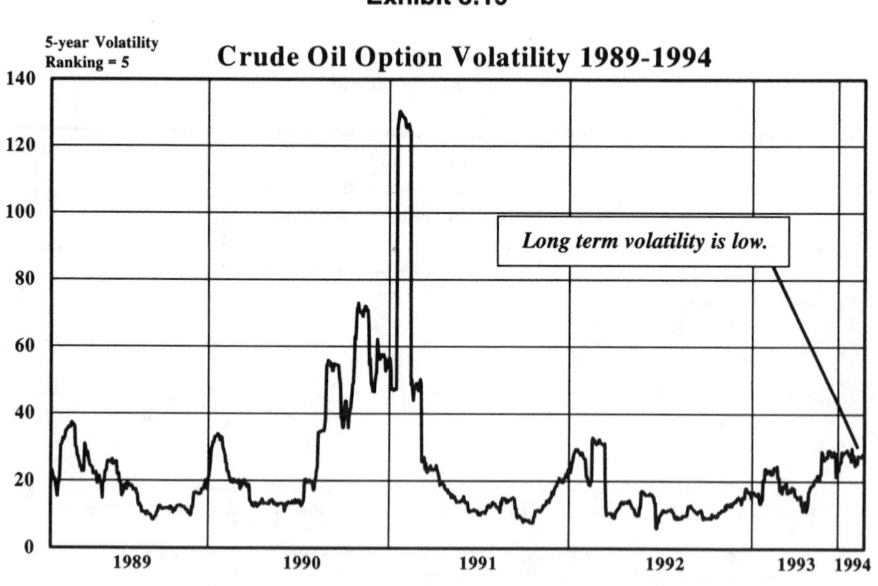
5-year Volatility
Ranking = 5
Crude Oil Option Volatility 1989-1994
140
120
100
80
60
40
20
0
1989 1990 1991 1992 1993 1994
Long term volatility is low.

Exhibit 3.20

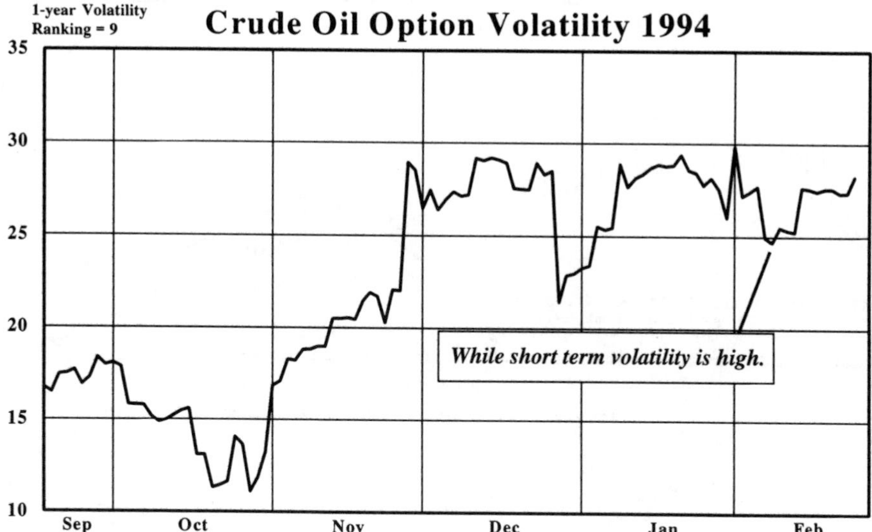

The option trader must not only similarly analyze the market, but also decide what strike price and month of options to use, whether options are to be bought or sold, or whether a combination of options is to be used (a strategy). One of the primary factors option traders use in deciding whether to buy or sell options, or which strategy to use is the volatility of the option market, as this will determine the premium paid or received for the trade.

There are times when looking at the underlying market volatility is equally important. The most dramatic example of this occurred in the foreign currencies over the last few years.

From December of 1988 through May 1989 the Swiss Franc declined from 7000 to 5500, a decline of 1500 points in seven months. During that time option volatility ranged from 12% in the beginning of the move to the 9% level in May and June.

In a similar price move, the Swiss Franc had increased from August through December 1988, from 6500 to 8000, a move of 1500 points in five months. However, option volatility differed dramatically from the first half of 1989, at times being twice as high (Exhibit 3.21).

Why did the option volatility vary so much when the underlying market movement was almost the same? In late 1987, the general attitude in the currencies was very bullish as the market was in the throes of a three-

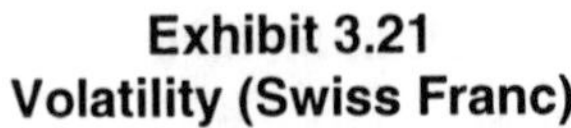

Exhibit 3.21
Volatility (Swiss Franc)

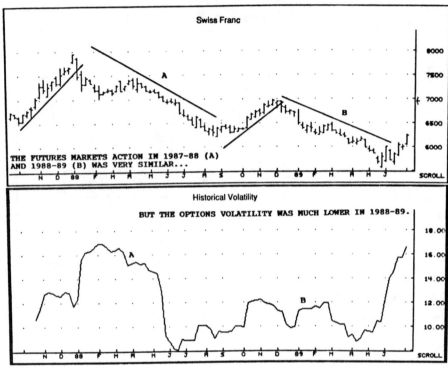

year bull move. In a bullish market, option premium is almost always higher than bear markets, since small public traders prefer to be long on a market rather than short, thus creating a demand for call options.

This great difference in option volatility means that you also must change your option trading strategies. With volatility at high levels at the end of 1987, selling options premium presented trades with high probabilities of profit. In fact, premium was so high at times, that on days of little activity, option premium shrunk for both puts and calls. However, in 1991, with option premium at levels 50% or more lower, option buying strategies were recommended.

In trading options one must learn to be flexible, using what the market gives you to your best advantage. Sticking to one strategy may not be appropriate for current conditions. Changes in volatility levels require the use of different option strategies, depending on both the relative level of volatility in the option or underlying market.

USING TRENDS TO YOUR ADVANTAGE

One of the first principles learned when I started trading was "The Trend is your Friend." I have found that to be one of the most important aspects of a trading plan. Attempting to fight the trend, guessing tops or bottoms, trading the correction, etc., is probably the biggest cause of losses in the marketplace. Most all traders have done this at one time or another—and paid the price.

Trends are important to option traders not only in determining market direction, but also in determining if option volatility is likely to move higher or lower. Volatility trends similar to price action. Volatility trends are just as reliable and long lasting as price trends, and like price action, when volatility hits low levels and begins to turn up (or high levels and turns down) it can continue to trend for several years (Exhibit 3.22).

Volatility trends in options are extremely important in determining the type of trading strategies that are most likely to be successful.

At the beginning of 1988, option volatility in the foreign currencies was extremely high, just coming off historically high levels in some of the foreign currency markets at the end of 1987. Similarly, option volatility was also near the high end of historical levels in the financial markets, in the treasury bond and Eurodollar option markets. With volatility continually declining during 1988, selling option premium presented trades with high probabilities of profit. This is because the daily shrinkage of time value of option premium was accelerated by the decreasing volatility. In fact, during that period, there were many days and weeks that option premium for both puts and calls moved lower. This type of action, obviously, was very beneficial for Neutral Option Positions (Exhibit 3.23).

Similarly, the 1982 through 1984 period was excellent for option sellers. The markets had just come off of large movements in the metals and grains, and traders' perceptions were that these conditions would continue. Additionally, options on futures were new, and disparity in pricing occurred more often, since traders were inexperienced in their use and pricing.

One of my favorite positions during this time was *ratio spreads* because the out-of-the-money calls were overvalued as compared to the closer-to-the-money calls. By using ratio spreads, I was able to take advantage of this comparative overvaluation.

In 1990, the markets were characterized by not only relatively low option premium but, in fact, option premium that was very low in some markets compared to the daily movement in the futures markets as we discussed above. For example, in 1990 option volatility in the metals, financials, and grains was at the low end of historical levels (Exhibits 3.29 and 3.30). In the currencies, option volatility was neither high nor low histori-

Exhibit 3.22
Treasury Bond Options

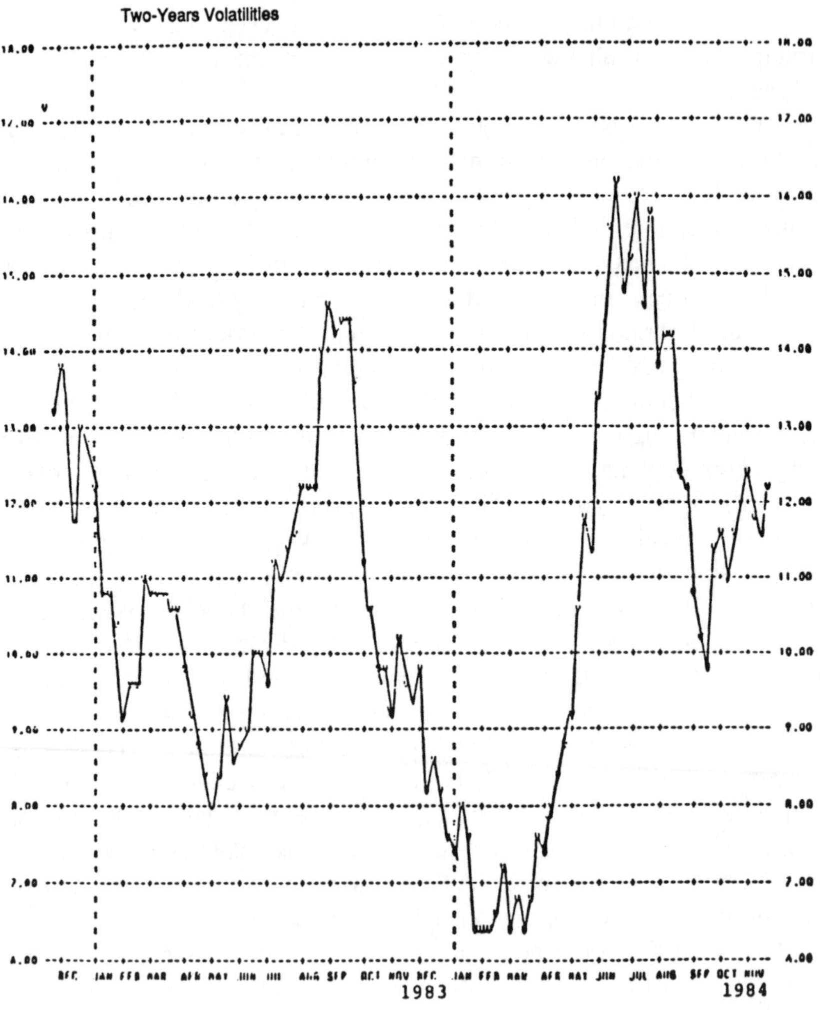

The above chart of Treasury Bond Option Volatility shows a historical two-year low occurring in the first quarter of 1984. This corresponded to the end of a two-year bear market in Treasury bonds and the commencement of a major rally. Statistically, there is over 80% correlation between extreme volatility changes and being able to predict market movement.

Exhibit 3.23

Cotton

CALLS

Mth		Strike	Vol.	Open Int.	Week's High	Week's Low	Week's Last	Net Chg.	Futures Close
Oct	91	74.00	21	70	5.60	4.15	4.65	+ 0.62	76.90
Oct	91	75.00	38	116	5.10	3.85	4.00	+ 0.58	76.90
Oct	91	76.00	8	142	5.60	5.60	3.45	+ 0.35	76.90
Oct	91	77.00	21	306	3.55	3.00	2.95	+ 0.40	76.90
Oct	91	78.00	83	185	4.20	2.45	2.50	+ 0.20	76.90
Oct	91	79.00	197	583	2.65	2.00	2.10	+ 0.10	76.90
Oct	91	80.00	137	594	3.30	1.70	1.75	+ 0.05	76.90
Dec	91	71.00	0	462	0.00	0.00	3.44	− 0.40	73.96
Dec	91	72.00	5	732	4.65	4.65	2.96	− 0.44	73.96
Dec	91	73.00	31	276	4.25	3.45	2.60	− 0.46	73.96
Dec	91	74.00	77	557	3.70	3.00	2.25	− 0.28	73.96
Dec	91	75.00	70	1,128	3.25	2.70	1.95	− 0.29	73.96
Dec	91	76.00	17	613	2.70	2.50	1.70	− 0.25	73.96
Dec	91	77.00	8	374	2.40	2.40	1.50	− 0.25	73.96

PUTS

Mth		Strike	Vol.	Open Int.	Week's High	Week's Low	Week's Last	Net Chg.	Futures Close
Oct	91	74.00	17	394	1.80	1.15	1.76	− 0.43	76.90
Oct	91	75.00	66	474	2.40	1.65	2.13	− 0.46	76.90
Oct	91	76.00	30	144	2.40	1.70	2.55	− 0.61	76.90
Oct	91	77.00	31	95	3.00	2.25	3.05	− 0.68	76.90
Oct	91	78.00	8	201	4.10	2.55	3.60	− 0.80	76.90
Oct	91	79.00	49	232	4.45	4.05	4.20	− 0.86	76.90
Oct	91	80.00	12	392	4.75	3.60	4.85	− 0.91	76.90
Dec	91	71.00	22	155	2.55	2.25	3.45	− 0.05	73.96
Dec	91	72.00	21	213	2.90	2.90	3.95	+ 0.00	73.96
Dec	91	73.00	10	160	3.50	3.40	4.60	+ 0.05	73.96
Dec	91	74.00	13	302	3.80	3.40	5.25	+ 0.15	73.96
Dec	91	75.00	20	108	4.65	4.15	0.00	+ 0.12	73.96
Dec	91	76.00	2	180	4.50	4.40	0.00	+ 0.17	73.96
Dec	91	77.00	9	42	5.10	4.40	0.00	+ 0.17	73.96

Calls Volume 2,225; Open Int 16,013
Puts Volume 1,116; Open Int 15,535
Volume figures reflect Friday through Thursday.
Open interest figures as of close of business Thursday.
High, Low and Close through Thursday.

Swiss Franc

S-FRANC CALL

JLY	91	620	100	100	—	—	2.25	+ 225	.6423
JLY	91	630	160	165	1.59	1.06	1.32	− 28	.6423
JLY	91	635	22	131	1.57	.60	.90	− 34	.6423
JLY	91	640	213	153	1.23	.38	.56	− 37	.6423
JLY	91	645	862	699	.98	.21	.31	− 37	.6423
JLY	91	650	1084	845	.75	.11	.16	− 32	.6423
JLY	91	655	123	353	.54	.05	.08	− 25	.6423
JLY	91	660	781	808	.35	.02	.04	− 18	.6423
JLY	91	665	249	268	.20	.02	.02	− 12	.6423
JLY	91	670	142	606	.13	.02	.01	− 9	.6423
JLY	91	675	75	96	.08	—	CAB	− 7	.6423
JLY	91	680	212	479	.06	—	CAB	− 5	.6423
JLY	91	685	102	229	.01	—	CAB	− 4	.6423
JLY	91	690	6	289	.01	CAB	CAB	− 3	.6423
JLY	91	695		250	—	—	CAB	− 1	.6423
JLY	91	700		200	—	—	CAB		.6423
JLY	91	705		249	—	—	CAB		.6423
JLY	91	710		55	—	—	CAB		.6423
JLY	91	715		546	—	—	CAB		.6423
JLY	91	720		177	—	—	CAB		.6423
JLY	91	730		20	—	—	CAB		.6423
JLY	91	740		65	—	—	CAB		.6423
JLY	91	760		34	—	—	CAB		.6423
JLY	91	770		50	—	—	CAB		.6423
AUG	91	625		1	—	—	2.20	− 17	.6423
AUG	91	635		1	—	—	1.49	− 23	.6423
AUG	91	640	1	18	1.69	1.01	1.20	− 24	.6423
AUG	91	645	2	2	1.41	.69	.96	− 23	.6423
AUG	91	650	34	50	1.27	.62	.75	− 21	.6423
AUG	91	655	16	16	.94	.42	.60	− 19	.6423
AUG	91	660	237	349	.77	.37	.46	− 18	.6423
AUG	91	665	13	21	.46	.36	.35	− 15	.6423
AUG	91	670	112	155	.50	—	.27	− 13	.6423
AUG	91	675		93	—	—	.20	− 12	.6423
AUG	91	680	175	218	.29	.11	.15	− 9	.6423
AUG	91	685		23	—	—	.11	− 8	.6423
AUG	91	690		18	—	—	.08	− 7	.6423
AUG	91	695		9	—	—	.07	− 5	.6423
AUG	91	700		128	—	—	.06	− 3	.6423
AUG	91	705		195	—	—	.05	− 2	.6423
AUG	91	710	10	190	.05	—	.04	− 1	.6423
AUG	91	720		31	—	—	.03		.6423
AUG	91	740		10	—	—	CAB	− 1	.6423
SEP	91	625		1	—	—	2.41	− 22	.6423
SEP	91	630		33	—	—	2.08	− 22	.6423
SEP	91	635		117	—	—	1.78	− 22	.6423
SEP	91	640	67	112	2.06	1.30	1.51	− 22	.6423
SEP	91	645	270	268	1.78	1.10	1.26	− 22	.6423
SEP	91	650	77	329	1.56	.93	1.06	− 20	.6423
SEP	91	655	4	10	1.36	.80	.87	− 20	.6423
SEP	91	660	307	467	1.14	.63	.72	− 18	.6423
SEP	91	665	11	30	.69	—	.58	− 18	.6423
SEP	91	670	408	489	.83	.42	.47	− 16	.6423
SEP	91	675		16	—	—	.37	− 15	.6423
SEP	91	680	78	576	.53	.28	.30	− 14	.6423
SEP	91	690	1	513	.36	—	.18	− 11	.6423
SEP	91	700	32	475	.24	—	.10	− 9	.6423
SEP	91	710	20	292	.10	—	.07	− 6	.6423
SEP	91	720	26	222	.06	—	.05	− 3	.6423
SEP	91	730	1	311	.05	—	.02	− 3	.6423
SEP	91	740	2	230	.04	—	.01	− 2	.6423
SEP	91	750		90	—	—	CAB	− 1	.6423
SEP	91	760		29	—	—	CAB		.6423
SEP	91	770		68	—	—	CAB		.6423
SEP	91	780		142	—	—	CAB		.6423
SEP	91	790		195	—	—	CAB		.6423
SEP	91	800		44	—	—	CAB		.6423
SEP	91	810		79	—	—	CAB		.6423
SEP	91	820		42	—	—	CAB		.6423
SEP	91	830		47	—	—	CAB		.6423
SEP	91	840		42	—	—	CAB		.6423
SEP	91	850		3	—	—	CAB		.6423
DEC	91	630	1	10	2.86	2.49	2.64	− 15	.6401
DEC	91	650	26	51	1.79	1.60	1.70	− 13	.6401
DEC	91	660	11	32	1.69	—	1.34	− 12	.6401
DEC	91	670	4	184	1.15	—	1.05	− 9	.6401
DEC	91	680	30	142	.83	—	.80	− 9	.6401
DEC	91	690	8	191	.75	—	.62	− 7	.6401
DEC	91	700	9	149	.48	.40	.47	− 5	.6401
DEC	91	710	15	91	.36	—	.35	− 6	.6401
DEC	91	720		51	—	—	.26	− 5	.6401
DEC	91	730		34	—	—	.19	− 4	.6401
DEC	91	740		13	—	—	.14	− 4	.6401
DEC	91	750		3	—	—	.10	− 4	.6401
DEC	91	760		3	—	—	.09	− 1	.6401
DEC	91	770		2	—	—	.07	− 1	.6401
MAR	92	660		20	—	—	1.78	− 7	.6392

S-FRANC PUT

JLY	91	600	5	306	.02	—	.01	− 1	.6423
JLY	91	610	151	151	.01	—	.02	+ 2	.6423
JLY	91	620	19	210	.14	—	.03	− 10	.6423
JLY	91	625	18	18	.20	—	.05	− 14	.6423
JLY	91	630	445	506	.33	.10	.09	− 19	.6423
JLY	91	635	878	368	.45	.17	.17	− 25	.6423
JLY	91	640	360	1168	.64	.27	.33	− 28	.6423
JLY	91	645	251	306	.91	.42	.58	− 26	.6423
JLY	91	650	200	762	1.29	.64	.93	− 20	.6423
JLY	91	655	15	199	1.73	.96	1.35	− 13	.6423
JLY	91	660	3	389	1.94	—	1.80	− 7	.6423
JLY	91	665	50	53	2.40	—	2.29	− 1	.6423
JLY	91	670	3	343	2.83	—	2.78	+ 3	.6423
JLY	91	675		69	—	—	3.27	+ 5	.6423
JLY	91	680		148	—	—	3.77	+ 7	.6423
JLY	91	685		32	—	—	4.27	+ 6	.6423
JLY	91	690		10	—	—	4.77	+ 9	.6423
JLY	91	695	6	27	5.14	—	5.27	+ 10	.6423
JLY	91	700		3	—	—	5.77	+ 10	.6423
JLY	91	710			—	—	6.77	+ 10	.6423
AUG	91	600	1	46	.15	.10	.10	− 5	.6423
AUG	91	610	60	81	.19	—	.18	− 8	.6423
AUG	91	620	42	177	.46	.34	.33	− 11	.6423
AUG	91	625	300	300	—	—	.44	+ 44	.6423
AUG	91	630	163	595	.77	—	.58	− 14	.6423
AUG	91	635		3	.92	.73	.76	− 14	.6423
AUG	91	640	40	56	1.16	—	.97	− 14	.6423
AUG	91	645	20	17	1.44	1.11	1.23	− 13	.6423
AUG	91	650	52	44	1.77	—	1.53	− 10	.6423
AUG	91	655		13	—	—	1.86	− 7	.6423
AUG	91	660		75	2.35	—	2.21	− 5	.6423
AUG	91	665		20	—	—	2.61	− 3	.6423
AUG	91	670		100	—	—	3.02	− 41	.6423
AUG	91	675		93	—	—	3.45	+ 5	.6423
AUG	91	685		20	—	—	4.36	+ 7	.6423
AUG	91	690		3	—	—	4.82	+ 7	.6423
SEP	91	600	52	2006	.29	.22	.22	− 7	.6423
SEP	91	610	346	746	.48	—	.37	− 9	.6423
SEP	91	620	535	596	.75	.50	.56	− 12	.6423
SEP	91	625	6	14	.84	—	.71	− 12	.6423
SEP	91	630	351	664	1.08	.72	.87	− 13	.6423
SEP	91	635	27	28	1.27	.93	1.06	− 13	.6423
SEP	91	640	185	419	1.52	1.07	1.28	− 12	.6423
SEP	91	645	260	302	1.79	1.29	1.53	− 12	.6423
SEP	91	650	55	424	2.08	1.50	1.81	− 9	.6423
SEP	91	655	2	5	2.20	—	2.12	− 8	.6423
SEP	91	660	7	469	2.65	—	2.45	− 7	.6423
SEP	91	665		1	—	—	2.81	− 5	.6423

Many weeks both put and call options decline in value, regardless of the direction of the underlying futures market.

cally, but in light of the large daily movement in the futures markets, option premium was extremely low. Because of this lower volatility the majority of my trades were option purchases with the objective of turning them into *free trades.*

In summary, these are two distinct types of trends:

1. Price action
2. Volatility

One of the advantages of options is the flexibility of the many different types of strategies. This allows you to pick an option strategy, or design a position to fit the market, not vice versa. Flow with these trends in volatility—don't struggle against them.

HOW OPTION VOLATILITY CAN HELP YOU DETERMINE WHICH OPTION STRATEGY TO USE

Which Option Strategy Is the "Best One" and When Should It Be Used?

In *The Option Secret,* we compare trading to playing poker in many areas. This analogy was not meant to be cute, but rather because they are quite similar in many ways. Also, it may be the easiest way to visualize when and why we should be trading. (Similar to trading, gambling analysts have stated that 80% of poker players lose, and professional players, although they may lose occasionally, year after year come out ahead.)

One of the biggest mistakes and money losers for beginning poker players is playing too many hands. These players tend to like the "action" and are not discerning enough about when a hand should be played or dropped. The expert player, on the other hand, plays only when he finds the odds significantly in his favor. He may adjust his style according to the other players in the game (loose versus tight; expert versus amateur, etc.). However, in general, he will not put his money in the "pot" unless he feels that there is a good reason to do so. The expert player knows that eventually the cards will turn in his favor and better hands will come up to provide him with his best playing opportunities.

This is exactly the same for the trader. Beginning traders are normally excited, wanting to get involved in the "action." Positions are taken without adequate planning. The professional option trader does not get involved without being able to obtain a significant opportunity. He analyzes option volatility levels, the technical pattern of the market, the trend of the market, and the market's current reaction to fundamental news to determine whether volatility is high, low or there are disparities in option premium. The trader then decides the best trading strategy to take advantage of both the volatility levels and the technical pattern and plans his trade accordingly.

IF THERE IS NO SIGNIFICANT ADVANTAGE OR TRADING OPPORTUNITY, THE TRADER WILL STAND ASIDE.

The trader knows there will be other days and other markets that will provide "better playing hands" for him.

We first analyze the underlying futures market to find a directional "bias" for our options positions. As we said earlier, you cannot trade options in a vacuum. That means you must know what is going on in the underlying market as well as the option market.

Again, this is similar to playing poker. Three aces is generally considered a very good hand. However, in a situation where there are many other players in the "pot" betting strongly, it could be the right move to throw that hand away. Not playing borderline hands, and not trading in inappropriate situations are probably the two most important things new poker players and traders must learn.

After analyzing the technical pattern of the market, we then examine option volatility levels. We prefer to look at "comparative" volatility levels, ranking markets on a 1–10 scale depending upon their current "implied" volatility levels, relative to periods in the past (Exhibits 3.24–3.25).

Then we combine the comparative volatility level with the technical pattern of the underlying market to determine whether a "special circumstance" or "favorable situation" exists. We can significantly increase our probability of profit and/or risk/reward ratio by purchasing/selling either an option or a combination of options (option spread strategy). This information is of such critical importance that its proper use can at times allow us to be inaccurate in our market views and still be successful; while improper use (such as buying high priced, out-of-the money options) can lead to losses even when the market moves significantly in your favor!

The following outlines virtually all the trades that we consider for the different volatility levels. (This information is directed at the off-floor trader. Floor traders have the ability to use these positions plus other, more "arbitrage" type positions because of their speed of execution and low trading costs. Floor traders tend to use many *"delta neutral" positions to squeeze out premium from options on a short-term basis. This includes not only the Neutral Option Position and "Ratio Spreads,"* which are our favorite (delta neutral) positions, but positions matching futures and options in almost any configuration to provide them with an advantage including "boxes," "conversions," etc.)

The following are the only positions we use in our own trading portfolio 99% of the time:

Exhibit 3.24
Volatility Composite Index

New Highs or Lows are Gray	Two Year Range	Six Month Range	Jun 27	July 26	May 27	Volatility Trend	Ranking 1 = Low 10 = High
Cattle	9.2 - 21.2	10.8 - 21.2	20.8	16.4	21.2	UP	8
Cocoa	19.2 - 46.8	19.2 - 46.8	37.1	38.1	46.8	UP	8
Corn	11.5 - 31.8	15.2 - 31.0	31.0	15.2	28.7	DOWN	2
Copper	11.8 - 33.0	17.0 - 33.0	26.2	21.7	33.0	DOWN	3
Crude Oil	14.9 - 42.4	16.2 - 42.4	30.9	33.5	28.9	- -	5
Deutsche Mark	8.9 - 12.6	8.9 - 12.0	12.1	12.0	10.6	UP	8
Euro-Dollar	10.8 - 39.2	10.8 - 23.2	20.2	17.5	22.9	- -	5
Gold	8.3 - 21.4	11.7 - 18.6	13.8	11.7	13.1	DOWN	3
Japanese Yen	7.5 - 16.1	9.2 - 13.0	13.0	12.3	9.2	- -	5
S & P 500	10.2 - 16.7	10.2 - 15.1	15.1	12.0	10.4	- -	6
Silver	14.5 - 39.6	22.7 - 35.2	27.6	22.7	30.3	DOWN	2
Soybeans	10.5 - 34.4	13.4 - 34.4	25.7	21.8	23.9	- -	6
Sugar	23.0 - 44.5	26.7 - 43.1	31.8	26.7	30.4	DOWN	2
Swiss Franc	9.8 - 17.7	9.8 - 14.6	12.2	12.2	11.6	- -	5
Treasury Bond	8.0 - 12.9	8.4 - 12.9	12.9	11.0	12.5	- -	7

We track option volatility on a historical basis, and compare it to past levels. That way we can know whether volatility is relatively high or low.

Source: *Opportunities in Options* Newsletter.

1. **NEUTRAL OPTION POSITION**—*High-medium option volatilities/trading range market* (sell out-of-the-money put and out-of-the-money call in the same expiration month). The "Neutral Option Position" is best used in markets that have extremely high premium (by selling far out-of-the-money options), and trading range markets at any volatility level that have little likelihood of significant movement.
2. **FREE TRADE**—*Low option volatility trade/trending market* (buy close-to-the-money call or put, and if the market moves in the direction intended, later sell much further out-of-the-money call or put at the same price). The "free trade" is used in trending markets to purchase options of low to medium volatility that are close to the money (particularly on pullbacks or reactions against the trend), and further out-of-the-money options which can have much higher volatility levels are sold on rallies to complete the "free trade."
3. **RATIO OPTION SPREAD**—*Premium disparity between option strike prices, high volatility in out-of-the-money options/mildly*

Exhibit 3.25

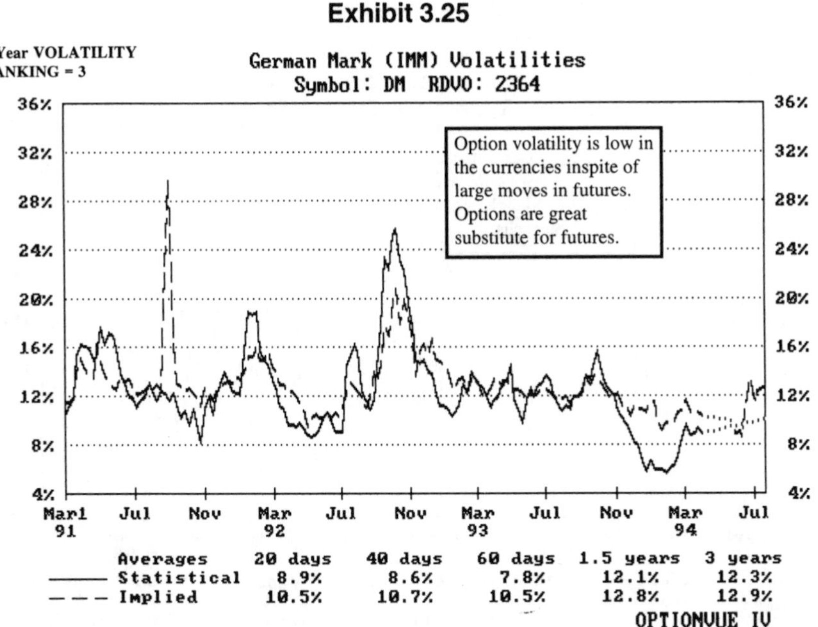

Option volatility charts can tell us important information about the underlying market and the best strategy to use.

Source: *Opportunities in Options* Volatility Chartbook.

trending market (buying close-to-the-money options and selling two or more further out-of-the-money options). The "ratio spread" is used when disparity in option premium exists. This generally occurs in extremely high volatility markets such as those that occur in silver and soybeans during rallies. In this case the close-to-the-money option is purchased and two or more further out-of-the-money options which can have up to twice as high option volatility levels are sold.

4. **CALENDAR OPTION SPREAD**—*Premium disparity between option months, high volatility in close-to-expiration options* (sell close-to-expiration month, buy deferred month in the same market). The "calendar option spread" is used to take advantage of disparities in volatility between different contract months of the same option. The trend is not as significant for this position as long as we feel the option we sell will probably not be "in-the-money" at expiration.

Exhibit 3.26

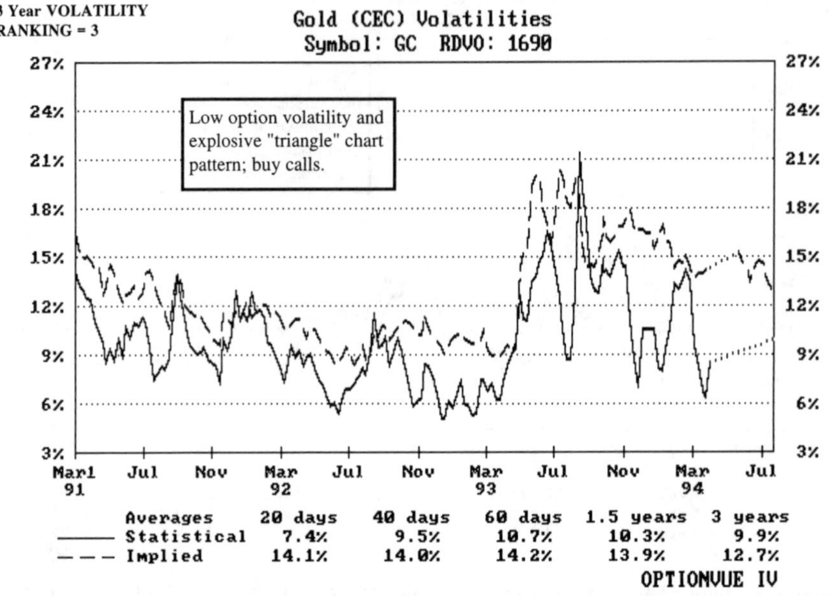

Exhibit 3.27

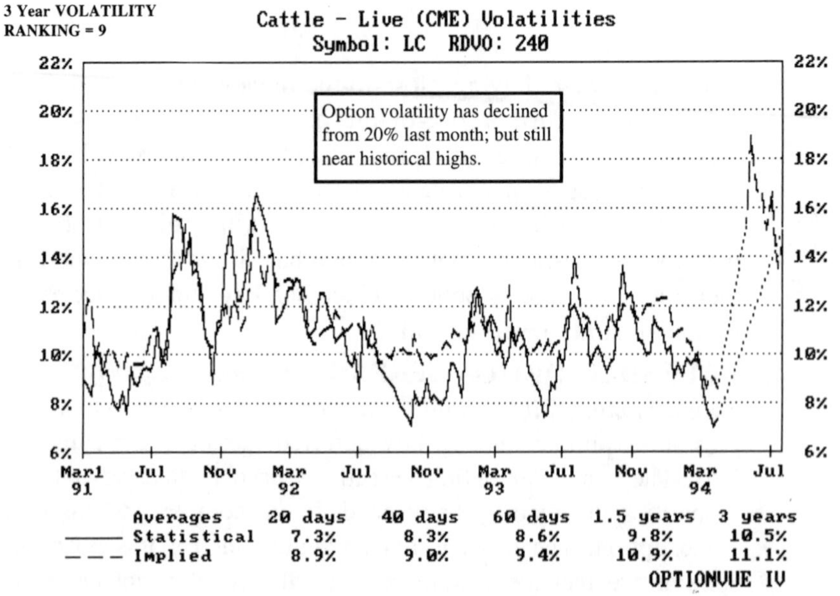

Exhibit 3.28

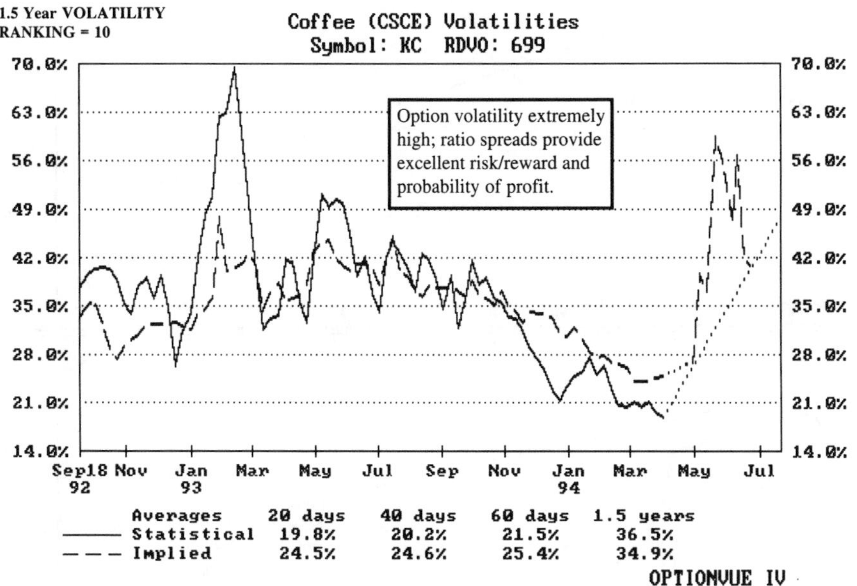

5. **IN-THE-MONEY DEBIT SPREAD**—*Premium disparity between strike prices/trending market* (buy in-the-money, or at-the-money option and sell further out-of-the-money option). The "in-the-money-debit spread" is initiated in volatile markets that are trending. Again, similar to the "ratio spread," the at-the-money option which is more fairly valued is purchased and the further out-of-the-money "overvalued" option is sold.
6. **NO-COST OPTION**—*Higher option volatility in out-of-the-money options/ take advantage of strong technical support and resistance levels* (buy near money option, sell out-of-money put and call). The "no cost option" allows us to purchase an option with the premium we receive from selling other option premium to pay for it.

That is it and that is all there is. You may want to use other positions yourself. You may want to invent complicated multi-legged positions, but we have found these to be the only consistently effective ones that can be practically used and provide a significant advantage.

There are three easy-to-use rules for using volatility:

Exhibit 3.29

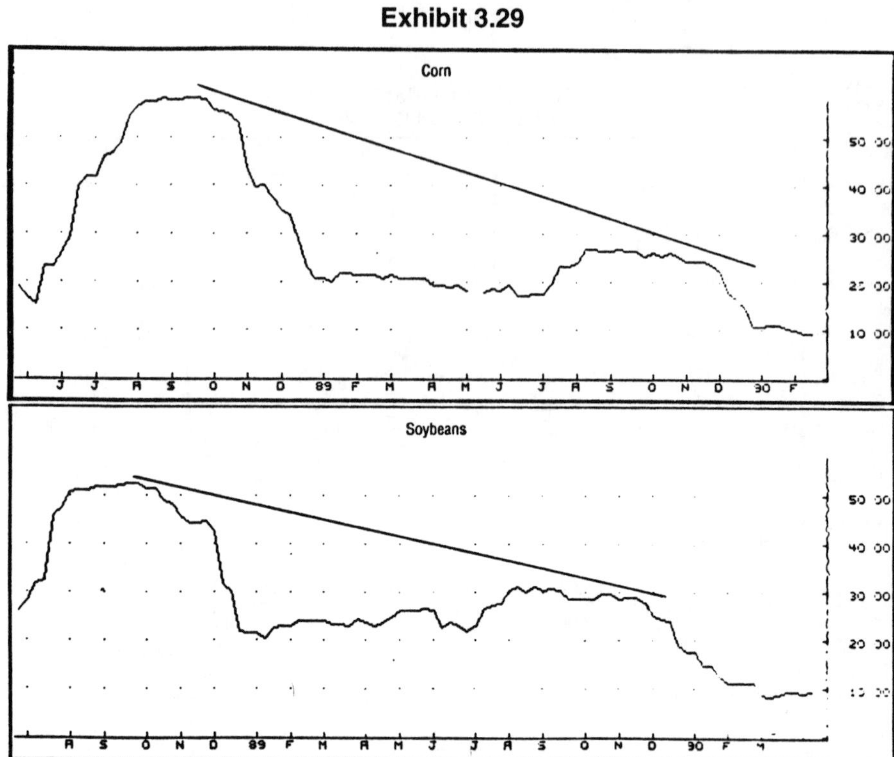

1. Low Volatility (but beginning to rise)
   Look for a trend change upon a breakout of the six-month trendline, and then purchase options (*free trades*) or initiate *synthetic futures positions*.
2. High Volatility (but beginning to decline)
   Expect a trading range market which will be excellent for *neutral option positions* because of high option premiums.
3. High Volatility (and market trend almost vertical)
   Look to initiate *ratio option spreads*, as out-of-the-money options will normally be extremely overpriced as compared to close-to-the-money options.

Knowing these factors of volatility can give you an overwhelming advantage in trading. Being able to sell overvalued, high-priced options that are near expiration can allow you to profit even with an incorrect view in the market. Similarly, being able to purchase low-priced options that will lose little if the market remains stable or moves slightly against you, gives

Exhibit 3.30

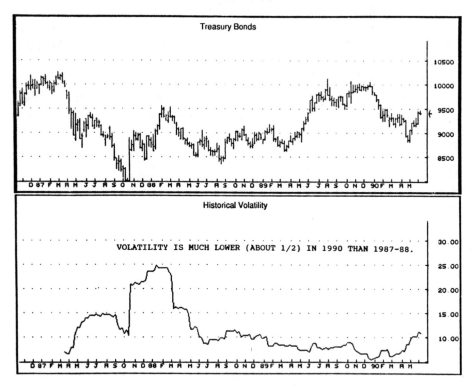

you great holding power. Consideration of these factors can be very important to a trader's pocketbook at the end of the year.

EXAMPLE OF USING OPTION VOLATILITY TO YOUR ADVANTAGE IN TRADING

I was contacted in May 1992 by a market commentator for a financial publication to discuss the effect the rise in crude oil had on option volatility. He expected me to tell him that option volatility had risen to very high levels.

In fact, although crude oil option volatility had risen over 30% in one day based on this market move, it was still almost 500% lower than previous readings (volatility was in the 18–20% range; during the Gulf War option volatility was as high as 100–130%).

This is where our newsletter's Volatility Composite Index chart becomes important (Exhibit 3.31). By looking at the six-month range and two-year range that we include in every issue, you can determine whether option volatility is at relatively high or low levels.

Where this market commentator was probably going to recommend that his readers sell crude oil options, by looking at our Volatility Composite Index we can see that option volatility was in fact at historical lows, and not at good levels for selling options.

Conversely, when we saw out-of-the-money soybean calls rise in May of 1992 to 30–40% volatility levels from half that level earlier, this helped us identify the potential for "ratio spreads."

Exhibit 3.31
Volatility Composite Index

	TWO-YEAR RANGE	*SIX-MONTH RANGE*	*MAY 30*	*MAR 30*	*APR 30*	*VOLA-TILITY TREND*	*RANKING 1 = LOW 10 = HIGH*
BRITISH POUND	9.1 – 16.7	9.1 – 15.7	9.9	12.5	9.1	DOWN	2
CATTLE	9.0 – 17.6	9.1 – 16.6	12.7	11.5	11.4	DOWN	3
CORN	14.5 – 48.3	14.5 – 28.6	28.6	16.5	17.6	UP	6
COPPER	11.8 – 41.8	11.8 – 34.2	23.6	11.8	11.9	UP	6
CRUDE OIL	18.9 – 98.2	18.9 – 34.8	18.9	22.8	22.3	DOWN	1
DEUTSCHE MARK	9.2 – 17.7	9.2 – 17.7	10.6	12.9	9.3	DOWN	2
EURODOLLAR	10.4 – 28.8	10.4 – 21.0	16.8	21.6	19.7	—	5
GOLD	8.9 – 34.3	8.9 – 14.2	8.9	11.3	10.8	DOWN	1
JAPANESE YEN	7.5 – 17.5	7.5 – 13.6	9.1	10.0	7.5	DOWN	3
S&P 500	13.8 – 33.8	13.8 – 31.8	13.8	15.0	14.5	DOWN	1
SILVER	14.5 – 46.4	14.5 – 22.4	14.5	20.6	16.5	DOWN	1
SOYBEANS	13.2 – 58.5	13.2 – 21.7	21.7	17.0	16.0	UP	5
SUGAR	22.7 – 44.2	24.2 – 44.2	34.8	27.0	44.2	UP	8
SWISS FRANC	10.0 – 18.8	10.0 – 16.8	11.3	12.8	16.0	DOWN	2
TREASURY BOND	7.4 – 12.4	7.4 – 10.3	10.0	9.5	8.7	DOWN	3

VOLATILITY COMMENTS FOR MAY—New six-month lows in volatility for crude oil, S&P 500, and the precious metals, and highs for the grains.

CHAPTER 4

Option Strategies

STRATEGIES TO GAIN A TRADING EDGE

Trading options is difficult to learn and even harder to learn to use properly. The advantages of option trading can provide an extra "trading edge," which in many cases can mean the difference between a successful trade and a losing situation. These advantages include:

1. *Limitation of risk* when purchasing options. This allows staying power, the ability to withstand any adverse market move without a margin call no matter how far the market may move against a trader's position. The option buyer can hold his position without being stopped out, or having the potential of unlimited losses, in anticipation of resumption of the market moving in his favor.
2. *The ability to sell* options and profit from the time decay of the option premium. This allows you to sell an out-of-the-money option, by predicting only where the market *isn't* going, and to profit if the market moves in the direction anticipated, stays neutral, or even moves slowly against you.

Option strategies can be designed by combining these two items. When two or more options are combined into a strategy, it is called an option spread. Option spreads can reduce the risk and raise the probability of profit on a trade. Option spread strategies may be used to take advantage of bull, bear, flat, or volatile markets. Spreads may vary from a simple vertical spread, with the purchase of a close-to-the-money option and the sale of a further out-of-the-money option, to complex arbitrage spreads which must be adjusted daily to remain "delta neutral."

When determining whether a spread strategy is appropriate, several factors must be present to cause you to go to the time and extra expense (commissions) to employ the spread:

1. *Limitation of risk.* Although risk is already limited by merely purchasing an option, you can further limit risk by employing an option spread strategy. For example, instead of purchasing a December gold 320 call for $2,000 (your risk of loss), purchase a December gold 320 call for $2,000 and sell the December 340 call for $1,000, thereby lowering your risk on this trade to $1,000 (Exhibit 4.1).
2. *Time decay.* The second reason to use option strategies is to be able to benefit from the time decay of the options sold. As noted earlier, many times options will lose value even if the market moves in their favor.
3. *Disparities in option premium levels.* Strategies are also employed to take advantage of disparities in option premiums which

Exhibit 4.1
A Bull Spread vs. Outright Call Buy

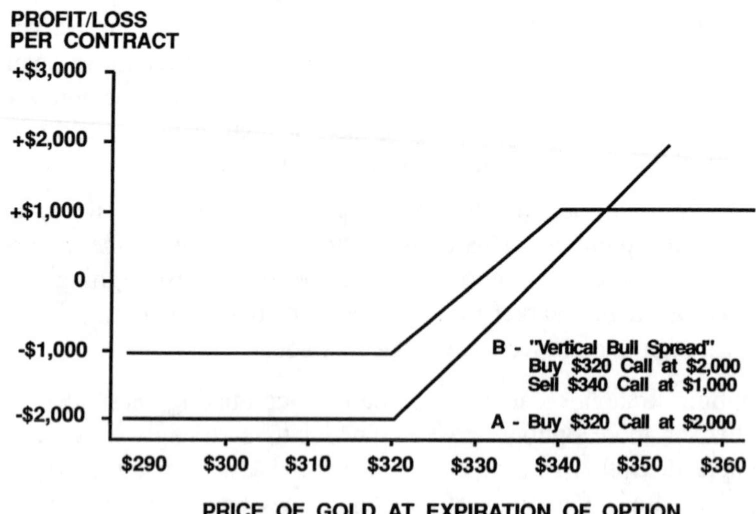

The 320–340 bull spread reduces the risk as well as the profit compared with an outright call buy.

occur from time to time. For example, during extended rallies or declines, out-of-the-money options can be overvalued, as the public usually wants to participate in these markets by obtaining great leverage, which can only be found in out-of-the-money options. This drives up the prices of these out-of-the-money options. Spreads formulated by selling these options can then be employed with high probabilities of profit. (These and other important benefits of option strategies are discussed in greater detail in Chapter 6.)

Exhibit 4.32, later in this chapter, provides a summary of the most common option strategies and their characteristics. The following positions are those that I use most of the time in my own actual trading that provide me with the most significant advantage ("trading edge"):

1. Free Trade (Option Purchase and Later Hedge)
2. Synthetic Futures Position
3. Ratio Spread
4. Neutral Option Position
5. Reverse Ratio Spreads
6. In-the-Money Debit Spread
7. Calendar Spread

To avoid unnecessary duplication in explaining these strategies, examples use "call" options only. Of course, all of these positions can also be initiated with puts. For example, in discussing a bullish call option ratio spread (buy a close-to-the-money call—sell two or more out-of-the-money calls) by substituting the word "put" for call, the position becomes a bearish put option ratio spread.

CHOOSING AND PURCHASING OPTIONS

Indiscriminate option purchasing is one of the biggest causes of losses in trading, since the odds are against the indiscriminate option purchaser because of the "time decay" principles. Therefore, a solid plan is necessary.

The reason most often given for using options (from books, advisors, brokers, and in fact, the Exchange's own pamphlets) is the limited risk factor in purchasing options. Do options truly provide limited risk to the investor? The answer is yes; however, this exists only for a limited period of time. (Options always expire at a definite time, and if "rolled" to a further expiration, a new premium cost must be paid.) This means not only can you lose money if you are incorrect in your market judgment, you can also lose money when your view of the market is correct. As discussed in

Chapter 1, there are many times when a trader who bought options lost money even though the market virtually exploded in his favor. Purchase of the wrong option or purchasing options at the wrong time will cause this type of loss. Again this is why the correlation of option traders winning or losing is exactly the same as with other traders. Perhaps the option buyers' only consolation seems to be with a degree of comfortableness in that they know, in advance, how much they are going to lose.

Three circumstances in which buying options is recommended include, when:

1. The option contains very little time value either by virtue of being close to expiration, and/or close-to-the-money (for short-term moves only).
2. The volatility (premium cost) of the option is at a relatively low level.
3. The trader feels that a substantial market move is imminent.

The trader must also make an appraisal of both the timing and the strength of the move. This does not have to be done with exactness; he must only determine whether a move will occur in a week, month, three months, six months, etc., and whether the move will be gradual, or sharp and immediate. This appraisal will greatly effect the month and strike price of the option recommended.

If the market were to make a sharp move, the nearest to expiration option will appreciate the quickest; but it will also lose its value the fastest unless this immediate move occurs.

Let's assume, for example, that in May 1995, with the bond market at 9200, we were considering the purchase of a Treasury Bond call option. The June contract has three days until expiration, the September contract three months until expiration, and the December contract six months until expiration.

If you purchased the June 94 call (approximately two points out-of-the-money), a move up of four points prior to expiration would cause this option to move from $250 to $2,000, a gain of 8 to 1, while the September and December options would merely double in value. (This can be determined by the use of computers—see Chapter 7.) If you had a very strong feeling that the market was going to move quickly, obviously the leverage and profits would be greatest in using the June options (Exhibit 4.2).

However, the amount of risk that one wants to take is another consideration in purchasing an option. Although the risk is always limited to the amount of premium that you pay for the option, and can be controlled even more by selling the option you buy prior to expiration, generally the closer-

Exhibit 4.2
Purchase Options

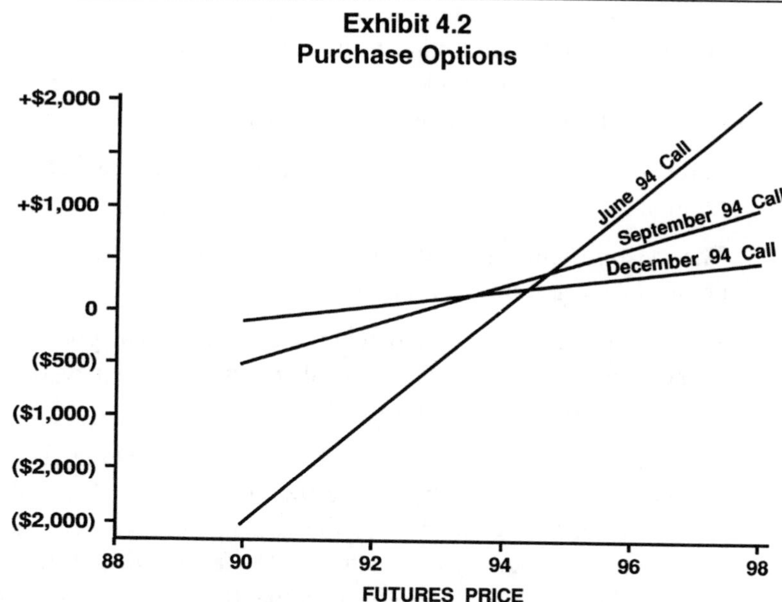

If the market makes a fast move higher, the close-to-expiration June option will gain the most.

to-the-money the option is, the more expensive it is, and the more risk it will have. That means that even though the June call discussed above has the potential for the longest quick gains, it will also lose value faster if the market fails to move.

Assume you decide to purchase an at-the-money bond call in June, September, and December, and one month later the market is unchanged; the June option will lose about $350, the September option will lose $250, and the December option will lose $100. However, if the market were to move up four points, the June option would gain almost $4,000 in value, the September option about $2,600 in value, and the December option about $2,000. On a move down of four points the June call would lose $500, the September call $350, and the December call $250.

How do you balance all of these conflicting factors of trying to keep risk low, while increasing leverage, and applying sound money management principles? The following specific rules can be used for purchasing options:

1. Never purchase an option with less than 60 days until expiration, unless you expect a very quick, sharp move. Never risk more than $500 per option on this type of purchase, and most important,

have a plan of either taking profits on the option at a pre-set level or selling a higher-up option to turn this into a "free trade." (We will discuss the "free trade" in the next section.) This is to make certain that you do not watch your profits "waste away."

2. Purchase options having between three and six months before expiration.
3. The most difficult factor is determining which strike price to purchase. Two rules are important here:
   a. Never purchase an option more than three strike prices from the money. This is because further out-of-the-money options are unlikely to become profitable.
   b. Look at the risk-reward of purchasing various options. For example, in deciding between the 92 and 94 September call, by comparing the actual cost of the two options, you can determine that it would cost an extra $1,000 for the 92 call, for only an additional $2,000 profit potential (a 2 to 1 risk-reward). However, in deciding between the 94 or 96 September call, there is only a $500 difference between these two calls and therefore a 4 to 1 risk-reward. Use 4 to 1 as your break-point in determining which option to purchase; if the risk-reward is higher than 4 to 1, purchase the closer-to-the-money option; at 4 to 1 or less, purchase the farther-away-from-the-money option.

This principle not only provides for sound money management, but also improves your risk-reward ratio, and allows the purchase of the most fairly valued option. Many times, as in the treasury bond example above, the choice of options to purchase is a very close one, and, in fact, either could be correct. At other times, one option can cost only $25 or $50 more and give you an additional $2,000 or more profit potential. Clearly, in that case, the higher priced option is the correct one to purchase.

PROFIT OBJECTIVES IN OPTION TRADES

An often overlooked subject, when purchasing an option, is that of the profit objective of the trade. Without a plan, a trader can watch an option quickly run up in value only to soon see his profit and even the entire premium value of the option disappear. By using the following rules for sound money management, this is less likely to occur:

1. When purchasing an option for a short-term move, sell half of your position if the price of the option doubles. This allows for both flexibility and protection. Many times markets will have a pullback or a consolidation. During these times, the price of the option you purchased, especially one that has a short time to expiration, will plunge rapidly (See Exhibit 4.3). By taking partial profits you not only protect yourself against this type of loss, but are also in a position to purchase additional options on a pullback without increasing your risk. During the two weeks prior to an options expiration, severe moves can produce unbelievable returns in short periods of time. For example, options on Treasury Bonds can be purchased for leverage of over 6,000 to 1, providing returns of 1,000% or more in less than two weeks. There have been cases where a low-priced option has risen over $1,000 during a single day and where bond options rose 10 times in value within two weeks prior to expiration (See Exhibit 4.4).

   These examples are exciting—but, of course, it's not as easy as it looks. The three hardest parts of this trade are knowing when to use it, which option to use, and how to determine when to take profits and losses.

   First, let's look at when a short-term option trade should be initiated. When a trader buys an option in the last several weeks of trading just because it is very low priced and provides substantial leverage, it is almost certain to lead to losses. Your trading plan should allow you to only trade with the trend of the market, and then to only initiate trades on a pullback against that trend to obtain the most favorable entry point. If this opportunity falls within the last two weeks of trading and you feel an immediate move will occur, then you can initiate action to buy the appropriate option. Although purchasing options two or three strike prices out-of-the-money cheaply may seem attractive, unless the market makes a large move, these options will not gain much in value.

   The best option to purchase for short-term moves is the option that is at-the-money or just out-of-the-money by one strike price. These options have a higher probability of profit by being more likely to gain in value if the market moves in your favor.

   Since purchasing short-term options is very speculative and volatile, take profits on half of your position if the options double in value, thereby giving you a "free trade" for the balance of the options. On the rest, there are no set rules, but let the markets

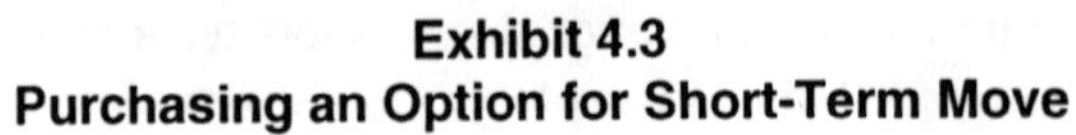

Exhibit 4.3
Purchasing an Option for Short-Term Move

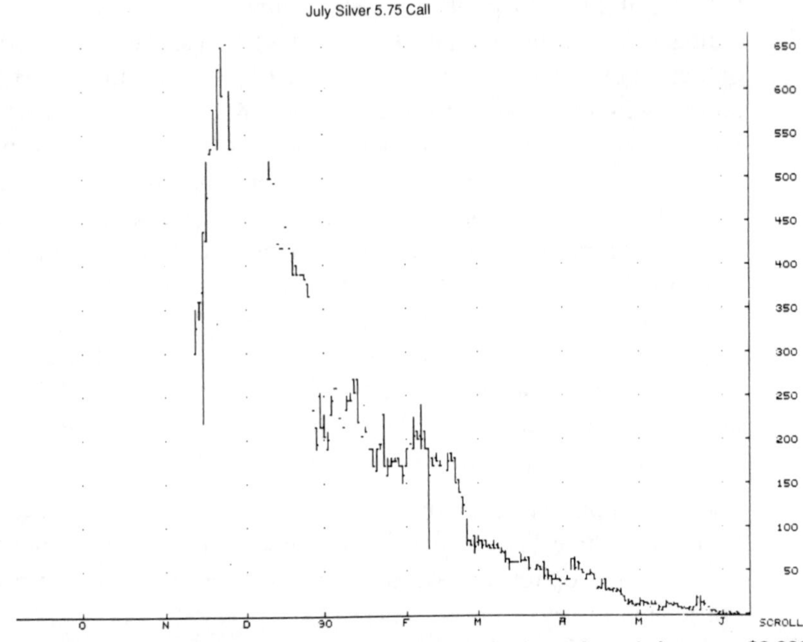

We watched this call (July 575 silver call) that we had purchased rise over $3,000 per option, only to plummet eventually to $0. (Fortunately, we followed our plan of taking profits on some of the position as the market rose and turning others into free trades to protect profits and capital.)

"tell you" when to take profits. Since option prices quite often spike up during big rallies or declines, always be on alert during these spikes to gain a favorable exit price.

2. There are two rules for taking profits with a longer-term option purchase:

   a. If the option purchased goes into the money by more than two strike prices, take profits. This is both for money management reasons, and because the option then becomes illiquid and difficult to trade. Additionally, at that point, usually so much premium is built up in the option, it is cheaper (from a margin standpoint) to take a futures position.

   b. Pick the strike price which corresponds with the resistance on the futures contract, and put an order in to sell an option at the same price for which you purchased your original option (to

Exhibit 4.4
Severe Moves Increase Premiums

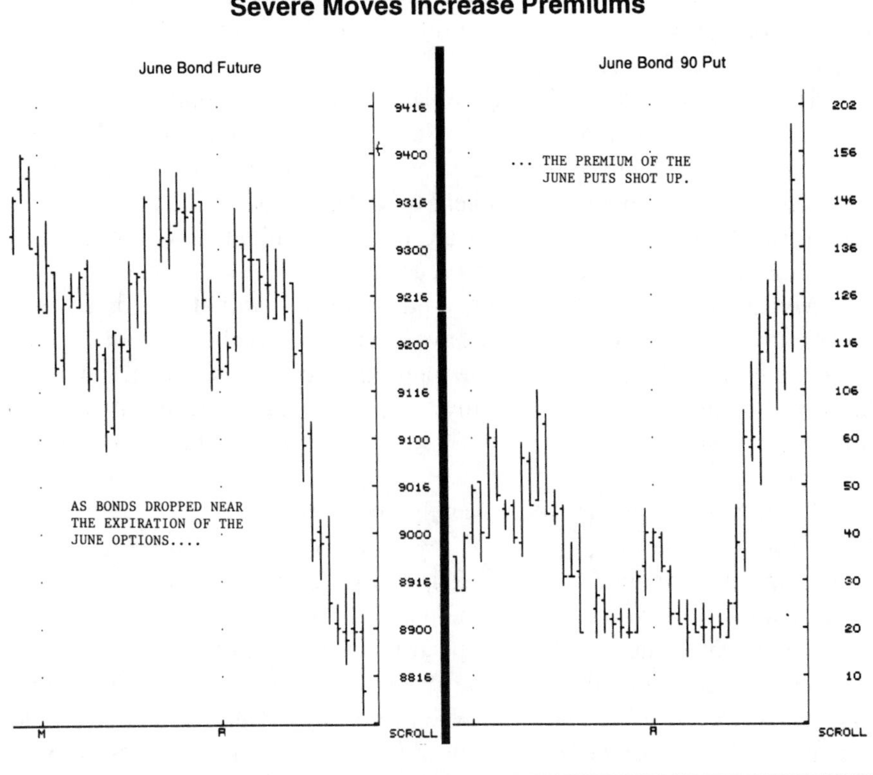

turn the trade into a "free trade"). Doing this both increases your probability of profit and risk-reward ratio, and allows you to put on additional positions on a pullback. This will be discussed in detail in the next section.

SELECTING THE BEST OPTION TO PURCHASE BY ANALYZING YOUR VIEW OF THE MARKET

Some traders decide which option is the best one to purchase based on either the amount of money available in their trading account or their broker's recommendation. Obviously, neither of these are excellent methods for making this decision.

I recently had the occasion to do work on these principles when I decided to purchase silver call options. It was an easy decision to eliminate all but four options from consideration (the July silver 4.25 and 4.50 call, and the September silver 4.75 and 5.00 calls). This was because in-the-money options provided little leverage, further out-of-the-money options were too speculative, requiring the market to make an extremely large move before providing significant profits, and far from expiration option months were too illiquid to trade.

However, after several hours of analysis, I could find no reason to favor any of these four options over the other. They were all well priced, and provided excellent risk/reward. This prompted me to do a computer study of how these options would behave under various price and volatility changes in the future. The results were not only enlightening, but allowed me to fine tune my option selection process.

My first choice before doing computer analysis would have been September silver $5 call which could have been purchased for about 8 cents ($400). I based this on both the low premium cost and the fact that I felt that even if the market moved to my "stop out" point, I would be able to hold this option for several weeks at a loss of not more than 3 cents ($150) per option.

What was distressing to me was that if the market moved up 30 cents during this time period (a move of 8% of the contract value) this option would only gain about 5 cents ($250), really not much of a reward for a fairly significant move in a short time period.

On the opposite end of the spectrum was the July silver 4.25 call. This option would initially cost about $600 (50% more than the September $5 call). However, if the market moved to my stop point, this option would lose almost four times as much as the March $6 call, losing two-thirds of its value or $400, in a three-week period. On the bright side, this option would gain 15 cents ($750) on a 30 cent move up. In comparing these four options the general principles I found were the following:

1. Closer to expiration options will appreciate faster if the market moves in your favor; however, because of their time decay, they will lose much faster if the market remains stable or moves against you;
2. Deferred month options will hold their value well in adverse conditions, but will not appreciate as rapidly (unless a major move occurs);
3. Close-to-the-money options cost more; however, they have a better chance to profit in normal market moves;
4. Further from-the-money options provide greater leverage, but require a larger move to profit.

What this all means, is that you must not only analyze market direction, but also have a general idea on market timing and velocity of the move. If you feel the market is likely to make a major move within a short time period, the best option to purchase would be close to expiration options. Conversely, if you feel the market is going to make a slow move up over a long period of time, select deferred month options. In major market moves, larger quantities of out-of-the-money options are a better choice; while in most normal moves, closer-to-the-money options should be selected.

HOW TO DETERMINE WHAT THE BEST OPTION POSITION IS FOR TRENDING MARKETS

Why do we recommend "free trades" in some trending markets, and "synthetic positions" or "in-the-money debit spreads" in others? For example, earlier in 1994 we were recommending "in-the-money debit spreads" in the corn and soybean markets; but later we switched to option purchases ("free trades").

There are three factors to consider when determining which position is the best: the aggressiveness of the position; the technical pattern of the market; and option volatility levels. While these positions all have different characteristics and advantages, they all have an important place in a trader's portfolio at the proper time. (While we have discussed these positions in detail in both of our books *The Option Advantage* and *The Option Secret,* the following should help you determine which of these positions is the best for a particular market or situation.

In the beginning stages of a market trend, we often recommend "free trades." In this case, option premium is normally low and the potential for an explosive market move high; so there is no reason to limit our profit by selling an out-of-the-money option. We also do not want to take the chance of using the more aggressive "synthetic option position" because the market is unproven and could cause a larger loss, if the market then turns around and heads against us. Our objective in the "free trade" is to sell a further out-of-the-money option to entirely pay the original premium cost of the option purchased after the market moves as we predicted. (If it doesn't, although your risk is limited to the premium plus commissions and fees, we recommend setting stricter limits.)

The more aggressive positions of the "synthetic option position" are used after a market's trend is formed and the market is resting above heavy support levels (bullish markets) or below resistance levels (bearish markets). In this case we will sell options beyond those support or resistance levels that are not likely to be breached, to pay most or all of the costs of the options that we have purchased. This option sale provides protection for the option purchases if the market does not make an explosive move, but merely stays within the existing range, making small moves in either direction; and also additional profits if the market moves as we expected.

In this position, our follow up procedure is similar to the "free trade" in that our option purchase is hedged by the sale of a further out-of-the-money option if the market moves in our favor, and the short option we had originally sold is repurchased and profits taken.

The "in-the-money debit spread" is initiated by purchasing an in-the-money option and selling a more overvalued out-of-the-money option. It is best used in more mature stages of a trending market or where premium for out-of-the-money options has begun to expand. In this case, although profits are limited, we are protecting ourselves from the potential consolidation of this more mature market by receiving the time decay for the out-of-the-money option.

The "ratio spread," is one of our favorite option positions. It is a position that when initiated at the proper time has a large range of profitability, as well as high probability of profit. This position is similar to the "debit spread" described above, except multiple further out-of-the-money options are sold. This position is recommended after explosive moves have occurred and the option premium for far out-of-the-money options is 50 to 150% higher than the at-the-money options. We recommend only initiating these positions at a credit, and closing them out if the price of the underlying market approaches the strike price of the options sold.

As you can see, these strategies have significant differences among them, both in the technical pattern of the market and the aggressiveness of the position. However, they all have an important place in a trader's portfolio at the proper time.

THE MOST OVERLOOKED OPTION BUYING STRATEGIES

Or Don't Trade Another Future until You Read This!

1. THE IN-THE-MONEY DEBIT SPREAD

The "in-the-money debit spread" consists of purchasing an in-the-money option and selling an out-of-the-money option of the same expiration month. It is a position that requires that we pay a premium—the cost difference between the option we purchase and the option we sell—in exchange for the potential for receiving the difference between the two strike prices.

For example, currently the September S&P is trading at 455. A trader who is bearish on the S&P 500 could purchase the September 465 put for 1,300 points ($6,500) and sell the 445 put for 500 points ($2,500) for a net cost or debit of $4,000. The potential profit on this position is the difference between these two strike prices: 465 minus 445 2,000 points ($10,000).

As uninspired as this position may seem, it actually has substantial benefits over a short futures position including:

1. Lower cost
2. Limitation of risk
3. Ability to take advantage of premium disparity

As we described above, the cost or debit of the September S&P in-the-money debit spread is $4,000. However, the exchange minimum margin for initiating a short futures position is almost three times higher at over $11,000. This allows a trader to commit less of his capital to any one trade.

The second, and probably more important advantage, is limitation of risk. While a short futures position burdens the trader with unlimited risk, the risk of the "in-the-money debit spread" is absolutely limited to the amount paid for the spread plus commissions and transaction fees. This can be more of a substantial benefit than most traders realize. Even though many traders feel that their risk when trading futures they can limit by the use of "stops," what is not taken into account is that many times the futures traders can be "stopped out" because of the risk of taking a large loss in a market that has begun to make a big move against this position, only to then later see the market reverse and move in their favor. With the "in-the-money debit spread" the trader knows that not only is his risk limited, but actually he is hedging some of his losses by the gains on the option he sold.

These factors can be very important, especially to a trader whose ability to predict market direction is good; however, who is emotionally and financially unable to handle the normal market "noise" of corrections even when the market is trending in his favor. This psychological advantage of knowing that your losses are absolutely limited can make the difference between a winning or losing trade.

The third advantage of this position is being able to take advantage of disparity in option premium. In the debit spread described above, the volatility of the 465 put was 10% and the 445 put 13%. This means that we were selling an option that was trading at a volatility of 30% higher than the option we were purchasing, providing another significant benefit for the trader.

The advantages of this position seems so overwhelming that one wonders why anyone would trade futures. There are several disadvantages that should be considered by all traders before they initiate this position. The

Exhibit 4.5
Option Action Chart

Market Direction	Option Volatility	Strategy	Advantages	Disad-vantages
UP	LOW-AVERAGE	BUY CALL (to initiate Free Trade)	Profit/loss ration usually exceeds 10–1; no margin required or loss potential when free trade is completed.	Premium decay of "Time Value."
UP	AVERAGE-HIGH	SELL PUT	Can profit if market moves sideways, higher, or even slightly lower. Allows us to buy commodity at lower price. (Not recommended strategy except to complete "Free Trade".)	Unlimited loss potential.
UP	HIGH	RATIO-SPREAD (BUY CALL-SELL 2 OR MORE HIGHER CALLS)	No loss if market remains stable or moves against you.	Can lose if market continues to move substantially higher
UP	AVERAGE	IN-THE-MONEY DEBIT-CALL SPREAD	No margin; can take advantage of market trend, time decay, and price disparities of options.	Loss occurs if market moves opposite of predicted direction.
SIDEWAYS-NEUTRAL	AVERAGE-HIGH	NEUTRAL OPTION POSITION	Only strategy that can profit in flat or choppy markets; can be successful without having to determine market direction; has high probability of profit; decay of time value for both options works in your favor.	Limited profit but unlimited loss potential.

Exhibit 4.5 (Continued)

Market Direction	Option Volatility	Strategy	Advantages	Disad-vantages
SIDEWAYS-NEUTRAL	AVERAGE	REVERSE RATIO SPREAD	Can be successful without having to determine market direction.	Loss occurs unless market moves in either direction.
DOWN	LOW-AVERAGE	BUY PUT (to initiate Free Trade)	Profit/loss ratio usually exceeds 10–1; no margin required or loss potential when free trade is completed.	Premium decay of "Time Value."
DOWN	AVERAGE-HIGH	SELL CALL	Can profit if market moves sideways, lower, or even slightly higher (not a recommended strategy except to complete "Free Trade").	Limited profit but unlimited loss potential.
DOWN	HIGH	RATIO SPREAD BUY PUT SELL 2 OR MORE LOWER PUTS	No loss if market remains stable or moves against you.	Can lose if market continues to move substantially lower.
DOWN	AVERAGE	IN-THE-MONEY DEBIT-PUT SPREAD	No margin; can take advantage of market trend, time decay, and price disparities of options.	Loss occurs if market moves opposite of predicted direction.

Exhibit 4.6
Options Trading Fact Sheet

OPTION	EX-CHANGE	TICK VALUE	TRADING MONTHS	TRADING HOURS (CST)	LAST TRADING DAY (Subject to Change)
FINANCIAL					
TREAS-URY BONDS	CBT	01 = $15.63	ALL	7:20–2:00 5:00–8:30	Friday (12:00 CST) which precedes contract month by at least 6 business days
TREAS-URY NOTES	CBT	01 = $15.63	ALL	7:20–2:00 5:00–8:30	Friday (12:00 CST) which precedes contract month by at least 6 business days
EURODOL-LAR	IMM	01 = $25.00	ALL	7:20–2:00	First Monday preceding third Wednesday of contract month
S&P 500	CME	05 = $25.00	ALL	8:30–3:15	Third Thursday of contract month (Quarterly) Third Friday of contract month (Serial)
NYFE	NYFE	05 = $25.00	ALL	8:30–3:15	Third Thursday of contract month (Quarterly) Third Friday of contract month (Serial)
NIKKEI	CME	05 = $25.00	ALL	8:00–3:15	Second Friday of contract month (Quarterly) Friday preceding third Saturday of contract month (Serial)
TOPIX	CBT	1/100 = ¥2,000	H, M, U, Z	7:00–2:00 5:40–8:15	Second Thursday of month
JAPANESE GOVT BONDS	CBT	1/2pt = ¥2,500	H, M, U, Z	7:00–2:00 5:40–8:15	Friday (12:00 CST) of month preceding contract month by at least 6 business days
METALS, CURRENCIES, AND OILS					
COPPER	CMX	05 = $12.00	ALL	8:25–1:00	Second Friday of month preceding contract month
GOLD	CMX	01 = $10.00	ALL	7:20–1:30	Second Friday of month preceding contract month
SILVER	CMX	01 = $5.00	ALL	7:25–1:25	Second Friday of month preceding contract month
PLATINUM	NYMEX	05 = $5.00	ALL	7:00–1:30	Friday preceding first Saturday of contract month
SWISS FRANC DEUTSCHE MARK BRITISH POUND JAPANESE YEN	IMM	01 = $12.50	ALL	7:20–2:00 5:00–8:30	Second Friday preceding third Thursday of contract month

Exhibit 4.6 (Continued)

OPTION	EX-CHANGE	TICK VALUE	TRADING MONTHS	TRADING HOURS (CST)	LAST TRADING DAY (Subject to Change)
CANADIAN DOLLAR	IMM	01 = $10.00	ALL	7:20–2:00	Second Friday preceding third Thursday of contract month
U.S. DOLLAR INDEX	NYCE	01 = $25.00	ALL	7:20–2:00	Second Friday preceding third Wednesday of contract month
CRUDE OIL HEATING OIL UNLEADED GAS	NYMEX	01 = $10.00	ALL	8:45–2:10	Second Friday of month preceding contract month
AGRICULTURE AND LIVESTOCK					
SUGAR	CSC	01 = $1.20	ALL	9:00–12:43	Second Friday of month preceding contract month
ORANGE JUICE	NYCE	01 = $1.50	ALL	9:15–1:45	First Friday of month preceding contract month
COTTON	NYCE	01 = $5.00	H, K, N, V, Z	8:30–2:00	First Friday of month preceding contract month
COCOA	CSC	01 = $10.00	H, K, N, U, Z	8:30–1:15	First Friday of month preceding contract month
COFFEE	CSC	01 = $3.75	H, K, N, U, Z	8:15–12:50	First Friday of month preceding contract month
WHEAT (HARD, RED, WINTER)	KC	1/8 = $6.25	H, K, N, U, Z	8:30–1:15	Friday which precedes contract month by at least 10 business days
CORN	CBT	1/8 = $6.25	H, K, N, U, Z	8:30–1:15	Friday (12:00 CST) preceding contract month by 6 business days
SOYBEANS	CBT	1/8 = $6.25	F, H, K, N, Q, U, X	8:30–1:15	Friday (12:00 CST) preceding contract month by 6 business days
LIVE CATTLE	CME	2.5 = $10.00	ALL	8:45–1:00	First Friday of contract month
FEEDER CATTLE	CME	2.5 = $10.00	F, H, J, K, Q, U, V, X	8:45–1:00	First Friday of contract month
LIVE HOGS	CME	2.5 = $7.50	ALL	9:10–1:00	First Friday of contract month
PORK BELLIES	CME	01 = $2.50	G, H, K, N, Q	9:10–1:00	Friday which precedes contract month by at least 3 business days

first is that since we are initiating a spread of two positions instead of one there is an extra commission for each trade. Second, orders should always be placed at a specific limit price to avoid slippage that can occur with less liquid options. Third, profit on a "Debit Spread" is limited, as opposed to the unlimited profit potential of futures positions. However, we feel that these disadvantages are a small price to pay for the benefits that accrue from this type of position, that could make the difference between a profitable or unprofitable trade.

2. OPTION STRADDLE PURCHASE

This strategy is also a greatly overlooked "nondirectional" option strategy. The "option purchase straddle" is a purchase of a put and a call of the same month and underlying market. In this strategy, we recommend as in all option purchasing strategies, that at-the-money or close-to-the-money options be used. Similar to the "in-the-money debit spread," risk is absolutely limited to the premium paid for the options, plus commissions and transaction fees. However, not only is the potential profit unlimited, but we can also profit by a move in either direction. This is why we call it a "nondirectional" option strategy—we don't care which way the market moves, as long as it moves.

Since this strategy will only be unsuccessful if the market does not make a significant move in either direction, we limit the times we recommend initiating this position to the following:

1. Before important reports, meetings, and other releases of information that could substantially affect the market in either direction;
2. When option volatility (premium cost) is low; or
3. When the market's technical pattern suggests that a large breakout is imminent.

This strategy was successfully initiated in July 1994 when a Deutsche Mark straddle was recommended just prior to the G-7 meetings. We expected these meetings to have a severe impact on the market, either by action or disappointment from nonaction. Further, the option volatility in the D-Mark was near historically low levels in spite of large daily moves that were occurring in the underlying future market. This strategy was immediately successful as the D-Mark jumped almost 200 points the day after the meetings concluded, allowing traders who initiated this position to turn their call purchases into "free trades." In fact, since the market began to turn around right after this jump, the puts began to gain significantly in value, and on a continued move down, traders were in a position to turn the puts into a "free trades" also. This is the ultimate of all positions, to have "free trades" in both directions, and be able to profit without having to pick market direction!

This position is also highly recommended when the market has moved itself into a explosive chart pattern. Our favorite type of chart pattern for this position is the "triangle" pattern, where the market has made lower highs and higher lows over an extended period of time. The market then "coils" itself into a tighter and tighter trading range from which a large breakout always occurs (as we discussed in our *Gold Market Comments*). However, the problem is in guessing which way this move will happen. The option straddle removes this question, allowing the trader to profit by a large move in either direction. Further, this is normally an opportune time to purchase options as volatility often moves to very low levels as the market "quiets down" and moves into this trading range. Then, after the breakout, not only does the option gain from the price movement, but volatility can increase substantially (coffee option volatility moved from 20% to over 100% on the breakout), thereby also further increasing the value of the options that you purchase.

We have found that these two positions are not only the most overlooked option purchasing opportunities, but they are two strategies that can provide the trader with significant advantages in the right circumstances—a substantial "trading edge" over the markets.

THE MOST OVERLOOKED OPTION SELLING STRATEGIES

We have often discussed the benefits of the Neutral Option Position (which is our favorite option strategy for choppy, flat, or nontrending markets) and the "ratio option spread," which is our favorite option strategy, when out-of-the-money option premium is extremely overpriced (which we often find in severely trending bull markets, or when weather scares occur in the grains during the summer months). However, two positions that have great benefits in many diverse situations, "covered call writing" and "calendar spreads" are often overlooked by most traders. These overlooked strategies can provide a trader with some overwhelming advantages when used in the right circumstances.

1. COVER CALL WRITING—ADDITIONAL INCOME ON EVERY TRADE

This strategy is one of the best methods of increasing your returns without any additional risk, margin, or capital necessary. This strategy is initiated by selling an out-of-the-money option against a long futures position. For example, a trader purchases silver futures contracts at $5 and at the same time sells $6.50 calls for $500 each. There is no additional cost or margin for this position (except commissions and fees) since the calls you sell are "covered" by the long futures contract. Thereafter, the market can react in four ways:

1. It can move lower;
2. It can remain stable;
3. It can move higher, but remain below $6.50;
4. It can move above $6.50 (an increase of 30%).

In the first three instances the net effect of initiating the covered call would be to add $500 to our account to either lower our losses in situation 1, or increase our profits in situations 2 and 3. However, even in situation 4, which is the only scenario that writing a call would be detrimental to us, the only loss here is that of limitation of potential profits above the $6.50 price. Our initial profits of $7,500 in a futures contract plus the $500 we received for selling the option would be ours to keep; we would just receive no additional profits if silver futures really took off and continued to move substantially above $6.50.

However, there are several ways to even lessen the impact of this situation. First of all, the likelihood of this happening (a move over 30% before the option expires) is very rare, occurring less than 5% of the time. Secondly, the consequences of this occurring are not "account threatening," as a substantial profit has already been made on this trade; third, an astute trader can decide to close out the "covered call" at any time when he sees the market beginning to make a large move. In doing this, the trader is back in the same situation he was originally of a long futures position with the potential of unlimited profits.

All in all, this is a strategy that has an extremely high probability of success with little risk and no additional capital necessary. All traders should initiate this strategy in almost every case of purchasing (or selling) a futures or stock position.

There is also variation of "covered writing" that can provide the trader with a more aggressive position, and additional profits in a trending market situation. In this case, after purchasing the silver futures contract with silver at $5, you also purchase a $5 silver call and sell two 650 silver calls at even money. Our existing position now would be long one silver futures contract at $5, long one silver $5 call, and short two silver 650 calls. In this situation, our maximum profit level would be $15,000 if December silver expired at the 650 level, instead of the $7,500 that we would make alone if we had only purchased the silver futures contract without the aggressive option strategy. In fact, silver would have to go all the way from $5 to $8, a move of over 60% for us to make as much money with the silver futures alone as we had made with the aggressive option strategy. In fact, only above $8 does this strategy become detrimental to us, as profits will be limited above this level.

In summary, with this aggressive option strategy, the scenario is as follows:

1. If silver were to move under $5 there would be no detriment from this strategy (except for extra commissions, fees, and premium debit, if any);
2. If silver were to move above $5, all the way up to $6.50, our profits would be double what we would make with a futures contract alone;
3. There would be additional profits for traders while silver was between $6.50 up to $8 above those that would be made on a silver futures contract alone; and
4. Only above $8 would profits be limited (however, we would have now made $15,000 for each position).

2. CALENDAR OPTION STRATEGY—TAKE ADVANTAGE OF DISPARITIES IN FUTURES AND OPTIONS

The "calendar option spread" is initiated by purchasing a deferred month option and selling a closer to expiration option. The initial advantage of this position is taking advantage of the steep time decay that close to expiration, out-of-the-money options undergo. This in itself is enough to bring a substantial advantage to a trader. However, in addition, there are two other situations when this trade turns the odds overwhelmingly in favor of the option strategist. The first situation is when option volatility for the closer to expiration months is trading at substantially higher levels than the deferred contract. This often happens in volatile markets as there is an increased demand for these "more active" options for speculation and hedging. Often, we find that the deferred month options are "forgotten" and trading at volatility levels of 50% or more lower than the active front month contract. Examples of this occurred earlier in 1994 in the cocoa and coffee option markets when they began to breakout; in the grains during the rally attempt at the beginning of the summer where the front month options were 20–30% higher in premium; in live cattle in May and June after cattle had experienced a severe decline of 1,000 points in two months, option volatility in the August contract rose up to 24% for the out-of-the-money options while the deferred month December contract was trading at 15%, almost 40% lower.

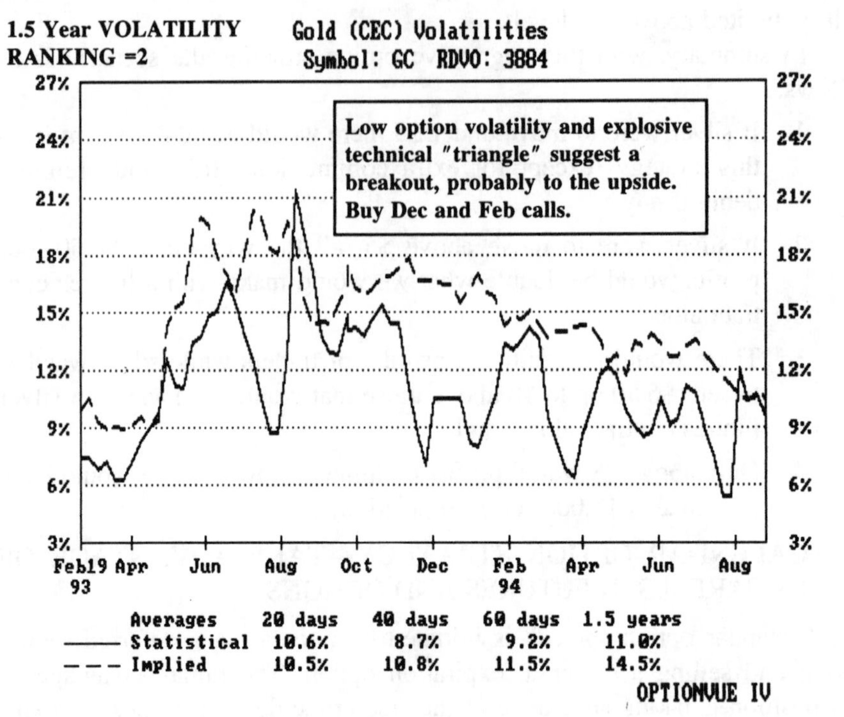

However, one of the best instances of the benefits of this strategy occurred in August in the live hog option market. In that market, the spread between February and October live hogs had moved from February being 100 over October in the beginning of June to February being more than 150 under October in July. Our research had shown that this did not happen often and many times this disparity in the futures contracts was quickly corrected. Additionally, because of the volatility in the live hog market, the February calls were 20% less expensive than the October calls. Therefore, we recommended an excellent calendar spread of purchasing in-the-money February call options, while selling out-of-the-money October options that were close to expiration and entering the period of their most severe time decay. Additionally, the February contract corrected in late August moved back towards parity with the October, thereby further increasing the value of the February calls in relation to the October. This trade combined the best of all worlds of the calendar spread, allowing:

1. The trader to take advantage of the undervaluation of the deferred month futures contract;

Exhibit 4.8

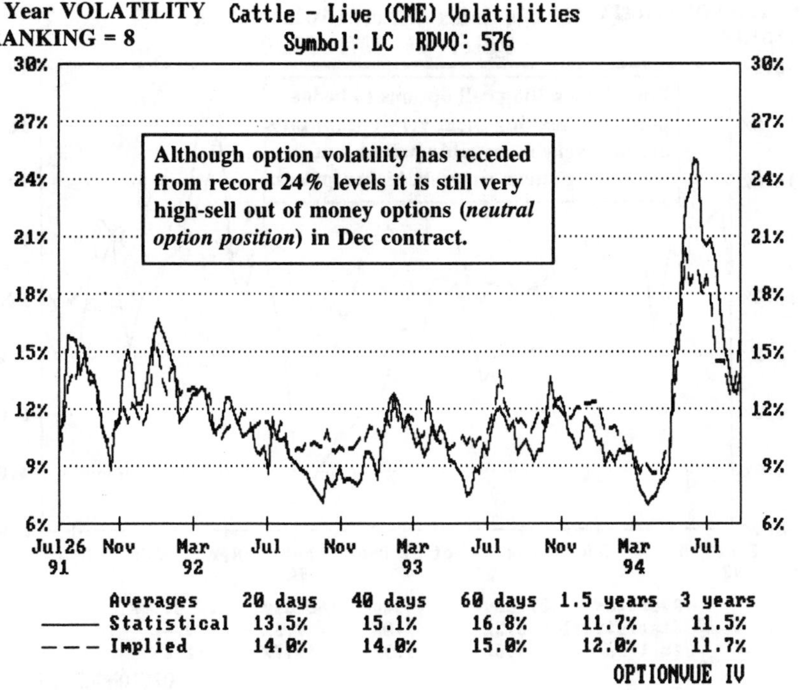

2. The overpricing of the close to expiration option; and
3. The rapid time decay of the close to expiration options.

THE FREE TRADE

The "free trade" is an option position that, when completed, is more commonly known as a vertical spread (bull or bear spread) (Exhibits 4.11, 4.12). In a vertical spread, both options are bought and sold at the same time. In the "free trade," first an option is purchased, and then at a later time, the out-of-the-money option is sold. This change makes a major difference in the risk-reward ratio for this position.

I do not usually recommend vertical spreads since I require that any trade initiated have a 10–1 risk-reward ratio and/or a 75% probability of profit. Most vertical spreads have no better than a 50% probability of profit and a 3–1 risk-reward (unless you sell an option that is almost worthless—which defeats your purpose of doing this position).

Exhibit 4.9

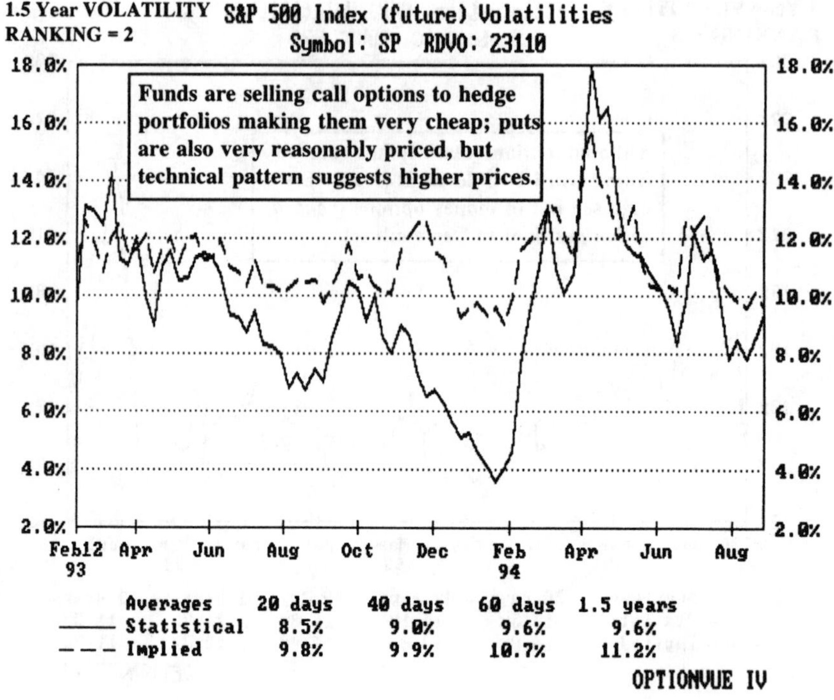

For example, being bullish the bonds, in May 1990, I purchased the September 94 call at 42 points ($656). I assigned a risk level of $300 to this position. (I would close it out if the option declined to 23 points or $359.) My objective was to sell a September bond 100 call on a rally, also at 42 points for a profit objective of $6,000. This would provide a risk-reward ratio of 300/6,000 or 20–1.

If I had considered a bull spread instead at that time, I could have purchased the 94 call and sold the 96 call for about 32 points ($500). This would have given me a risk-reward of only 500/2,000 or 4–1.

Another benefit of the "free trade" is that after it is completed there is no margin, or capital, necessary or potential loss. This accomplishes several objectives.

First, it keeps your account intact if the market turns against you. For example, I completed free trades in corn and soybeans in April and May 1990, as the grain markets heated up. However, as quickly as they rose, they began to fall. Even though most of my original call purchases were at a loss, "free trade" positions provided protection from loss, because the option I sold was losing more!

Exhibit 4.10

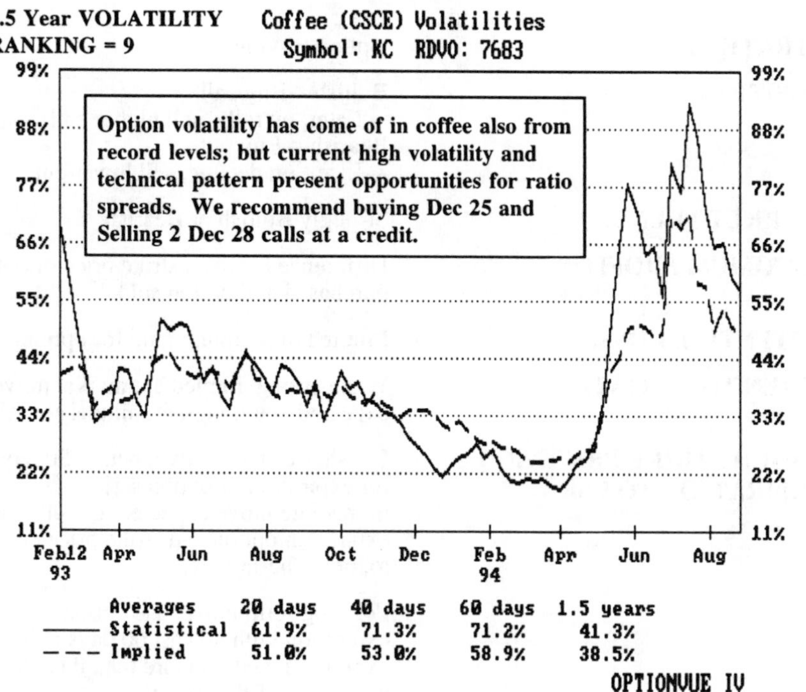

Second, the "free trade" gives you time to unemotionally examine your position, without the panic other traders may be in as their profitable positions begin to nose-dive. With the protection of the "free trade," you can wait for emotions to subside and the market to give you a better indication of its next move. You can then decide whether you want to hold your position for your full profit potential (knowing you are completely protected from loss), or cash out and take your existing profits (Exhibits 4.13, 4.14).

The third benefit is that when these "free trades" are completed, since your original capital is protected, you can turn your attention elsewhere. You may find opportunities in other markets or even take advantage of a pullback in the market in which you have completed "free trades" to add more positions. This can now be accomplished without increasing original risk—since your first "free trades" are now risk-free!

It is difficult to closely monitor more than two or three net positions, especially in volatile markets. The "free trade" allows you to concentrate more fully on other situations and meet your objective of getting a "trading edge" over the markets by using options.

Exhibit 4.11
Free Trade

STRATEGY:	Option Buying.
POSITION:	Bullish—Buy call —Later, on rally, sell higher call. Bearish—Buy put —Later, on decline, sell lower put.
MARKET TREND:	Strongly Bullish or Bearish.
MAXIMUM PROFIT:	Difference between strike price of option purchased and option sold.
POTENTIAL LOSS:	Limited to premium paid for option.
WHEN TO INITIATE:	When strong, immediate market move is expected and option premiums are low.
WHICH STRIKE PRICE AND EXPIRATION TO USE:	For shorter-term move, within 30 days for expiration of option series; if immediate move expected, use closest to expiration option and strike price closest to, or in-the-money. For long-term move, use option expiration with at least 60 days before expiration, and no more than three strike prices out-of-the-money.

After the "free trade" is completed, there are three possible alternatives:

1. Hold your position until expiration, and exercise your long option if it is in the money;
2. If the market has moved against you, allow both options to expire worthless; or
3. You may decide at any time to close out your position and take profits.

Your decision of which position to choose must be determined through your own trading plan and current view of the market.

The only "complaint" that I have heard about the "free trade" is that you are limiting your potential gain by hedging with the sale of the out-of-the-money call. Your profit is limited; however, this detriment is more than offset by the "no loss" aspect of this trade. And, you can continue to add on to this position in the further out months on the next pullback. In effect,

Exhibit 4.12
Examples of Chart Pattern to Look for in Underlying Future

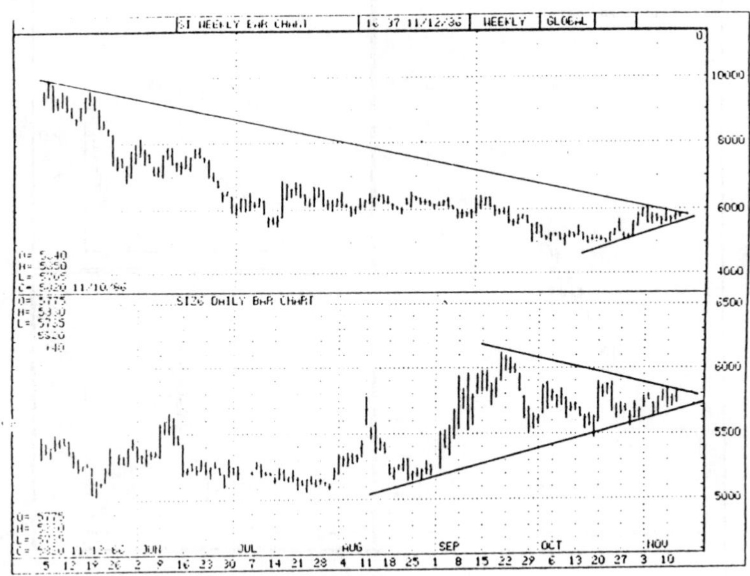

Option buying recommended as markets are likely to make big move in either direction.

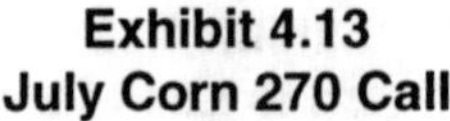

Exhibit 4.13
July Corn 270 Call

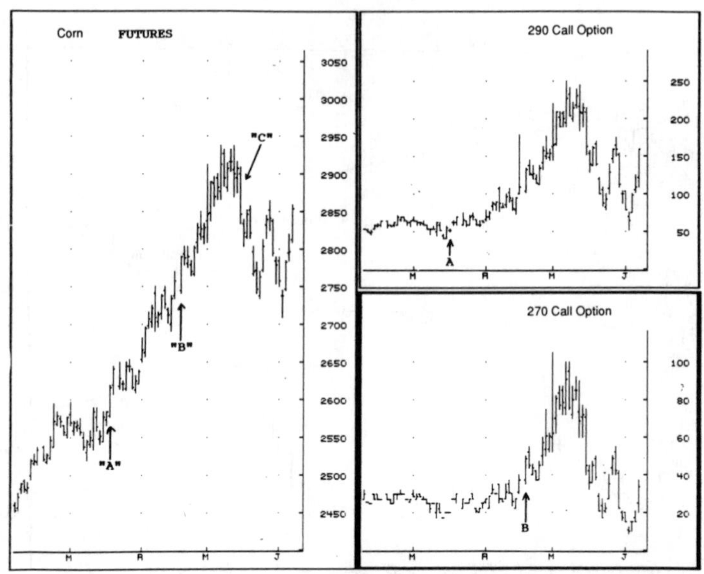

On March 14 at "A," we purchased the July corn 270 call at 4½. After the market rallied to "B" on April 19, we sold the July corn 290 call at 4¾ to complete the free trade, because we were able to hold the position through the break in the market at "C." Also of importance is that the 270 call gained in value 20 cents during the April rally and 10 cents in June, while the 290 call gained only 8 cents and 2 cents.

you can keep building this position without increasing your initial risk. This can allow for as much or even more profit than just holding your original position.

EXAMPLE OF FREE TRADES IN THE GRAIN MARKETS

The expiration of the July grain options at the end of June brought to our attention how well the "free trade" works. In the middle of March, we purchased the July corn 270 call and the July soybean 650 call, expecting a substantial rally. In April, as the market began to move in our favor and option premiums increased, we were able to turn both of these positions into "free trades"—in corn by selling the 290 call and in soybeans by selling the 675 call at the same price we had purchased our options for. We then had no risk of loss, margin, or capital required for these trades. Sub-

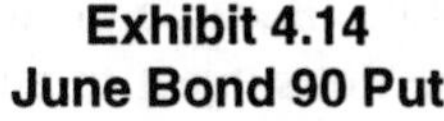

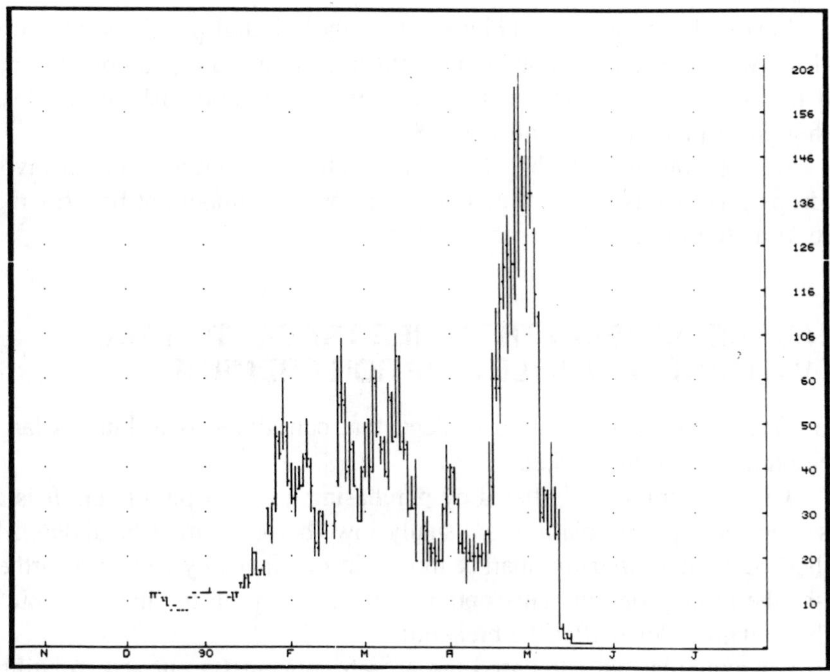

Within two weeks to expiration, this put first gained almost 800% in less than two weeks, before plunging the same amount the next week, showing the importance of our rule for profit-taking.

sequently, although the corn market did continue higher, and soybeans collapsed, the results of both trades show the benefits of our "free trade" strategy.

In corn, although, we turned this into a "free trade" well below the highs, because we took advantage of the volatility of the market and the time value of the out-of-the-money option, we were able to make not only close to 300% on our option purchase, but also were able to collect the entire amount of premium on the option we sold to hedge this position. Further, in spite of the market's severe decline of 20 cents in May, we were able to hold this position without risk of loss until the market subsequently rallied in June. This holding power without risk of financial loss or emotional pressure is, we feel, the main benefit of the free trade.

In soybeans, the market also rallied, allowing us to turn this position into a "free trade" and, similar to corn, the market then declined in May. However, the markets then diverged and soybeans never recovered before the expiration of the July option. Because of this, both options then expired worthless. However, we were not subject to any loss on this trade because of our strategy.

Finally, because of our ability to turn these initial positions into "free trades," we were able to initiate and still have two more positions in corn and one more in soybeans, that are free trades, without risk of any loss, with a profit potential of almost $3,000.

As you can see, whether the market stalls out, continues in our favor, or drops precipitously, the "free trade" can provide important benefits that give us a "trading edge" over the markets.

EXAMPLE OF USING THE "FREE TRADE" TO TAKE ADVANTAGE OF THE LOW OPTION PREMIUM

The "free trade" is an exciting strategy that can allow us to build a large position in a trending market.

The "free trade" is initiated by purchasing a call or put option. It is at this time that option volatility is usually low (before market breakouts). It is then completed after the market moves in our favor by selling a further out-of-the-money option. This option will normally be trading at a much higher volatility level after the breakout.

For example, we purchased the March copper 105 put at a volatility level of 18.6. One month later, after the market plummeted, we were able to sell the March copper 100 put at a volatility level of 27.8%. This returned to our account all of the money we had paid to purchase the 105 put, and provided us with a position that had no margin or debit. Our profit objective is always the difference between the strike prices of the options bought and sold. In the example above, our profit potential would be 105 minus 100 or 500 points ($1,250).

The "free trade" allows us to take advantage of these volatility disparities to our advantage.

SYNTHETIC FUTURES POSITION

By using a combination of puts and calls, you can create a synthetic option position with a profit potential that will closely approximate a futures contract or stock purchase with many benefits over just a net futures or options position. A bullish synthetic option position is created by purchase of a call and the sale of a put, and a bearish synthetic is just the opposite. This position can be created to reflect both your views on the market and the amount of money you care to risk on the trade. When a credit is received from initiating this spread, in addition to this credit and potentially unlimited profit if the market moves in your favor, one can profit if the market remains neutral, and in some cases, even if the market moves against you! (See Exhibit 4.15.)

For example, in the beginning of October 1985, I recommended a synthetic bullish options position in the December S&P of purchasing the 195 call and selling the 175 put (Exhibit 4.16). I used these options because my trading plan called for closing out this position if the S&P closed below the 180 level (area of heavy support), and this position would have the least risk if that happened. (In any strategy containing an option sale, risk limits must be set to prevent potentially unlimited losses.) At that point, the loss in this position would be about $250. Additionally, I decided to use the 195 call and the 175 put because the combination of this position would give me a credit of $300, that would be our profit even if the market maintained its current trading range.

Exhibit 4.15
Synthetic Futures Position

STRATEGY:	Synthetic Futures Position.
POSITION:	Bullish—Buy call, sell put. Bearish—Buy put, sell call.
MARKET TREND:	Potential of change of trend (previous trend broken); or upon reaction (pull-back) in already trending market.
MAXIMUM PROFIT:	Unlimited.
POTENTIAL LOSS:	Theoretically unlimited. (Place $500 stop loss instructions with broker.)
WHEN TO INITIATE:	Market basing (topping) and unlikely to go substantially lower (higher).
WHICH STRIKE PRICE AND EXPIRATION TO USE:	Options that have 60 days or more before expiration. Buy option nearest-the-money. Sell option below last low (bullish) or above last high (bearish).
COMMENT:	Excellent position to take advantage of market trend, as short option pays for cost of long position; if initiated at credit, profit will be made even if it moves slightly against you.

Exhibit 4.16
Examples of Chart Pattern to Look for in Underlying Future

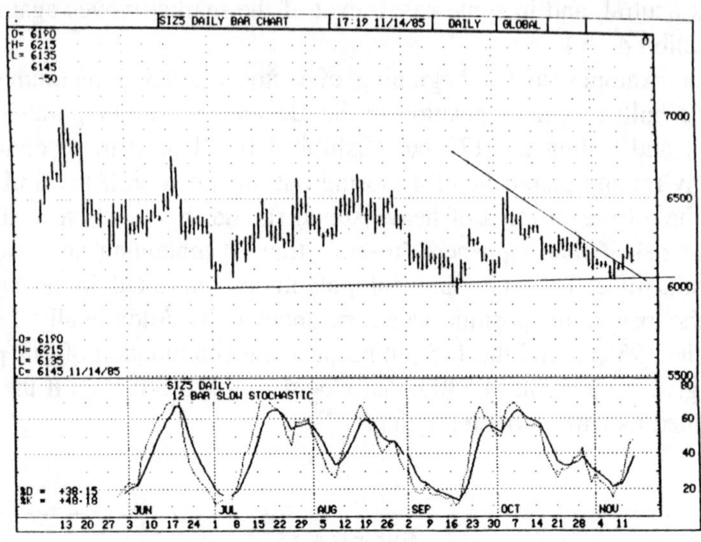

Bullish synthetic futures position initiated of long 7 call, short 6 put at credit, as market has potentially triple bottomed and broken out of downtrend.

Synthetic futures position (long call, short put) initiated at credit as market analysis shows 75% + probability of trading range or higher prices.

This position had a 75% probability of profit because I would profit in three out of four situations: (1) if the market moved higher; (2) if it remained neutral; or (3) if it moved slowly lower. Only if the market dropped suddenly would this position lose money.

This spread is a flexible strategy that can be changed to meet your views of the market. It is an excellent position when a futures contract is at heavy support or resistance levels.

Follow-up action should be taken on this strategy:

1. If the market moves against you, this position should be closed out prior to your short option being in the money (to prevent unlimited loss) or at a set loss level not exceeding $500; and
2. If the market moves in your favor, profits should be taken on the short put, and the long option turned into a "free trade" pursuant to the guidelines in the last section.

NEUTRAL OPTION POSITIONS

Selling options is a strategy that most public traders have stayed away from, both for a lack of understanding and a fear of potential loss (unlimited) that can occur. The professional trader, on the other hand, employs the option sale quite frequently (Exhibits 4.17, 4.18).

Statistical research in this area is very interesting. Over 90% of the public when speculating in options purchase options; and the public loses in option trading over 90% of the time. Conversely, professional traders, who are the biggest sellers of option premium, profit a majority of the time.

The mathematical odds strongly favor the option seller. An option is a wasting asset (Exhibit 4.19). This is because an option is comprised of time value premium. The longer an option has until expiration, the more value it should have. However, each day the option will lose some of its time value. Therefore, if one buys an option, even if his assessment of the market is correct, each day the time value of his option will be decreasing. In fact, as discussed in Chapter 1, the time decay of out-of-the-money options is so great, that sometimes even a large move in favor of the option buyer will not produce a profit.

The neutral option strategy is initiated by the sale of an out-of-the-money put and call of the same month of an option. Since both options are out-of-the-money, and both contain only time value premium, each day time value is lost by both options. There are four significant factors in a trading plan for Neutral Option Positions:

Exhibit 4.17
Option Sale

STRATEGY:	Neutral Option Spread.
POSITION:	Sell out-of-money put and call.
MARKET TREND:	Neutral.
MAXIMUM PROFIT:	Credit received when initiating position.
POTENTIAL LOSS:	Unlimited, if either strike price is exceeded. (Place stop loss order with broker.)
WHEN TO INITIATE:	Trading range markets with high volatility.
WHICH STRIKE PRICE AND EXPIRATION TO USE:	Use closest to expiration option and strike prices at least two futures moves out-of-the-money.
COMMENT:	Best initiated 15–45 days prior to expiration (period of maximum decay). Close out if underlying market approaches either strike price or 70% of premium collected.

1. The probable range of the future contract underlying the option prior to the expiration of the option;
2. Comparison of the relative volatility level of the option;
3. Calculation of the options that have the most disparity (overvaluation), which will determine which combinations of options have the highest probability of profit (and least likelihood of loss), and the most favorable risk to reward ratio; and
4. Principles of money management.

The first element of a strategy is determination of the probable range of the futures contract. Also considered at this point is the long- and short-term trend of the market and contract support and resistance.

The second factor is the relative volatility levels of the option. This is to determine whether the option contract has relatively high or low volatility (premium value). When high volatility occurs over an extended period of time, it is mathematically probable that the market will enter a trading range or consolidation period. It is, in fact, during severely trending markets that we experience the greatest discrepancies in option premium, as

Exhibit 4.18
Neutral Option Positions

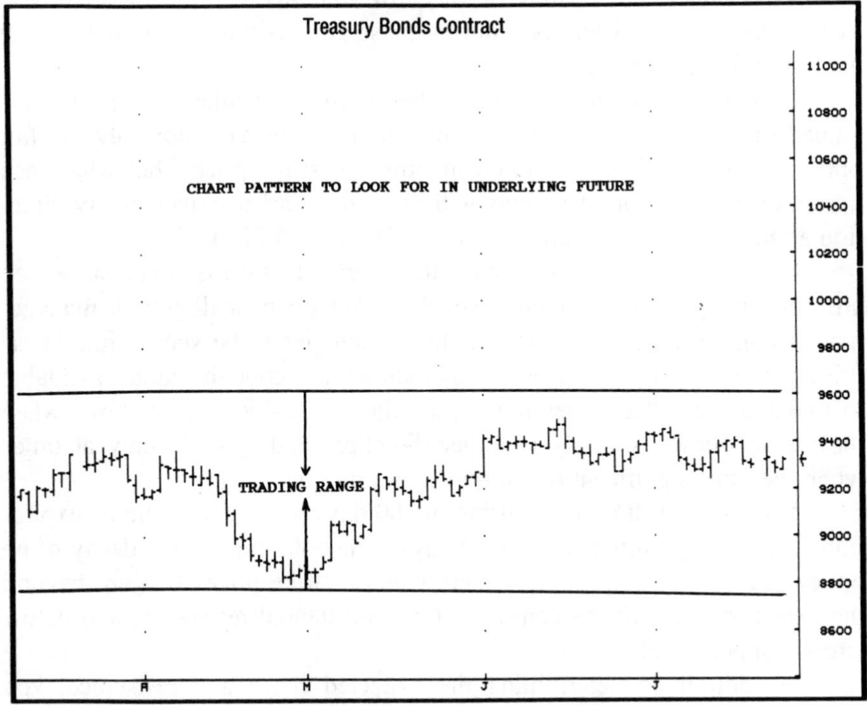

Exhibit 4.19
Neutral Option Position in June Bonds
(Short 86 Put and 96 Call)

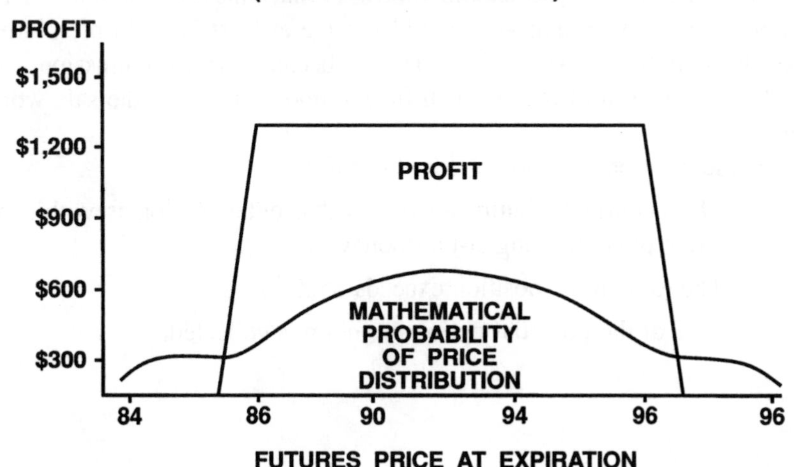

the option premium of out-of-money options can rise far in excess of their fair valuation, providing some of the best opportunities. Conversely, research has shown that in times of very low volatility, the market is likely to make a large move. Therefore, during these periods you should not initiate neutral option positions.

Computer generated charts are then used to calculate the most overvalued options. "Trade sheets" are prepared that provide not only the fair option value for all of the option months and strike prices, but what each option or combination of options will do, if the market moves in any direction at any time in the future (Exhibits 4.20, 4.21, 4.22, 4.23).

Finally, proper money management methods are essential. Since you are not attempting to be predictive of market price or direction, management techniques are necessary for these strategies to be successful. These principles of money management include having enough margin available to maintain your "delta neutrality," to adjust a position up or down when the market moves strongly in either direction, and to trade only at times when the most significant opportunities are present.

You should sell options during the 60 days prior to an option's expiration (particularly during the last 30 days), since the time value decay of an option accelerates quite rapidly then. Choose strike prices that are beyond the expected range of the contract, above substantial resistance, and below strong support levels.

In addition to determining the expected range and resistance, you should also look at the risk-reward in selling an option. For example, if an option can be sold that is $2,000 more out-of-the-money with only $100 less premium received, your risk-reward in this trade is increased by 20 to 1 by choosing the further out-of-the-money option.

A final rule that you should follow is that unless an option has less than 30 days to expiration you should receive at least $250 in premium to make the option sale worthwhile. This is because with commission costs and slippage, you must receive a sufficient amount to make the sale worthwhile.

These positions should be closed out if:

1. The underlying future moves so that either option is within one strike price of being at-the-money;
2. The loss on the position exceeds $500; or
3. 75% of the potential option premium is collected.

Exhibit 4.20
Future Expected Value of September 74 Treasury Bonds Put at Different Futures Prices as It Approaches Expiration

VOLATILITY = 12.475%
INTEREST RATE = 8.5%
EXERCISE PRICE = 74

	++++++++++++++++++++++++PUTS+++++++++++++++++++++++++						
DAYS LEFT:	19	16	13	10	7	4	1
72'09	1'62	1'59	1'56	1'52	1'49	1'47	1'46
DEL	-.78	-.80	-.83	-.86	-.90	-.96	-1.00
72'13	1'56	1'52	1'49	1'46	1'42	1'39	1'38
DEL	-.76	-.79	-.81	-.84	-.89	-.95	-1.00
72'17	1'49	1'46	1'43	1'39	1'35	1'32	1'30
DEL	-.75	-.77	-.79	-.82	-.87	-.93	-1.00
72'21	1'44	1'40	1'36	1'32	1'28	1'24	1'22
DEL	-.73	-.75	-.77	-.80	-.85	-.91	-1.00
72'25	1'38	1'34	1'30	1'26	1'22	1'17	1'14
DEL	-.71	-.73	-.75	-.78	-.82	-.89	-.99
72'29	1'32	1'28	1'24	1'20	1'15	1'10	1'06
DEL	-.69	-.70	-.73	-.75	-.80	-.86	-.99
73'01	1'27	1'23	1'19	1'14	1'09	1'03	'62
DEL	-.67	-.68	-.70	-.73	-.77	-.84	-.98
73'05	1'22	1'18	1'13	1'08	1'03	'61	'55
DEL	-.64	-.66	-.68	-.70	-.74	-.80	-.96
73'09	1'17	1'12	1'08	1'03	'61	'55	'47
DEL	-.62	-.63	-.65	-.67	-.71	-.76	-.93
73'13	1'12	1'07	1'03	'62	'56	'49	'40
DEL	-.60	-.61	-.62	-.64	-.67	-.72	-.88
	++++++++++++++++++++++++PUTS+++++++++++++++++++++++++						
DAYS LEFT:	19	16	13	10	7	4	1
73'17	1'07	1'03	'62	'57	'50	'43	'33
DEL	-.58	-.59	-.60	-.61	-.64	-.68	-.83
73'21	1'02	'62	'57	'52	'45	'38	'27
DEL	-.56	-.56	-.57	-.58	-.60	-.63	-.76
73'25	'62	'58	'53	'47	'41	'33	'21
DEL	-.53	-.54	-.54	-.55	-.56	-.58	-.67
73'29	'58	'53	'48	'43	'36	'28	'16
DEL	-.51	-.51	-.51	-.52	-.52	-.53	-.57
74'01	'54	'49	'44	'39	'32	'24	'12
DEL	-.49	-.49	-.49	-.49	-.49	-.48	-.47
74'05	'50	'46	'41	'35	'29	'21	'08
DEL	-.46	-.46	-.46	-.46	-.45	-.43	-.37
74'09	'46	'42	'37	'32	'25	'17	'06
DEL	-.44	-.44	-.43	-.42	-.41	-.39	-.28
74'13	'43	'39	'34	'28	'22	'14	'04
DEL	-.42	-.41	-.40	-.39	-.37	-.34	-.21
74'17	'40	'35	'31	'25	'19	'12	'02
DEL	-.40	-.39	-.38	-.36	-.34	-.29	-.14
74'21	'37	'32	'28	'23	'17	'10	'01
DEL	-.37	-.36	-.35	-.33	-.31	-.25	-.09

Exhibit 4.21
Daily Trade Sheet for June Treasury Bonds

Volatility= 11.9% Interest Rate= 8.5%										Days Out= 264 8-26-85						
++++++++++++++++CALLS+++++++++++++										++++++++++++++PUTS+++++++++						
	68	70	72	74	76	78	80	82		68	70	72	74	76	78	80
68'00	2'34	1'47	1'30	'47	'28	'17	'09	'05		2'40	3'45	4'63	6'28	8'01	9'45	11'29
DEL	.49	.36	.28	.20	.13	.09	.06	.03		–.45	–.56	–.65	–.73	–.80	–.85	–.88
DIV	'14	'13	'12	'10	'08	'06	'04	'03		'14	'14	'12	'10	'08	'06	'04
69'00	3'03	2'10	1'29	'61	'38	'23	'13	'06		2'13	3'11	4'23	5'46	7'15	8'56	10'38
DEL	.54	.43	.33	.24	.17	.11	.07	.04		–.40	–.50	–.60	–.69	–.76	–.82	–.86
DIV	'14	'14	'13	'11	'09	'07	'05	'03		'14	'14	'13	'12	'09	'07	'05
70'00	3'40	2'39	1'52	1'14	'50	'31	'19	'11		1'53	2'45	3'50	5'03	6'31	8'04	9'47
DEL	.60	.49	.36	.29	.21	.14	.09	.06		–.35	–.45	–.55	–.65	–.73	–.79	–.84
DIV	'13	'14	'14	'13	'11	'08	'06	'04		'14	'14	'14	'13	'11	'09	'07
71'00	4'16	3'08	2'14	1'34	1'00	'41	25	'15		1'32	2'18	3'16	4'28	5'50	7'18	8'58
DEL	.64	54	.44	.34	.25	.17	.12	.08		–.30	–.40	–.50	–.60	–.69	–.76	–.81
DIV	'13	'14	'14	'14	'12	'10	'07	'05		'13	'14	'14	'14	'12	'10	'08
72'00	4'58	3'44	2'44	1'57	1'18	'53	'34	'21		1'14	1'58	2'50	3'55	5'08	6'35	8'07
DEL	.69	.59	.49	.39	.29	.21	.15	.10		–.26	–.35	–.45	–.55	–.64	–.72	–.78
DIV	'12	'14	'15	'14	'13	'11	'09	'07		'12	'14	'15	'14	'13	'11	'09
73'00	5'40	4'20	3'13	2'19	1'38	1'04	'44	'26		'63	1'37	2'23	3'21	4'32	5'54	7'22
DEL	.73	.64	.54	.44	.34	.25	.18	.12		–.22	–.30	–.40	–.50	–.60	–.68	–.75
DIV	'11	'13	'15	'15	'14	'12	'10	'08		'11	'13	'15	'15	'14	'13	'10
74'00	–6'24	4'62	3'49	2'49	–1'61	1'22	–'57	–'37		'51	1'19	1'62	2'55	3'60	5'12	6'39
DEL	.77	.69	.59	.49	.39	.30	.22	.15		–.18	–.26	–.35	–.45	–.55	–.64	–.71
DIV	'10	'13	'14	'15	'15	'13	'12	'09		'10	'13	'14	'15	'15	'14	'13
75'00	7'10	5'44	4'24	3'18	2'24	1'42	1'08	'47		'40	1'03	1'41	2'27	3'26	4'37	5'58
DEL	.80	.73	.64	.54	.44	.34	.26	.19		–.15	–.22	–.31	–.40	–.50	–.59	–.67
DIV	'09	'12	'14	'15	'15	'14	'13	'11		'09	'12	'14	'15	'15	'14	'13
76'00	7'62	6'27	5'02	3'54	2'53	2'02	1'26	'60		'32	'54	1'23	2'03	2'60	4'00	5'16
DEL	.83	.76	.68	.59	.49	.39	.30	.22		–.12	–.19	–.27	–.36	–.45	–.56	–.63
DIV	'08	'11	'13	'15	'15	'15	'14	'12		'08	'11	'13	'15	'15	'15	'14
77'00	8'52	7'13	5'47	4'29	3'22	2'28	1'47	1'12		'25	'43	1'07	1'46	2'32	3'31	4'41
DEL	.85	.79	.72	.63	.54	.44	.35	.26		–.10	–.15	–.23	–.31	–.40	–.50	–.59
DIV	'07	'09	'12	'14	'15	'16	'15	'13		'07	'10	'12	'14	'15	'16	'15
++++++++++++++++CALLS+++++++++++++										++++++++++++++PUTS+++++++++						
	68	70	72	74	76	78	80	82		68	70	72	74	76	78	80
78'00	9'43	8'00	6'30	5'07	3'58	2'58	2'06	1'30		'19	'34	'58	1'27	2'08	3'00	4'05
DEL	.87	.82	.76	.68	.58	.49	.39	.31		–.08	–.13	–.19	–.27	–.36	–.45	–.54
DIV	'06	'08	'11	'13	'15	'16	'16	'14		'06	'09	'11	'14	'15	'16	'16
79'00	10'35	8'54	7'16	5'51	4'33	3'27	2'33	1'51		'15	'27	'47	1'11	1'50	2'37	3'36
DEL	.88	.84	.79	.71	.63	.54	.44	.35		–.06	–.10	–.16	–.23	–.31	–.40	–.50
DIV	'05	'07	'10	'13	'15	'16	'16	'15		'05	'08	'10	'13	'15	'16	'16
80'00	11'28	9'44	8'03	6'34	5'11	3'63	2'63	2'11		'11	'21	'37	'62	'132	'213	'305
DEL	.90	.86	.81	.75	.67	.58	.49	.40		–.05	–.08	–.13	–.20	–.27	–.36	–.45
DIV	'04	'06	'09	'12	'14	'16	'16	'16		'04	'07	'09	'12	'14	'16	'16

Daily trade sheet for June Treasury Bonds giving theoretical option values at different futures prices.
"DEL" is the percentage the option value will change as compared to the futures.
"DIV" is the amount the option value should change if volatility increases or decreases by 1%.
(Com-Tech Software)

Exhibit 4.22

Option: US	Valuation Date: 5/19/91	Interest: 8.75	Div/For: 0.00

Theoretical Profit and Loss

Futures	Time: 5/19/91	7/06/91	8/24/91
9000	-208	-147	-128
9020	-146	-117	-52
9108	-122	-53	-12
9128	-100	-28	28
9216	-46	-6	104
9304	-30	12	124
9324	-18	27	124
9412	-8	38	124
9500	-2	45	124
9520	0	48	124
9608	-1	48	124
9628	-5	43	124
9716	-13	34	124
9804	-24	22	124
9824	-38	5	124
9912	-55	-15	52
10000	-112	-38	12

Futures Prices

Sim	U	MY	Spread	Value
*	Y	M1		9518
	Y	U1	-26	9424
	Y	Z1	-23	9401
	Y	H2	-20	9313
	Y	M2	-17	9228
	Y	U2	-16	9212
	Y	Z2	-15	9129
	Y	H3		

Range: FUTURES
From: 9000
To: 10000

Contour: TIME
- - - : 5/19/91
— — : 7/06/91
——— : 8/24/91

Exhibit 4.23

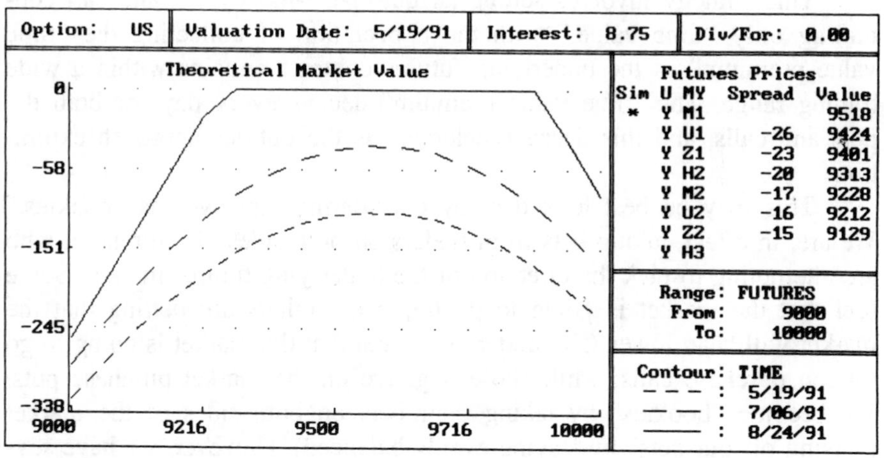

USING NEUTRAL OPTION POSITIONS TO TRADE "LIKE A BOOKIE" WITHOUT HAVING TO PREDICT MARKET DIRECTION

The Neutral Option Position is a trading strategy that provides the trader with many benefits over a long or short futures or options position. While option purchases and futures trades are only successful if the market moves in the direction predicted (without the trader being "stopped out" first); a Neutral Option Position can be successful in a non-trending or choppy market (studies have shown that markets are in a nontrending or sideways pattern over two-thirds of the time); or if the market moves slowly lower or higher. Only when the market makes an extreme move will this position be negatively impacted. In that case, this position still can be dynamically adjusted to match the movement of the markets.

In addition to allowing the trader to be successful without having to predict the direction of the market, the Neutral Option Position incorporates the advantages of:

1. Special circumstances
2. Price disparity
3. Option time decay
4. Mathematics
5. Probability
6. Money management

This strategy involves selling an out-of-the-money put and call containing only "time value," with the expectation of collecting the "time value premium" as the underlying futures contract remains within a wide trading range. The "time value premium" decays every day for both the puts and calls, and this decay accelerates as the options approach expiration.

This may be best looked at by considering ourselves as "bookies." We are, in effect, taking bets from traders on both sides of the market who are attempting to pick the direction of the underlying futures market. Some feel that the market is going to go up; while others are betting that the market will head lower. The traders who feel that the market is going to go up can purchase calls; while those negative on the market purchase puts. We become "bookies" by taking their bets on both sides of the market ("laying off our bets" by staying evenly balanced). However, we have several advantages that are not available to the house ("bookie") even in Las Vegas.

For example, if a "bookie" takes bets on a prize fight and "balances" his book properly, half the people betting will win and half will lose. He must pay off half these bets. The "bookie" derives his profit by establishing odds for the two fighters. (Assuming that the fighters are evenly matched, the "bookie" may quote 6 to 5 odds "pick 'em." This means that you can pick either fighter and receive a five dollar profit for every six dollars you bet.) Therefore, if a "bookie" is able to obtain bets of $600,000 on each participant in the fight for a total bet of $1,200,000, no matter which fighter wins he is obligated to pay off $1,100,000, for a profit of $100,000. However, the Neutral Option Position can allow us to do even better by allowing us to "win" on both sides of the "bet" (if the market stays within our predicted or "adjusted" trading range).

For example, with treasury bonds trading near 115, we can take the view that the market is going to remain within a range between 110–120, and sell the 110 put and the 120 call. These options are sold to other traders who are "betting" on their prediction of market direction—that the market is going below 110 (puts) or above 120 (calls). We are making no predictions other than it will remain in this wide trading range.

Neutral Option Position (110 Put—120 Call)

110 put gains	(Both options worthless at expiration)		120 call gains
120 call worthless	110 put ——— SAFE ZONE ———	120 call	110 put worthless

MARKET PRICE

100 105 109 110 115 120 121 125 130

Even if the market moves out of this range, the position can still be successful. This is because every day both options lose some of their time value. This continued loss of time value on both sides provides significant protection. Further, "adjustment" techniques are available, allowing us to "rebalance" this position when necessary (see analysis of *Continuous Option Position Envelope* attached).

The benefits of this position include:

1. Not having to predict market direction.
2. Being able to collect premium from both sides of the transaction—both the buyer of puts and buyer of calls.
3. Being able to take advantage of the "overvalued" time value of out-of-the-money options (although the amount of option premium changes from time to time, traders continue to buy options, thinking they can "beat the market").
4. We can use "special circumstances" to our advantage based on favorable market conditions (high option premium), and we have 40 different markets to choose from.
5. Finally, we have the ability to both adjust our positions and increase our position size. This is the reason that most casinos have limits on the amount of money you can bet, because it has been

mathematically shown that with an unlimited amount of money the odds of beating the "house" become significantly greater. However, we have that ability to increase our positions to a very high level, since the limits established by the CFTC are so large that unless we became very large or greedy, it would not affect us.

PUT TIME ON YOUR SIDE BY USING NEUTRAL OPTION POSITIONS

Whether you are in your twenties, thirties, forties, or above (my area of concern), every morning we awake and find we are fighting time a little bit. Whether it is the creaky back, bothersome knee, or fickle stomach, there always seems to be something that time has ready to make us remember that it is working against us.

In fact, every day it gets even a little worse. Assuming a life expectancy of 100 years (which all of us traders by our excellent eating, sleeping, and exercise habits are assured to obtain), a 10-year-old has 90 years of expected life. Therefore every day that goes by reflects a loss of 1/90 × 365, or about .00003 of his remaining life span. However, a 90-year-old's time is now going by more than 10 times as fast, since every day will be a loss of about .002 of his remaining life span. Even worse, this problem continues to accelerate every day without stopping.

As they said in the movie *Network*—"I'm sick and tired and I'm not going to stand for it anymore!" While we can't fight Father Time directly other than by staying healthy, we can fight him in our forum through our *(NOPS) Neutral Option Program.* By using Neutral Option Trading positions (selling an out-of-the-money put and call), we can use time in our favor. That is because these options contain only "time value" and each day as the option approaches expiration, this time value erodes. In fact, similar to our discussion of Father Time accelerating our percentage of time left adversely, the time value of option decay accelerates as the option approaches expiration providing an additional benefit for us.

As we have mentioned in our books, *The Option Advantage* and *The Option Secret,* the power of the decay of time value is so severe that often a market can move strongly in favor of your views, and an out-of-the-money option still will not gain value. An example of this occurred in the bond market in October 1993.

The out-of-the-money 124 call gained little during the bond rally as its *time value* was working against it. At the same time the out-of-the-money puts were dropping quickly, thereby providing additional benefit. They lost almost all of their value when the market declined. Therefore, time value works strongly in our favor on both sides of the market in this case without regard to the direction of the underlying market. In fact, if you check the end of the week prices in *Barron's* for options, often you will find option markets in which both out-of-the-money puts and calls drop in value during that week (Exhibits 4.24–4.26.

Using time value in the options market not only is my revenge on Father Time, but it is also a mathematically sound way of trading, along with having a less stressful way of looking at the markets by not constantly having us pick market direction. Because of the above, this is the basis for our *Neutral Option Trading Program.*

Exhibit 4.24

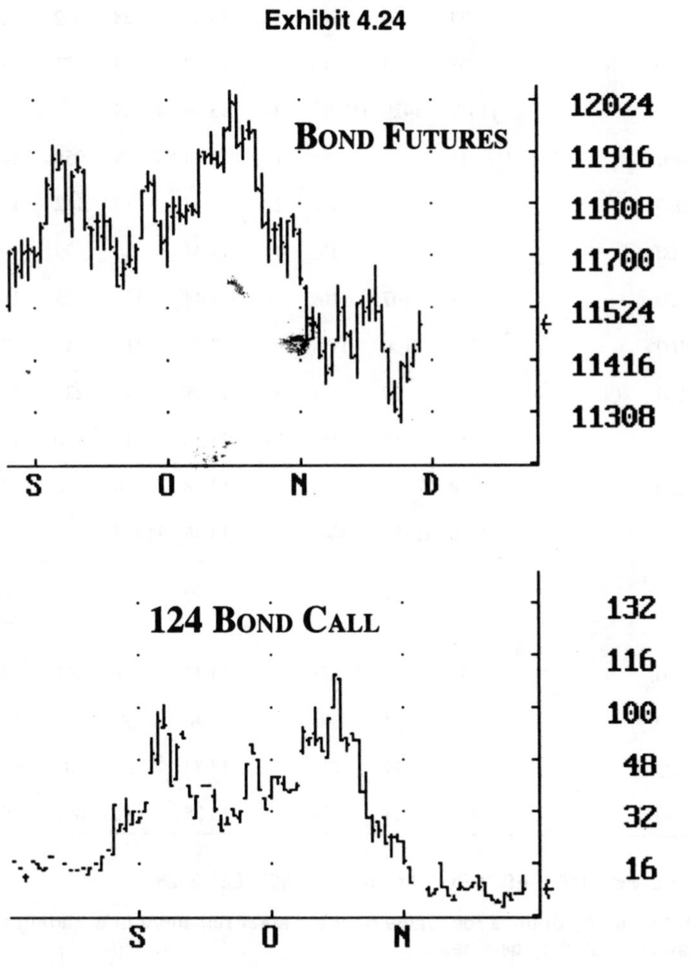

Exhibit 4.25

Contr	Str	Bid	Ask	high	Low	Last	Chg	Time	Prev1	Delta	DTE	ImpVol
PEDU3	9650			3	2	2s	1–	13:39	2	.201	37	.1712
PEDZ3	9600			11	9	10s	=	13:39	10	.323	128	.2275
PUSU3	1080			1	1	1s	=	13:43	1	.013	14	.1508
PUSU3	1100			2	1	1s	=	13:43	1	.017	14	.1134
PUSU3	1120			7	3	4s	=	13:43	4	.064	14	.0978
PUSU3	1140			30	15	20s	1–	13:43	20	.257	14	.0888
CUSU3	1140	140		146	112	139s	3–	13:38	139	.734	14	.0915
CUSU3	1160			34	16	28s	3–	13:38	28	.352	14	.0823
CUSU3	1180			138	3	4s	3–	13:38	4	.075	14	.0825
USU3				11517	11420	11509s	2–	13:46	11509			
PUSZ3	1060			11	9	9s	1–	13:44	9	.058	105	.0899
PUSZ3	1080			23	19	19s	2–	13:44	19	.112	105	.0873
PUSZ3	1100			48	37	38s	4–	13:44	38	.199	105	.0852
PUSZ3	1120			124	107	110s	2–	13:44	110	.325	105	.0859
CUSZ3	1160			119	100	112s	6–	13:38	112	.355	105	.0820
CUSZ3	1180			46	32	41s	3–	13:38	41	.224	105	.0819
CUSZ3	1200			19	14	18s	2–	13:38	18	.120	105	.0791
CUSZ3	1220			8	6	8s	2–	13:38	8	.060	105	.0797
USZ3				11410	11315	11404s	1–	13:46	11404			
PUSH4	1040		21	22	21	21s	=	13:44	21	.092	196	.0894
PUSH4	1060			41	34	38s	2–	13:44	38	.149	196	.0895
CUSH4	1220			24	17	21s	5–	13:38	21	.103	196	.0821
CUSH4	1240			13	11	12s	3–	13:38	12	.064	196	.0827

Charts courtesy of FUTURESOURCE, Lombard, IL (800) 621-2628.

All out-of-the-money options lost value as the market remained in a trading range during the day and volatility declined.

Exhibit 4.26

Contr	Str	Bid	Ask	High	Low	Last	Chg	Time	Prev1	DTE	Delta	ImpVol
PSSU3	600			3	2	3s	=	12:24	3	30	.015	.3236
PSSU3	625			6	4	4s	4–	12:24	4	30	.023	.2767
PSSU3	650			26	14	16s	10–	12:24	16	30	.066	.2782
CSSU3	650			820	700	820s	94+	12:23	820	30	.913	.2980
CSSU3	675			590	500	590s	60+	12:23	590	30	.852	.2656
CSSU3	700			440	350	434s	44+	12:23	434	30	.690	.3172
CSSU3	725			324	240	316s	36+	12:23	316	30	.545	.3520
CSSU3	750			230	170	224s	24+	12:23	224	30	.419	.3730
CSSU3	775			152	104	152s	2+	12:23	152	30	.311	.3839
CSSU3	800			104	80	104s	4+	12:23	104	30	.228	.3995
CSSU3	850			50	34	50s	2+	12:24	50	30	.119	.4286
CSSU3	900			22	12	16s	5–	12:24	16	30	.049	.4262
CSSU3	950			6	4	6s	2–	12:24	6	30	.023	.4445
CSSU3	1000			54	4	4s	1–	12:24	4	30	.014	.4872
OSU3				7310	7190	7302s	104+	11:40	7302			
PSSX3	600			17	14	14s	2–	12:24	14	93	.041	.2341
PSSX3	625			44	34	34s	6–	12:24	34	93	.083	.2366
CSSX3	700			584	510	576s	52+	12:24	576	93	.630	.2899
CSSX3	750			390	320	380s	30+	12:24	380	93	.459	.3206
CSSX3	800			260	218	254s	32+	12:24	254	93	.328	.3488
CSSX3	850			170	140	166s	16+	12:24	166	93	.230	.3675
CSSX3	900			104	80	104s	10+	12:24	104	93	.156	.3773
CSSX3	950			60	54	60s	=	12:24	60	93	.098	.3776
CSSX3	1000			50	34	40s	=	12:24	40	93	.068	.3924
SX3				7320	7190	7310s	100+	11:40	7310			

Charts courtesy of FUTURESOURCE, Lombard, IL (800) 621-2628.

Even though soybeans increased by 10¢ ($500 per futures contract) in one day—many out-of-the-money calls had little or no increase in value.

INITIATING AND ADJUSTING NEUTRAL OPTION POSITIONS

When we initiate a Neutral Option Position, we always include a recommendation that the position be readjusted or closed out if the option comes close to being in the money. (We normally say one strike price or, in the case of bonds, one to two points, etc.) This is for risk management purposes, so that we are not subject to extreme losses if the market begins to move strongly in either direction. Although in many cases these movements are only temporary and are eventually readjusted, we feel that safety is the better part of valor. We also readjust our positions when the option premium on one side is more than double the option premium on the other side. However, the exact method of adjustment leaves wide latitude for discretion. We look at the trend of the market and the option volatility levels of the various option strike prices in making our decisions. Perhaps the best way to discuss this matter is to look at our actual adjustments of our Neutral Option Positions in the bonds and S&P 500 in 1994.

In mid-April we entered the Neutral Option Position of selling the June bond 100 put and 106 call. Thereafter the market began to rally almost one full point a day and this position quickly became unbalanced. We initially rebalanced this position by selling 101 puts, however, the continued rally made this position still unbalanced. Therefore, when bonds moved above 104 we repurchased our short 106 calls and sold an equal number of 107 calls and 102 puts.

When bonds then moved above 105, we repurchased our short 107 calls and sold 108 calls and more 102 puts. The reason we sold 102 puts again instead of moving up to the 103 puts was that 102 puts were trading at a very high volatility level for bonds—above 13%, and we preferred to sell multiple 102 puts instead of the closer-to-the-money 103 puts which could be more adversely affected by a strong downward move.

This brings us to another very important point both in initiating and adjusting our positions. WE ALWAYS PREFER TO SELL MORE OF FURTHER OUT-OF-THE-MONEY OPTIONS WHEN CHOOSING WHICH STRIKE PRICE TO USE. For example, as I write this article, the June 102 bond puts are trading at 13 and the 103 puts are trading at 19. In this case, we would prefer to sell three 102 puts rather than two 103 puts to collect the same amount of premium. This is because the 102 puts are safer and will lose their premium quicker as the market moves up or remains stable, while gaining premium much slower if the market moves against them.

Then later, after bonds moved over 106, we repurchased some of our 108 calls and sold 109 and 110 calls for the same premium. We do not hesitate to repurchase short options and sell multiple further out-of-the-money options when we can get the same or more premium if the market is approaching the strike price of the options we have sold. However, to make certain that you have enough margin available to be able to do this, we strongly recommend that you trade with as large of an account as possible, so you don't run out of margin when adjusting your position, and that your initial position size be manageable. For example, in our $100,000 accounts, we initially used under $6,000 of margin. Even after adjusting the positions because of the unexpected large move in bonds, we were still using less than 20% of available margin. Always having enough margin available to adjust your positions when necessary is extremely important.

Neutral Option Positions in the S&P 500 during April 1994 presented an entirely different situation. In this case, put option premium was trading at levels of two-and-one-half to three times higher than the call options. Therefore, with the S&P 500 trading near the 445 level, we sold May 390 puts and 465 and 470 calls for approximately the same amount of premium even though the puts were much further out-of-the-money than the calls. In this case, so that these positions would remain neutral while the market stayed in the trading range we expected, we sold multiple puts for every call. Thereafter, the market quickly rallied to 452, and as expected, the highly priced 390 puts lost premium, dropping over 50% in less than two weeks. However, the interesting factor in this trade is that although the market rallied, the far out-of-the-money 465 and 470 calls that we had sold also lost their value, allowing this position to work on both sides.

This brings up another important factor in initiating "neutral option spreads"—knowing the characteristics of the various option markets when the markets begin to move. In the grain and metal markets, the out-of-the-money call options increase in value very quickly when the market rallies, while the puts move little on declines. In past years, out-of-the-money soybean and silver options have risen in volatility up to 400%, and often trade at levels 200–300% higher than the at-the-money options (providing our best "Ratio Spread" opportunities at those times).

However, the financial markets exhibit completely different tendencies. Volatility in the bond market is somewhat skewed towards the puts, which often run 10–20% higher than the calls. For example, in 1994 the out of the money June puts were trading at a 13% implied volatility rate, while the out-of-the-money calls we were selling were trading at close to 11%. This difference is magnified even more in the S&P 500. We find that on severe declines similar to the drop from 470 to 440 during the last two weeks of March, implied volatility for puts in the S&P 500 rose over 200%. This caused the far out-of-the-money puts to be trading at volatility levels of over 25% while the calls were between 10–12%. Therefore, to take advantage of this disparity, we sold multiple far out-of-the-money puts for every out-of-the-money call sold in our Neutral Option Positions.

The following article further explains our management of Neutral Option Positions by way of what we call the "Continuous Option Position Envelope."

THE CONTINUOUS OPTION POSITION ENVELOPE

The money management theory behind the Neutral Option Position is to have sufficient funds available to adjust this position continuously to any changes in the underlying market trend or trading range. For example, the Treasury bond 110 put and the 120 call is sold with the underlying market trading near 115 (Envelope-1). If the market stays within the range of 110 to 120 at expiration, both of these options will expire "worthless," and the entire premium received for selling these options will constitute profit (less brokerage commissions and fees).

However, if the market were thereafter to move to 120, it would create an "unbalanced" position that was now much more dependent on market direction (losses can accrue, if the market moves outside this range). Adjustment of this position would then be necessary to maintain a "neutral" stance. In this case, the 120 call could be repurchased and 124 calls sold to regain the same amount of premium as before. At the same time, to remain "neutral," the 110 put could be repurchased (the profits from which would, at least, offset some of the premium necessary to repurchase the 120 call) and additional 114 puts sold (Envelope-2 would now consist of the 114 put and 124 call).

These money management principles provide the trader with the ability to "Envelope" the market continuously, until the market trend coincides with the parameters of our Neutral Option Position and/or the out-of-the-money options expire worthless. In trading, it is easy to be able to make profits if the market moves in your favor. However, the difficult part is being able to hold a position that has moved against you. If it is financially possible to hold a position that has moved against you, you then put yourself in a position to benefit from a move in your favor. This is the purpose of the Continuous Option Position Envelope. Money management principles allow the trader to maximize the number of adjustments, if the market moves outside the predicted range to increase the probability of profit. In addition, the option time decay (which accelerates as an option approaches expiration) is causing both the put and call to lose "time value" every day. Therefore, the Continuous Option Position Envelope allows the Neutral

Exhibit 4.27

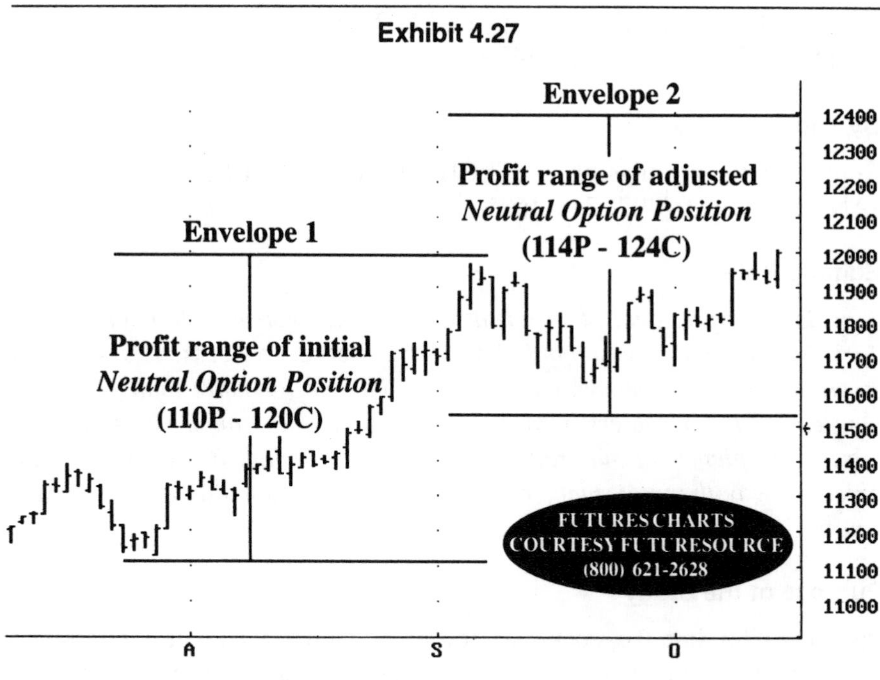

Option Position to be adjusted both up or down within the same expiration period or to further out contract months to rebalance and regain the original amount of premium.

The use of the Continuous Option Position Envelope allows the trader to let the market "tell us" where it wants to go without having to "guess" or pick market direction. It is similar to the theories used in the sport of judo where, instead of struggling with your opponent, his weight, movement, and force are used in your benefit as you "adjust" your throw or reaction in the direction of his attack.

The Neutral Option Position and the Continuous Option Position Envelope allow us to trade combining the benefits of the natural tendencies of the market to eventually maintain a trading range, and use the characteristics of options including price disparity and time decay; along with the sciences of mathematics, probability, and money management. The "weight" of these factors all used in our favor provide us with a "trading edge" over the markets.

One of the reasons we like Neutral Positions is that we have found that markets spend 50–75% of their time in a nontrending mode.

STUDY OF TIME SPENT IN TRENDING AND SIDEWAYS MARKETS

By Thomas Basso

Reprinted by permission of TECHNICAL TRADERS BULLETIN—JANUARY 1993, (407) 746–1605

Editor's Note

Tom Basso is president of Trendstat Capital management. He is profiled in Jack Schwager's newest book, The New Market Wizards. *His study of stock market price behavior recently has interest for more than just stock market and index traders because it reminds us of the importance of keeping the big picture of our trading expectations in mind. It also states in an objective way the importance of recognizing the personality of the markets you trade.*

Purpose of the Study

Investors who time the stock market are constantly faced with the prospect of becoming impatient when, over a shorter time frame, there doesn't seem to be value added by a timing strategy. Frequently, their excuse for throwing out an indicator or trading system is "it doesn't work anymore" or "I could have made more money with a buy and hold strategy."

Investor psychology is heavily at work here. The investor, at that point, does not remember why they developed or started using their trading strategy in the first place. Many times, I have seen investors forget what to expect in the best case, worst case, and expected case scenarios. I maintain that if the investor can understand exactly what to expect from a strategy, they will be less surprised when the timing strategy inevitably does exactly as expected.

Results

Statistic	1960s	1970s	1980s	1990s	Total
Number of up markets	5	7	10	2	24
Total value of up markets	34	84	117	20	255
Average up market	6.72%	11.96%	11.71%	10.15%	10.61%
Days spent in up markets	595	785	1,065	173	2,618
Number of down markets	2	4	4	1	11
Total value of down markets	18	49	47	15	129
Average down market	8.92%	12.15%	11.79%	15.13%	11.7%

Statistic	1960s	1970s	1980s	1990s	Total
Days spent in down markets	169	348	270	92	879
Number of sideways markets	48	98	88	26	260
Total value of sideways markets	–15	–98	–119	–34	–266
Average sideways market	–0.32%	–1%	–1.35%	–1.29%	–1.02%
Days spent in sideways markets	1,431	2,517	2,327	641	6,916
% Of time in up markets	27%	22%	29%	19%	25%
% Of time in down markets	8%	10%	7%	10%	8%
% Of time in sideways markets	65%	69%	64%	71%	66%
Total number of trades	56	109	102	28	295
Average trades per year	9.27	10.89	10.02	11.28	10.34

How the Study Was Done

To that end, I set out to define and measure worst, best, and expected case scenarios by measuring market character in terms of upwards, downwards, and trendless activity. I wanted to do this in a way that everyone could relate to. I applied a simple trend-following model on the S&P 500 index for the period January 1964 to July 1992. I used a simple five-day and 10-day exponential moving average crossover system to create signals. When the five-day average crossed the 10-day average to the upside, I rated that a buy signal. When the shorter average crossed the longer average to the downside, I considered it a sell.

I then broke all these signals into up, down, and sideways markets by assuming that an "up" market was any buy signal that created at least a 5% return. Any sell signal in which the market declined by at least 5% was considered a "down" market. If the market gave between a +5% and –5% return, I rated the move small enough to consider it a "sideways" market. I expressed the results both for the individual decades and for the entire test period.

Conclusions

1. Most of the time (66%) was spent in sideways markets, where trend-following adds little or negative value. However, the value lost on each trade was small (–1.02).
2. Value was added in both up and down markets (average +10.61% and +11.70% respectively).

3. Without exception, timing added value in every decade tested.
4. The market was "up" only 25% of the total time over 28.5 years.
5. The market was "down" only 8% of the total time over 28.5 years.
6. The five- and 10-day exponential crossover system measured about five round turns (10 trades) per year and that amount was consistent in each of the decades measured.
7. The results by decade were quite similar to each other and to the entire period itself.
8. So far, the 1990s have not added very much value and have the lowest up percentage of any period measured.

How Investors Can Profit from This Study

I believe that one of the keys to successful investing is being informed and knowledgeable about your investment strategy's expected performance. This study points out the need for investors to understand why timing is important. In every decade, measured value was added by this type of timing strategy. But in every decade measured without exception, 64–71% of the time was spent in sideways markets where, typically, trend-following does not add value.

If you are looking for a quick killing, you need to head for Las Vegas. But if you want a risk averse way to manage your investments that shows added value over almost four decades of statistics, you must have the patience to spend 60–70% of seeing negative value-added to enjoy the 30–40% of the time when you're glad you used a market timing strategy. If you are experiencing one of those negative value-added periods, remember that this is the expected performance. If it isn't broken, don't fix it!

Study by:

Thomas Basso
Trendstat Capital Management, Inc.
10805 Sunset Office Dr. #400
Saint Louis, MO 63127
(314) 822-3500

ADDITIONAL COMMENTS BY ADAM WHITE, CONSULTING EDITOR

As a rough rule, it seems like markets are trending less than they did before. Perhaps this is due to the prevalence of institutional money employing trend-following strategies. The crowd can never be overwhelmingly correct in their approach to the market simply because the crowd is the market. It is like the maxim applied to generals: they always fight to win their last war. Perhaps someday futures markets will change character after all traders are solidified into the camp that practices trading range strategies.

RATIO OPTION SPREAD

This position consists of buying an option that is close-to-the-money and selling two options further out-of-the-money (Exhibits 4.28, 4.29). It works particularly well in volatile markets, especially those that are bullishly oriented. The reason for this is that the options that are the far out-of-the-money options become overpriced because of the demand for "cheap" options in these types of markets.

An example of a ratio spread would be purchasing an April gold 440 call and selling (2) April gold 500 calls at a $300 credit. (This is the way you give the order to your broker.) The floor broker, for example, will purchase the 440 call for $2,400, while simultaneously selling (2) 500 calls at $1,350 each. You, therefore, pay out $2,400 but receive back $2,700, for a net of $300 credit. This $300 credit is very important in preventing losses if your prediction of market direction is wrong.

This trade would be profitable if gold moves down $440 or up over $110, for a range of profitability of over $550 (Exhibit 4.30). If April gold expires at any dollar value from $440 to $0, both the calls purchased and the calls sold are worthless. Therefore, you lose the $2,400 paid for the 440 call, however, make $2,700 you received for the (2) 500 calls, for a net profit of $300.

However, if the gold contract expires in the range between $440 and $500 (which is what you would be predicting in doing this spread) you are much more profitable. In that case, you still collect the $2,700 premium for selling the 500 calls as they are expiring worthless; you still lose the $2,400 premium paid for the 440 calls; however, you make $100 for every $1 gold closes above $440. The chart below also shows the amount of money that you will make in addition to the $300 credit at each price level, which ranges from $300 at the 440 level to $6,300 at the $500 level (Exhibit 4.31).

Now before everyone rushes out to put on this spread, let's look at the area where potential problems arise. (Remember, there is no "sure thing" in trading: if it looks too good to be true, it is!) There are only trades that are profitable over large ranges or have high probabilities of profits. Ironically, the problem in this trade arises if the market does even better than predicted. The chart also shows what happens to profits over the

Exhibit 4.28
Ratio Option Spread

STRATEGY:	Ratio Option Spread.
POSITION:	Bullish—Buy call, sell 2 or more out-of-money calls. Bearish—Buy put, sell 2 or more out-of-money puts.
MARKET TREND:	Neutral/slightly trending.
MAXIMUM PROFIT:	Difference between strike prices of long and short options.
POTENTIAL LOSS:	Unlimited if underlying futures contract exceeds strike price of options sold.
WHEN TO INITIATE:	Option premium high; market has made large move and is likely to continue to trend.
WHICH STRIKE PRICE AND EXPIRATION TO USE:	Buy strike price at least a limit move out-of-the-money; sell options at least 2 strike prices away. Use option expiration at least 3 months from strategy initiation. Excellent position to initiate after market has made a large move and option premiums are high, especially if credit is received, as spread will be profitable if market moves against you, remains neutral, or reacts as expected.

500 level, until finally at $560 per ounce you begin to lose money! In effect, you lose $100 for each $1 gold closes over $560 per ounce.

Because of this, strict risk management requires closing out the position if the price of the contract rises above the strike price of the calls sold. In this case, it would require closing the position if gold closed over $500 per ounce. If this were to occur quickly, say in one month after initiating, this would cause a loss. (However, if you were able to hold the spread for three weeks or more, the decay of the premium for the short options should act to prevent any loss in this position even if you were forced to close it out.)

Why does this spread work so well? Because the two options sold contain only "time value" which constantly decays each day as the option approaches maturity. In this example, the two 500 calls you sold will decay in value much quicker than the 440 call since the 500 calls are much further out-of-the-money.

Exhibit 4.29
Examples of Chart Pattern to Look for in Underlying Future

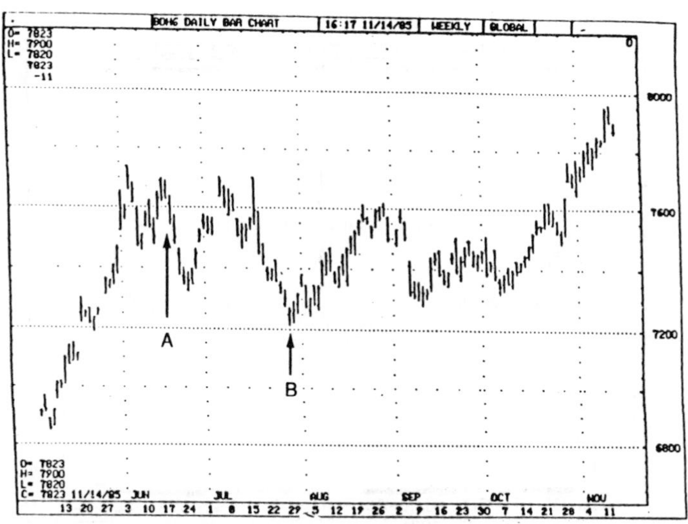

©1991 CQG, Inc. TQ 20/20

Treasury bonds had made a near vertical move of eight points in one month, causing out-of-the-money calls to expand greatly in premium valuation. The ratio spread of long 76 call and short 80 and 82 call, even though initiated at a small debit, had an excellent probability of profit.

©1991 CQG, Inc. TQ 20/20

The Swiss Franc moved up 1,000 points from May through October, and option premiums were very high. The ratio spreads of long the 46 call and short two 49 calls was initiated at a $200 credit. This spread has a very high probability of profit, and had a profit range from 0 through 5,200.

Exhibit 4.30
Range of Profit

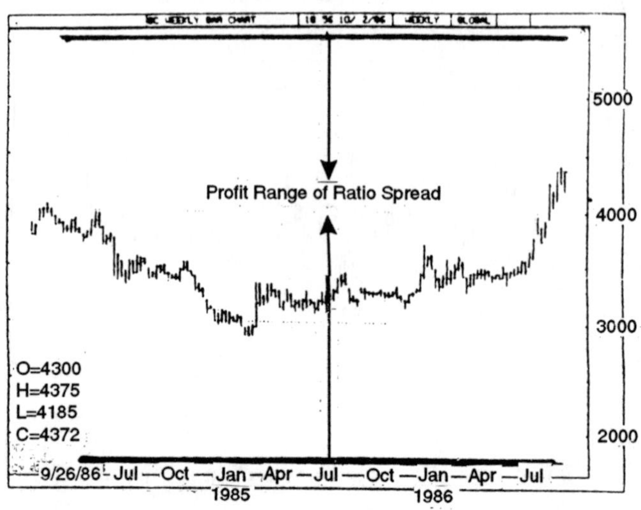

Exhibit 4.31
Profit/Loss of Gold Ratio Spread

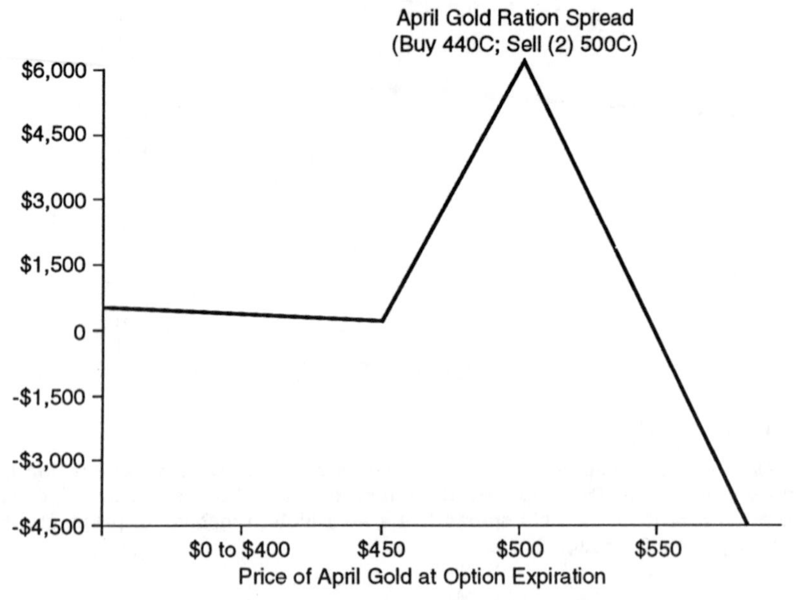

The chart formation we are interested in is always the same—a market making an almost straight up vertical move. This type of bullish formation is necessary since you are seeking to sell multiples of the furthest out-of-the-money options at the highest possible premium. This is the real *secret* of the best ratio spread—being able to obtain extraordinarily high premiums for the out-of-the-money calls that you sell, and this type of bullish market provides your best premiums.

For example, in 1990, with March copper trading at 115 (after moving almost straight up from 60) you could buy one March copper 120 call and sell two March copper 140 calls and receive a 100 point or $250 credit. The 140 calls at that time were the furthest out-of-the-money calls available, and could be sold at 700 points each. Being able to receive a large amount of premium not only provides more cash for your account, but also allows significant protection if the market consolidates or turns around and heads lower (Exhibit 4.32).

In the March copper ratio spread, the type of action you were looking for was a slow upward movement in the market with March copper expiring at the 140 level. This would provide you with a 20 cent ($5,000) profit on your long call; no loss on your short calls as they would expire worthless; and you would also collect your initial $250 credit.

The only problem area is when March copper begins to exceed the 140 level. Since you would be short two options and only long one, you begin to lose 2 cents on the options that you are short and gain only 1 cent on the long option for loss of 1 cent ($250) for every penny copper moves over $1.40.

It is for this reason that it is best to place mandatory stops on all ratio spreads at the level of your short calls. That is, if March copper were to exceed $1.40 at any time, you should close out the position. The amount of profit or loss on this spread at that point would depend on the time when copper reached this level. As seen in Exhibit 4.33, if copper did not reach this level until December 1, you would have a profit on this spread.

The reason for the amount of time for copper to exceed this level is important. The overvalued out-of-the-money calls will begin to quickly lose their value because of the time decay of these options as the contract approaches expiration. However, the opposite will happen to the long 120 call if the market makes a slow move up. This call would be in-the-money and start to gain in value. In fact, during the last 60 days before expiration of the option, with copper trading between 125 and 135, you could expect many days to see that the option purchased gains in value, while the out-of-the-money calls that had been sold lose value, thereby providing profit on both sides of the transaction.

Exhibit 4.32
Ratio Option Spread (Copper)

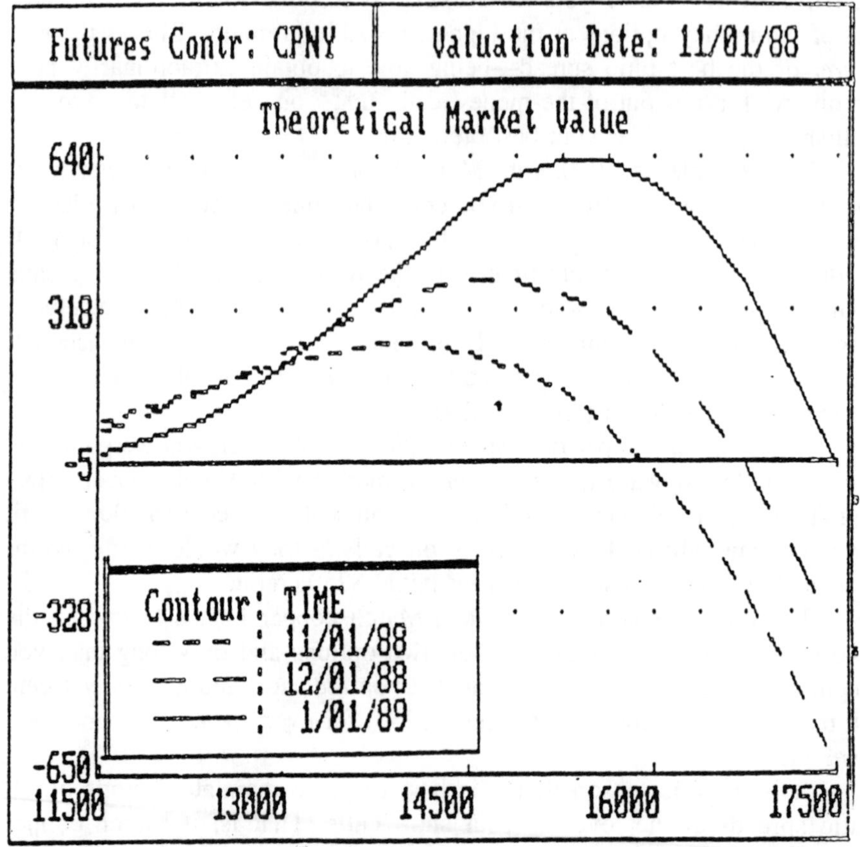

The only problem is when March copper begins to exceed the 140 level. Since we are short 2 options and only long 1, we begin to lose 2 cents on the options that we are short and gain only 1 cent on the long option for loss of 1 cent ($250) for every penny copper moves over $1.40. The chart illustrates how profits begin to erode to a point where at $1.60 we begin to experience losses.

The main benefit of this position is its flexibility in allowing you to profit without having to predict the exact direction of the market. It allows you to make maximum use of the overvaluation and disparity in price of the out-of-the-money options. Because of this, ratio spreads are one of our favorite option strategies.

Exhibit 4.33
Ratio Option Spread (Copper)

Futures Contr: CPNY	Valuation Date: 11/01/88		
	Theoretical Market Value		
Futures	Time:11/01/88	12/01/88	1/01/89
11500	92	67	24
11875	121	99	46
12250	152	138	82
12625	183	184	132
13000	212	233	199
13375	234	282	279
13750	247	327	368
14125	248	361	458
14500	234	381	540
14875	202	381	602
15250	149	358	636
15625	75	308	633
16000	-22	230	590
16375	-143	122	501
16750	-287	-15	368
17125	-453	-181	193
17500	-641	-375	-13

HOW TO FIND THE BEST OPPORTUNITIES FOR RATIO SPREADS, AND PICK THE BEST OPTIONS TO USE

The ratio spread is one of our best trading opportunities. The main benefit of the ratio spread is to take advantage of disparities between option strike prices. We find at times, that out-of-the-money options become greatly overvalued and the ratio spread is one of the best trading strategies to take advantage of this overvaluation. This is because the ratio spread has a LARGE RANGE OF PROFITABILITY.

There are two areas however, that seem to be the most difficult in considering this position:

1. How can a trader recognize opportunities for ratio spreads?
2. How can you determine which are the best strike prices to use?

With over forty futures markets that trade options and at least three trading months in each of these markets, it would be a tedious task of several hours per day to determine which options are overvalued; even if you had an on-line computer. Since the types of ratio spreads we like to take advantage of occur usually no more than a couple of times a year, even the most dedicated trader could soon lose interest after putting in months of hard work and not finding any trades.

Fortunately, the markets themselves usually tell us when the best ratio spread opportunities occur. Simply stated: a vertical move up, or any large break to the upside is our sign to begin watching that market for ratio spread opportunities. Why is this? We found that when a market begins to make a bullish move such as we had in the summer of 1992 in the soybean market, that small public traders have a demand for "cheap" options to purchase to be involved in this move.

In nontrending or slowly trending markets, the out-of-the-money options usually have somewhat of a higher volatility and are slightly overvalued as compared to the at-the-money options. For example, in gold, the October gold 340 call which was $2 in-the-money was trading at a volatility of 8.1% and the 350 call was trading at a volatility of 8.7%, while the 360 call was at 9.5%. However, contrast this with the November soybean market where the $6 call was trading at 27.6%, and the $9 call at 46.5%, an increase of over 59% over the at-the-money option!

This disparity of the price of the out-of-the-money options increasing on breakouts to the upside occur when markets move lower. Small public traders that are the call option buyers in bullish markets do not seem as interested in bear markets to allow the same discrepancy on the put side. There are exceptions, however, such as the October 1987 stock market crash, and the oil market during the Gulf War; both of these events even caused the out-of-the-money call options to greatly increase in volatility and provide ratio spread opportunities. Also, as a general group, the metals and agricultural markets tend to provide the best opportunities for ratio spreads. We have found our best ratio spreads over the last years to occur in silver followed closely by soybeans and then sugar and gold. However, in addition to these markets we have previously used ratio spreads in treasury bonds, S&P 500, Swiss Franc, Japanese Yen, and cotton.

Now that we have some idea of the best methods to locate the potential for ratio spreads, determining the contract month and strike price to use can be confusing. There are several points to look at here. First, and most important in constructing a ratio spread, we want to make certain (as much as possible) that we do not sell options that are likely to go "into the money."

For example, in the 1994 soybean market, soybeans moved up from 590 to 640 in the last three months with a 30-day range of 620–650. A ratio spread of long the November $6.50 call and short two $7 calls, would produce a credit of 20 cents premium (the net of the money we received for selling the two $7 calls minus payment for the $6.50 call we purchased). This money would be ours to keep if November soybeans expired under the current highs of 650. This position would also produce the best profits if soybeans expired in the range of $6.50 to $7, as again we would still receive the $1,000 credit plus 50 cents for every penny that November soybeans closed above $6.50 to a maximum of $2,500 at $7.

However, this position becomes dangerous if prices exceed $7. This is because even though we are at a 50 cent profit ($2,500) at $7, for every penny the market moves over $7 at expiration, we lose one cent ($50) of that profit. Therefore, at $8, we would lose back our initial credit and have a potential unlimited loss of $50 for every cent the market exceeded $8. This is particularly disconcerting—to have a bullish outlook and have the market move in our direction (although stronger than we expected), and still lose money.

Contrast this position with the ratio spread of buying the November soybean $8 call and selling two $9 calls at 4 cent ($200) credit. In this position if November soybeans close below $8 at expiration we collect $200. Although this provides much more protection than the previous position, the reward is also a lot less (80% lower). Also, if soybeans move up and close between the range of $6.50 to $8, there is no additional profit as there would be in the previous position. However, on the upside, if soybeans were to begin a runaway bull market, a maximum profit of $5,000 (plus our initial credit) can be made if beans close at $9 at expiration, and our profit range on this spread extends all the way to $18.

Therefore, in comparing these positions from a money management standpoint, we can come to simple conclusion. If our market perception is that soybeans are going to stay in the current range, move lower, or just slightly higher, the first, more aggressive position is the best one. However, if our concern is that the market may continue to move rapidly higher, and we want to have a conservative position that will make profits, whether the market moves lower, stays in the same range, or moves substantially higher (in this case up to $11), the second position is better.

To summarize, there are some absolute rules we use in looking for the best ratio spreads:

1. Look for markets that are beginning to have large bullish moves.

2. Use options between three and six months before expiration.
3. Always initiate the ratio spread at a credit (for complete downside protection).
4. Sell options as far as possible from the current price of the underlying market (while still obtaining a reasonable premium).
5. Make certain that there is a disparity in the premium between the options bought and options sold to provide you with a real advantage.

However, the discretionary part of this trade occurs in determining which options to use. As we mentioned above, some of this will come into play based on your view of the underlying market, and your decision whether to take a conservative or aggressive position. Whichever stance is taken, remember that these positions are flexible and can be modified at a later date very easily.

For example, if a market has a long period of consolidation or retracement after initiating the ratio spread, you may want to consider repurchasing one of the short options to allow for greater profits and less risk if the market begins to trend in your favor. (We often do this when the market shows some sign of life after this pullback.) On the other hand, if the market does begin to trend strongly and near the danger point of being close to the price of the options sold, you have the flexibility of either closing one of the short options or moving the entire position to higher strike prices.

REVERSE RATIO SPREAD

The reverse ratio spread is an excellent position to enter into in extremely volatile option markets such as coffee, orange juice, pork bellies, or cotton, and even in the currencies or financial markets in turbulent times or before major reports or events (Exhibits 4.34, 4.35).

This spread is initiated by selling an at-the-money put and call, and purchasing two or more out-of-the-money puts and calls. You would like to obtain a credit on the position, or at worst a break-even on the debits versus credits.

As seen in the profit/loss graph below, this position is profitable when the market makes a large move in either direction (Exhibit 4.36). It is similar to the Neutral Option Position in that it is unnecessary to determine the exact direction of the market, however in this case, you want to be able to deduce that a large move is about to occur. It is for this reason, this spread is particularly effective in the agricultural commodities during critical growing times, and the currencies during politically turbulent periods.

To give this trade time to mature, you should initiate the position using options having about six months to expiration. Since the maximum loss occurs at expiration if the underlying market fails to move substantially, you should close out this trade 30-45 days prior to expiration, if the expected move fails to occur.

IN-THE-MONEY OPTION DEBIT SPREAD

The "in-the-money option debit spread" is a position that can be used to take advantage of a trending market, and also provide significant benefits over a straight "long or short" future position (Exhibits 4.37, 4.38).

It is initiated by purchasing an in-the-money option containing intrinsic (real) value, and selling an out-of-the-money option containing only time value. If the market moves in the intended direction, the in-the-money option will gain value much faster than its out-of-the-money option, which,

Exhibit 4.34
Reverse Ratio Spread

STRATEGY:	Reverse Ratio Spread.
POSITION:	Sell at-the-money put and call. Buy two or more out-of-the-money puts and calls.
MARKET TREND:	Neutral—but likely to make large moves in either direction.
MAXIMUM PROFIT:	Unlimited.
POTENTIAL LOSS:	Difference between the strike prices of options bought and sold.
WHEN TO INITIATE:	Technical pattern of market suggests large move likely to occur, but direction is uncertain.
WHICH STRIKE PRICE AND EXPIRATION TO USE:	Options that have 60 days or more before expiration. Sell put and call options at-the-money; purchase 2 puts and 2 calls two strike prices out-of-the-money.
COMMENT:	When credit received, position will be profitable if market moves in either direction.

Exhibit 4.35
Reverse Ratio Spread (Treasury Bonds)

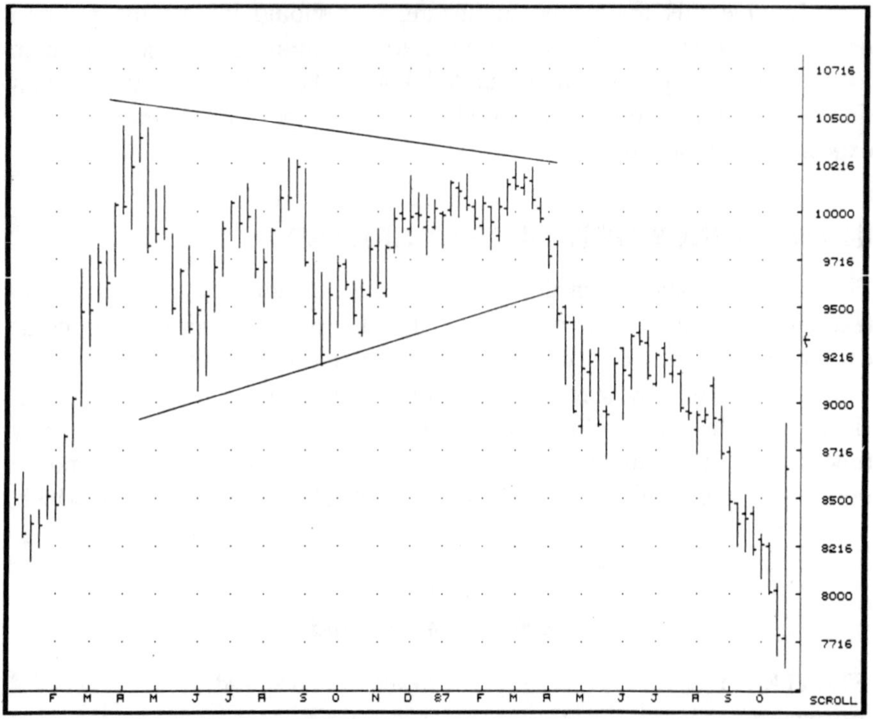

Bonds moved into a one-year consolidation triangle suggesting a large move in either direction and option volatility had dropped to historically low levels.

in fact, sometimes will lose its value, even as the market moves in its favor! It can also provide substantial protection in a neutral market, as you will collect premium from the declining value of the out-of-the-money option that you have sold.

Using in-the-Money Options to Take Advantage of Option Price Disparities

We have always recommended that option positions be used when they can provide us with an advantage ("trading edge") over futures. In conventional futures trading, after using our selected trading method (technical, fundamental, trend-following, etc.) to determine market direction, we then initiate our trade by purchasing or selling a futures contract. If the market does not move in the direction predicted, we lose money on this trade. (In fact, many times money is lost even when the market moves as predicted, after

Exhibit 4.36
Profit/Loss of Reverse Ratio Position

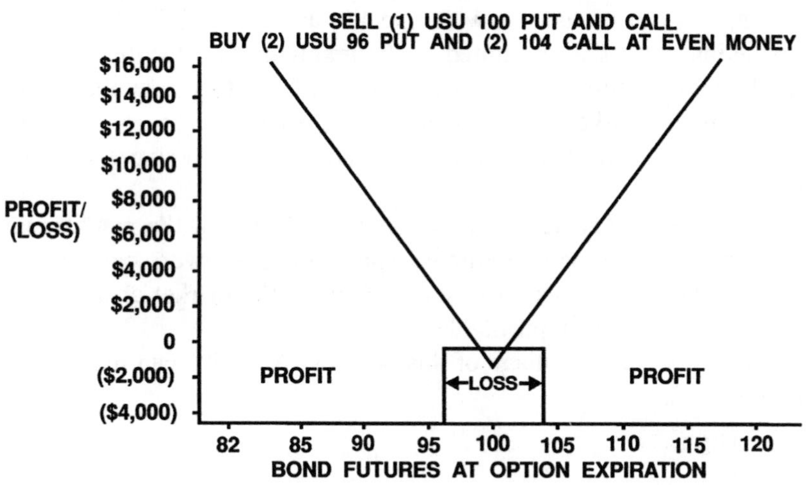

Exhibit 4.37
In-the-Money Option Debit Spread

STRATEGY:	In-the-Money Debit Spread.
POSITION:	Bullish—Buy in-the-money call, sell further out-of-the-money call. Bearish—Buy in-the-money put, sell further out-of-the-money put.
MARKET TREND:	Bullish or bearish.
MAXIMUM PROFIT:	Differences between strike prices of options.
POTENTIAL LOSS:	Limited to debit paid when position is initiated.
WHEN TO INITIATE:	Trending market with higher option premium (volatility) for out-of-the-money option.
WHICH STRIKE PRICE AND EXPIRATION TO USE:	Options that have 60 days or less before expiration. Buy option in or near the money. Sell most overvalued option.
COMMENT:	Excellent position to take advantage of market trend, disparity in option premium, and time decay of the out-of-the-money option.

first making a sharp move against us, thereby "stopping" us out of our position.)

This is where the proper use of options and option strategies becomes important, and can provide us with a real "trading edge." First, when buying an option since risk is limited to the premium paid for the option, we can trade without "stops," since we no longer have to worry about unlimited losses if the market moves against us. This can prevent us from losing our position (and our money) when the market makes a sharp, temporary, short-term move.

The in-the-money debit spread can be successful if the market moves in the direction that you predicted (put spread—lower; call spread—higher), or even if the market is stable! Only if the market changes direction will this spread be unprofitable.

This is another advantage of this position. A market can move only in three directions:

1. Higher
2. Lower
3. Neutral

This position is profitable both if the market moves in our desired direction (higher or lower), and if the market remains neutral; thereby creating a successful position in two out of three instances. Compare this with conventional futures trading where not only is our trade profitable only in one out of three of the same circumstances, but since we can also be stopped out at times even when we are correct on our market direction, our chances for success are closer to 25%.

However, our advantages do not stop here. In addition to more than doubling our odds of success on a trade, this position also allows us to take advantage of disparity in option pricing (overvaluation), and the time decay of option premium.

However, after extensive research we have determined that the benefits from using these in-the-money options can far outweigh the disadvantages.

We have found that by purchasing in-the-money options and selling one or more further out-of-the-money options we can construct a position that takes advantage of:

1. The trend of the market;
2. The overvaluation of the out-of-the-money options;
3. The time decay of the out-of-the-money options; and

Exhibit 4.38
Chart Patterns to Look for in Underlying Future (A Trending Market)

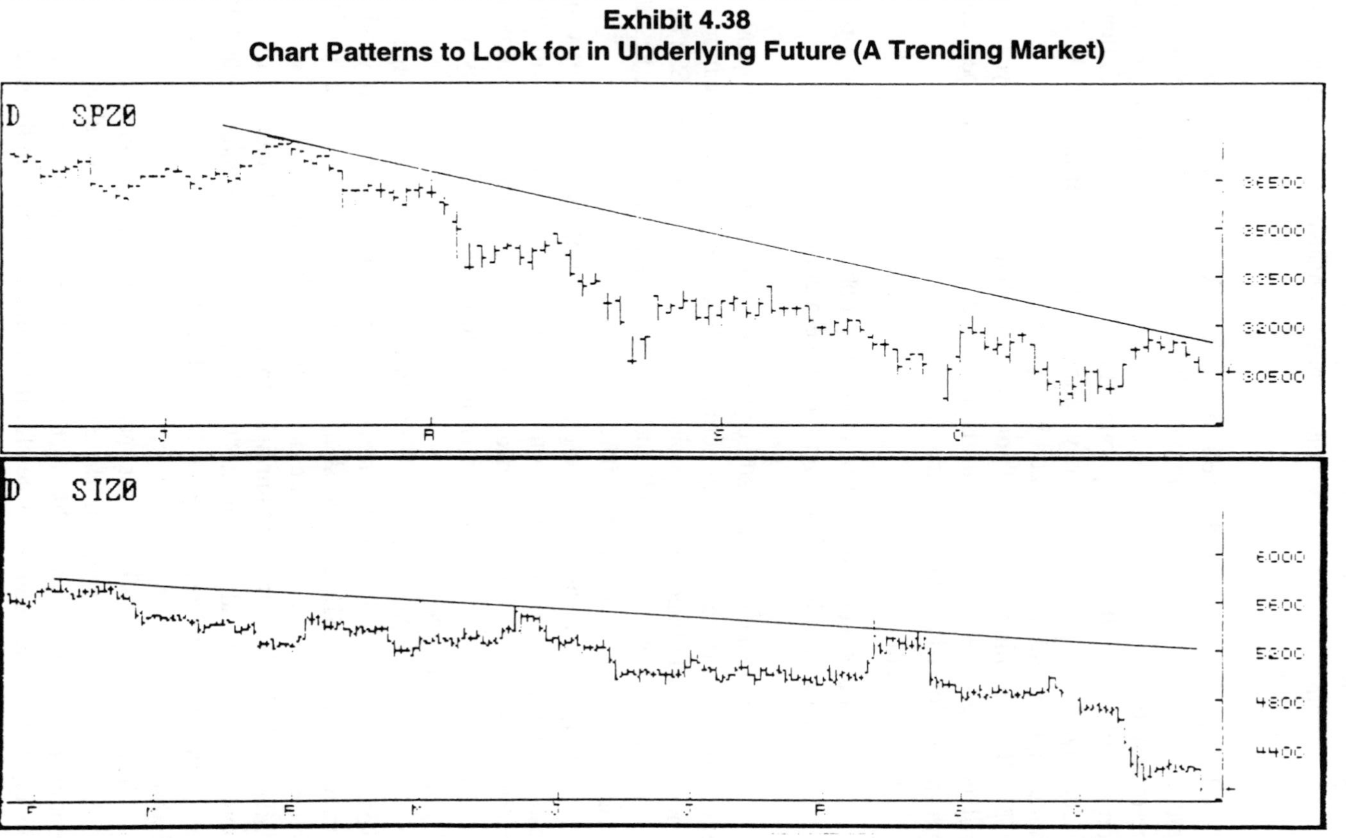

4. The tendency of the in-the-money options to hold their value better than the out-of-the-money options under most market circumstances.

This position also works well to help us take advantage of the overvaluation of out-of-the-money options. Many times we find that the out-of-the-money options are overvalued anywhere from 10% to 50% or more as compared to the in-the-money options. This means that the premium that a trader pays for the out-of-the-money option is much higher than the in-the-money option, and it will decay at a much faster rate.

After watching and researching these positions for the last year we will now begin recommending in-the-money debit spreads. The best circumstances for using this position are:

1. A trending market.
2. Markets where the out-of-the-money options are trading at a premium of at least 20% over the in-the-money options.

Another advantage of this strategy is the need for much less capital to enter a position, thereby allowing both more leverage and diversification of funds. While a bullish future's position in the S&P 500 requires $22,000 initial margin, our "debit spread" mentioned above requires only a $2,500 premium, a reduction of almost 90%.

Finally, this position can also effectively be used as a hedge for your cash or future portfolio. For example, if you own a stock portfolio, put positions can be constructed to hedge your downside risk at a minimum cost. Similar hedges can also be constructed to protect bond, currency, metal, and agricultural positions.

During Oct.–Dec. 1990 while the market was in a trading range between 315 and 330, although the market was neutral, an in-the-money debit spread of long the 315 call and short the 330 put would have been profitable and have collected the entire debit during this period. This is because while the 315 call contained "intrinsic" (real) value, the further out-of-the-money option (330 call) contained "time" value. The time value in the 330 call option decayed every day as the option moved closer to expiration (Exhibit 4.39).

Therefore, the 330 call lost much of its value on a continual basis, while the in-the-money option (the 315 call) lost little of its value since it contained very little time value to begin with. Because of these reasons, this type of position can be successful if the market moves in the direction that you predicted (put spread—lower; call spread—higher), or even if the market is stable! In addition to increasing your odds of success on a trade,

Exhibit 4.39
In-the-Money Debit Spreads (S&P 500)

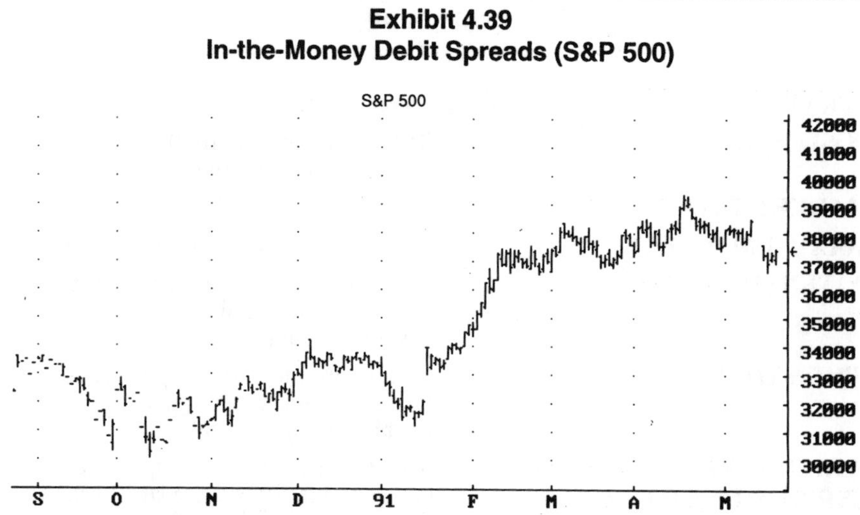

In-the-money debit spreads were recommended in late 1990 and early 1991 to take advantage of trending market and high premium for the out-of-the-money call options.

this position also allows you to take advantage of disparity in option pricing (overvaluation), and the time decay of option premium.

CALENDAR SPREAD

The calendar spread is initiated by selling an option of close-in-maturity and purchasing the same option of a later expiration (Exhibits 4.40, 4.41).

The option sold will lose its time value at a much greater rate as it approaches maturity. As decay of option time value accelerates in the final 60 days prior to expiration, this is the best time to initiate the calendar spread. At that time, this strategy has a high probability of profit because of the severe decay in time value. The objective of this position is to profit from the more rapid time decay of the close to expiration option.

For example, on November 1, 1990, a calendar spread could have been constructed in crude oil options by purchasing the January 36 call and selling the December 36 call at a debit of 50. Both options were out-of-the-money (with December crude being at 3300 and January at 3200), and contained only time value. However, since the December option had only 14 days until expiration, it would decay much faster, whether the market went higher, lower, or remained stable. This position had the further benefit of the December option having higher volatility than the January options.

Exhibit 4.40
Calendar Spread

STRATEGY:	Calendar Spread.
POSITION:	Sell near-month call (put). Buy far-month call (put).
MARKET TREND:	Neutral or trending.
MAXIMUM PROFIT:	Unlimited after short options expire.
POTENTIAL LOSS:	Unlimited (theoretically), but short option loss should, in most cases, be covered by gain in long option value.
WHEN TO INITIATE:	60 days prior to option expiration to take advantage of decay in option premium of option sold.
WHICH STRIKE PRICE AND EXPIRATION TO USE:	Sell closest-to-expiration option series, buy next furthest out; use strike prices depending on market outlook.
COMMENT:	Excellent spread to take advantage of option premium time value decay while still having protection from adverse move.

Exhibit 4.41
Calendar Spread (Swiss Franc)

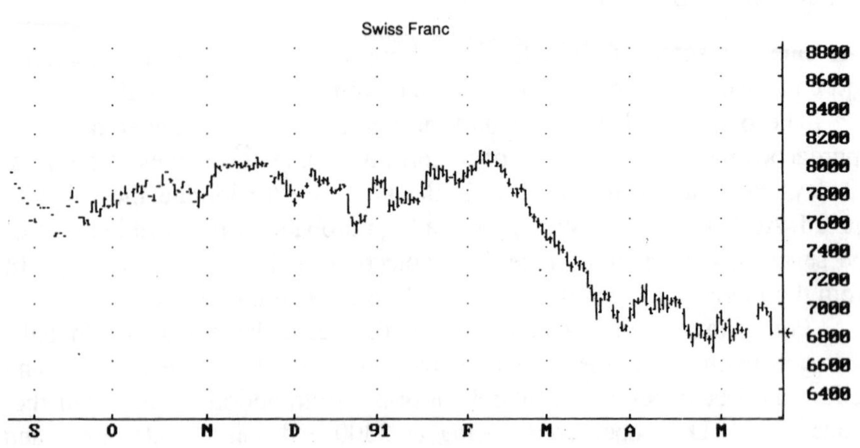

The calendar spread was recommended in March and April 1991 to take advantage of the high option premium in the expiring May Swiss Franc option contract.

Closer to expiration options frequently have higher volatility than further out options. In 1991 this occurred quite often in many markets, including the currencies, bonds, and cattle. Anytime volatility is 20% or more higher in the front months, calendar spreads should be considered.

After the expiration of the short option, you should then have an objective of turning the long option into a "free trade," if the market moves in your favor, or just close out the remaining option if it doesn't.

OTHER COMMON OPTION STRATEGIES

The benefits and disadvantages of many option strategies are outlined in Exhibit 4.42. (Although it is impossible to discuss all of the many different positions that can be created by combining or mutating other option strategies, the most commonly used strategies are summarized here.)

I am not going to discuss these strategies in detail for several reasons. First, I see no reason to duplicate the many fine books in our bibliography that describe these positions adequately; and second, I wish to consider only strategies that can give you an advantage ("trading edge") by presenting you with favorable risk/reward ratios or a high probability of profit.

HEDGING WITH OPTIONS

Hedging strategies have been commonly employed by farmers, producers, distributors, and institutions to lock in costs, profits, or limit potential losses. Prior to the introduction of options in the 1980s, the futures market was commonly used for these purposes.

For example, a jewelry manufacturer who needs to purchase silver in the next six months, could purchase a six-month silver futures contract at today's price to lock in his cost of silver. Similarly, a wheat farmer, with wheat trading at $3 per bushel and the cost of production at $2.25 per bushel, could sell his wheat on the futures market even though it would not be ready in the fields for several months, and lock in a profit of 75 cents per bushel. And, companies that deal with other foreign countries and must contract in advance would use currencies futures to make certain that fluctuations in the currencies market would not adversely effect them.

However, the introduction of options in the 1980s brought more tools and flexibility for hedgers' needs. For example, the wheat farmer instead of selling his wheat at $3, and not being able to participate in any further price rise, could then use put options to protect his profits, and still be in a position to make more money if the wheat market went higher.

Exhibit 4.42

MOST COMMON OPTION STRATEGIES FOR ALL MARKETS			
OPTION SPREAD STRATEGY	**POSITION**	**CHARACTERISTICS**	**BEST TIME TO USE**
NEUTRAL STRATEGIES			
STRANGLE	Sell out-of-the-money put and call.	Maximum use of time value decay.	Trading range market with volatility peaking.
GUTS	Sell in-the-money put and call.	Receive large premium.	Options have time premium and market in trading range.
ARBITRAGE	Purchase and sell similar options simultaneously.	Profit certain if done at credit.	Any time credit received.
CONVERSION	Buy futures, buy at-the-money put and sell out-of-the-money call.	Profit certain if done at credit.	Any time credit received.
BOX	Sell calls and puts same strike prices.	Profit certain if done at credit.	Any time credit received.
BUTTERFLY	Buy at-the-money call (put) sell 2 out-of-the-money calls (puts) and buy out-of-the-money call (put).	Profit certain if done at credit.	Any time credit received.
CALENDAR	Sell near-month, buy far-month, same strike price.	Near-month time value decay faster.	Small debit, trading range market.
MIXED STRATEGIES			
RATIO CALL	Buy call, sell calls of higher strike price.	Neutral, slightly bullish.	Large credit and difference between strike price of option bought and sold.

Exhibit 4.42 (Continued)

MOST COMMON OPTION STRATEGIES FOR ALL MARKETS			
OPTION SPREAD STRATEGY	**POSITION**	**CHARACTERISTICS**	**BEST TIME TO USE**
STRADDLE PURCHASE	Buy put and call.	Options will lose time value premium quickly.	Options under-valued and market likely to make a big move.
COVERED CALL	Buy future—sell call.	Collect premium on calls sold.	Neutral—slightly bullish.
COVERED PUT	Sell future—sell put.	Collect premium of puts sold.	Neutral—slightly bearish.
SYNTHETIC FUTURES POSITION	Buy call (put). Sell put (call).	Neutral, slightly trending market.	Receive credit, option sold far-out-of-the-money.
BULLISH STRATEGIES			
BUY CALL	Most bullish option position.	Loss limited to premium.	Undervalued option with volatility increasing.
SELL PUT	Neutral-bullish option position.	Profit limited to debit.	Small debit, bullish market.
VERTICAL BULL-CALLS	Buy call, sell call of higher strike price.	Loss limited to debit.	Small debit, bullish market.
VERTICAL BULL-PUTS	Sell put, buy put of higher strike price.	Loss limited to price difference.	Large credit, bullish market.
BEARISH STRATEGIES			
BUY PUT	Most bearish option position.	Loss limited to premium.	Undervalued option with volatility increasing.
SELL CALL	Neutral-bearish option position.	Profit limited to premium.	Option overvalued, market flat, bearish.
VERTICAL BEAR-PUTS	Buy at-the-money put, sell out-of-the-money put.	Loss limited to debit.	Small debit, bearish market.
VERTICAL BEAR-CALLS	Sell call, buy call of higher strike price.	Loss limited to strike price difference minus credit.	Large credit, bearish market.

These strategies are not limited to farmers, producers, and manufacturers. Any trader of a stock or commodity can also use options for hedging. Let's examine the three most popular methods of hedging:

1. Purchasing puts to protect a long position (or calls to protect the short position);
2. Selling calls to add income to an account; and
3. "No-Loss, Cost-Free" hedging.

1. Purchasing a Put for Protection

The main benefit of purchasing a put to protect a long position is that it will provide absolute price protection if the market begins to decline. For example, assume that a trader has purchased a June S&P 500 contract at 435 and the market has now moved up to 465 and begins to consolidate. A trader with a long position and profits of $15,000 per contract could be very concerned as to whether a severe correction is about to take place. Although a "stop" order could conceivably be used to protect his profits, many times a stop will not provide sufficient protection if events occur overnight or if the market begins dropping very rapidly. Further, it can be frustrating when the trader finds himself "stopped out" of a good position, which then begins to take off in his favor.

A better method here would be to purchase a S&P 455 put. By using less than 10% of the profits of the trade (about $1,000 in this case), a put can be purchased that will provide absolute price protection below the 455 level. This means that profits of $10,000 can be locked in, and unlimited profits are still available if the market continues to move higher (Exhibit 4.43).

2. Selling Calls for Income

Using the same example as above, the trader may decide that the market is again consolidating after moving from 435 to 465, and wish to add additional income to his account during this consolidation phase. To accomplish this, the trader would sell a 475 call and collect this premium for his account. The major benefit of this position over the purchase of put is that in a consolidating market, this strategy will add substantial income to your account on top of your profits, where the put will be a drain on your profits. However, the sale of calls provides no substantial protection against a large break in the market, unlike the put purchase.

Exhibit 4.43
Purchasing a Put for Protection (S&P 500—455 Put)

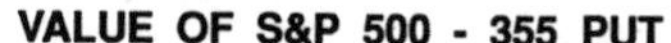

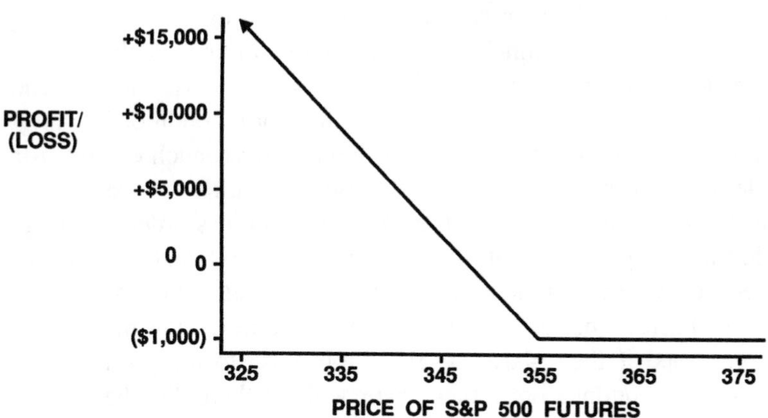

As the price of the S&P 500 *declines*, the put becomes more valuable and offsets any loss in the futures contract.

As the price of the S&P 500 *increases*, the futures contract becomes more profitable.

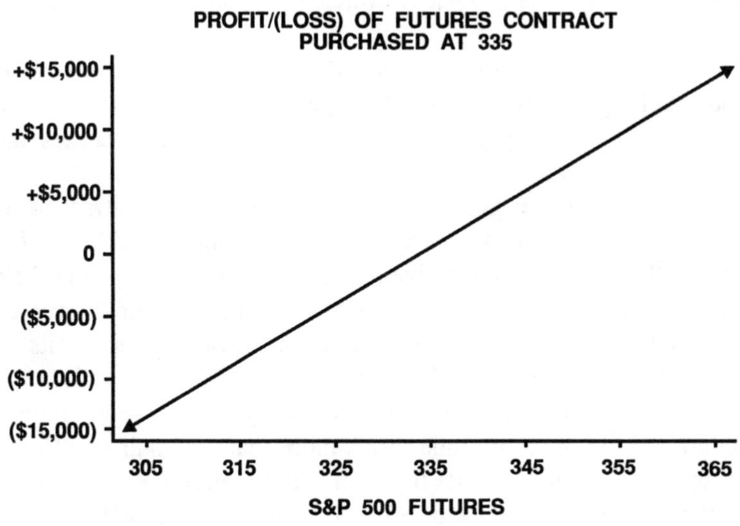

3. "No-loss Cost-free" Option Hedging

The best method of protecting positions is a combination of number 1 and 2 through a "No-Loss Cost-Free" hedging method. This allows you to use benefits of both strategies.

Quite often in the markets we are faced with tough decisions regarding giving up a "sure thing" for a potentially more valuable prize. For example, after the crude oil exploded, traders had profits of thousands of dollars per position. However, because of the world conditions, many were concerned about not only being able to hold onto as much of this profit as possible, but protecting their capital in case the market dropped as quickly as it had risen. They also were insecure with stop loss orders, feeling they provided little protection against a drop in the market, since the oil market is subject to extreme overnight moves, based on political conditions around the world. Further, because of the explosive nature of the market, traders were concerned if they placed a "stop" too close to the position, only to see the market continue on in their favor without them. On the other hand, placing a stop order far away from the market could subject them to much larger losses.

Fortunately, there was a much easier way to protect profits, while still allowing them to make additional profit if the market continued in their favor. And, all of this could be accomplished for no additional out-of-pocket expense! Imagine being offered a free insurance policy to cover all of your assets from any potential problems or disaster without costing you any additional money. This is what is available to you by the proper use of options.

How do you accomplish this? In the case of the crude oil market, where you are long a futures contract (expecting the price to go higher) you first purchase a put option. Remember a put option becomes more valuable as the price goes lower.

Let's assume that you purchased a crude oil futures contract at $20, and after it rose to $40 you purchased the 35 put option for $1,000. If oil were to drop, this would provide absolute protection of any profits below your put's strike price of $35. Since you had purchased your futures contracts at under $20, you are in effect "locking in" most of your profits with no chance for loss no matter what happens.

Let's assume that overnight large previously undiscovered fields of oil are found and the price of crude drops more than one-half to $15. This would cause your original contract that you had purchased at $20 to have a loss of 500 points × $10 a point or $5,000. However, your $35 put would now be worth $20,000 ($35 strike price minus $15 actual price or $2,000 × $10 a point or $20,000). Even this type of catastrophic event leaves you with a profit of $15,000. And, the best part is if oil continues higher, you will still be able to profit from the appreciation of the market.

The second factor of the protective option strategy, "no-loss, cost-free hedging," is to sell a call to pay for the put purchased. If you continue to just pay for the protection by way of the puts, it can eventually become pretty expensive if the market stays in a trading range. This is because the options expire in a definite amount of time, and if the market just remains in a trading range, as markets often do, you will have to continue purchasing new puts and paying substantial amounts in premium.

Therefore, to pay for the put you purchased, I recommend selling an "out-of-the-money" crude oil call option. In this case you could sell a $45 call, which would not only entirely pay for the purchase of the $35 put, but still allow you $5,000 of additional profit if the market continued moving in your favor. Profits are limited to $45, if the market continued past that level. However, since the market had already moved over 100% from its lows at the beginning of the year, and you were still allowing for another more than 10% rise in prices, this small risk of having future profits somewhat limited is well worth the financial and emotional protection this position provides.

"No-loss, cost-free hedging" therefore provides for a win-win trade no matter what happens. If the market goes down, your capital and a percentage of your profits are protected from loss.

Using the same example as in number 1, after the S&P 500 rises from 435 to 465, you institute the no-loss cost-free hedging by purchasing the 455 put and selling the 475 call. In this instance, you are able to purchase the put for 350 points and sell the call for 450. By doing this you have locked in your profits of $10,000, similar to number one above; however, instead of having to pay $1,500 for the option, you are in fact paid $500 which is yours to keep on top of your profits. This is through the sale of the 475 call. You are also still able to receive an additional $5,000 in profits from this position if the market continues to rally.

The only negative that can be said about this trade at all is that your profits are limited to the 475 level. However, since the market had already made a substantial move and you are still allowing for another 1,000 point price rise, the small risk of having futures profits somewhat limited is well worth the financial and emotional protection this position provides. Further, if the market began to show substantial signs of breaking out from this consolidation, the position could be closed out, allowing for unlimited profits again.

With "No-loss, cost-free" hedging, if the market goes down, all of your capital and a good percentage of your profits is protected from loss. If the market moves sideways, you have neither gained nor lost from your strategy, since you received a credit when you initiated this position. And finally, if the market moved in your favor (although this insurance turned out to be unnecessary) at least you did not pay for it, you were not "stopped out" of your position as you could have been with a stop order, and you were still able to make additional profits on your trades (and in all cases, you were able to sleep well at night knowing your capital and most of your profits were protected).

Exhibit 4.44 examines the results of these and other possible hedging strategies in different market scenarios.

Exhibit 4.44
Results of Using Hedge/Income Strategies on Stock Portfolio

Standard & Poor's Futures with 30 Days to Expiration = 460; 450 Put = $850; 460 Put = $1,750; 460 Call = $1,750; 470 Call = $850

STRATEGY	STRATEGY CHARACTERISTICS	REQUIREMENT FOR PROFIT	ACTION	MARKET MOVEMENT	STRATEGY PROFIT/LOSS	STRATEGY GAIN/LOSS
Put Purchase	High cost/risk is loss of option premium; reward limited to prevention of loss of stock or bond portfolio value; requires good skill in timing and premium evaluation.	Loss of premium results unless significant downside move occurs.	Buy 2 460 Puts	Flat Decline to 450 Increase to 470	–3,500 +3,000 –3,500	–14% 12% –14%
Call Sale	Reward limited to amount of premium; limits profit potential of underlying portfolio, requires good skill in timing and premium evaluation.	Will add income to portfolio in flat or bear market, but can limit profit of underlying positions in bull market.	Sell 2 470 Calls	Flat Decline to 450	+1,700 +1,700	+6.8% +6.8%
Sell Future	Unlimited risk/reward requires maximum skill in timing.	Can provide hedge against loss in declining market, but can limit profit of underlying positions in bull market.	Sell 20 Futures	Flat Decline to 450 Increase to 470	0 +5,000 –5,000	0 +20% –20%
Neutral Option	Reward equal to amount of premium collected. Does not require prediction of market direction; requires good market monitoring and premium evaluation skill.	Underlying future remains in trading range of puts and calls sold; however, can be "rolled up or down."	Sell 2 450 Puts and Sell 2 470 Calls	Flat Decline to 450 Increase to 470	+3,400 +3,400 +3,400	+13.6% +13.6% +13.6%
Buy Put Sell Call ("No-Loss Cost-Free")	Eliminates downside risk without premium cost; does not require prediction of market direction or monitoring.	Excellent strategy for portfolio after significant market rally to lock in profits.	Buy 2 450 Puts Sell 2 470 Calls	Flat Decline to 450 Increase to 470	0 0 0	0 0 0
Ratio Write	Reward equal to premium collected; high probability of profit; requires some monitoring.	Best used after significant rally to add return to portfolio.	Buy 2 460 Calls and Sell 5 470 Calls	Flat Decline to 450 Increase to 470	+850 +850 +4,350	+ 3.3% + 3.3% +16.8%

CHAPTER 5

The Option Trading Plan

ORGANIZING YOUR PLAN

How can an option trader organize his research most effectively? This can seem quite confusing. In every market the trader is faced with three months of actively traded options containing approximately 10 actively traded strike prices each month for both puts and calls; and countless numbers of combinations and strategies that can be initiated between these options. To the new option trader, this can look like an insurmountable task. But, with proper organization and a few simple rules, order can be made out of this chaos.

First, use the process of elimination to pare down the amount of research and work that you plan to do each week. Illiquid option markets are dropped from consideration. (Any option market that does not trade an average daily volume of more than 1,000 contracts.)

Second is the elimination of all but seven types of option strategies. The strategies eliminated include all of the so-called arbitrage strategies including box spreads, conversions, butterflies, etc. As discussed before, although these spreads are great for floor traders and firms that specialize in arbitrage, the commissions and slippage on these trades make them economically unfeasible for everyone else. This leaves only seven positions (our "trading edge" strategies) to consider:

1. Option Purchase ("Free Trade")
2. Synthetic Futures Position
3. Neutral Option Position
4. Ratio Option Spread
5. Reverse-Ratio Spread
6. In-the-Money-Debit Spread
7. Calendar Spread

Then consider two final elements of importance—option volatility and the technical pattern of the market.

- In considering option volatility, compare current volatility readings with those of the last several weeks, months, and years to both determine the trend in volatility and see whether current option volatility is relatively high, low, or mediocre. High volatility readings alert us to potential option selling strategies, and with low volatility, option purchases should be considered.

- Finally, review the technical pattern of the market to determine whether there is any recognizable chart pattern that has been reliable in the past. Look at the short, intermediate, and long-term trends, and support and resistance levels.

You can then combine these factors to use the benefits of option strategies with the most reliable chart patterns. There is no denying that option strategies are initially more work than trading only futures; however, the benefits and advantages of option strategies which are unavailable anywhere else (taking advantage of under- and overvalued options, the time-value decay of options, and using neutral positions for flat markets) can be very effective for the knowledgeable option trader.

Before any trade is initiated several questions must be answered:

1. Where is the underlying market going (or not going)?
2. Is option premium relatively high (signifying option selling opportunities); relatively low (option buying opportunities); or is there disparity in option premium between different months or strike prices presenting potential for initiation of option strategies by purchasing undervalued and selling overvalued options?

Once these questions are answered we must then determine the most important question of all: is there a "special circumstance" that provides us with a "trading edge"?

We Initiate Trading Positions Only if a Combination of These Factors Indicate That We Can Get a "Trading Edge" over the Markets.

An example of this on the option buying side occurred in 1993 in the gold and silver option markets. The market had previously broken out of its one-year downtrend in April and quickly moved 20% higher over the next several months. However, the market had gotten ahead of itself and during July and August, and retreated down to near its original breakout point. In fact, this correction had extended so far that gold and silver were the most oversold of any markets that we had seen in the last several years. Option volatility had also declined to low levels. The combination of these factors provided one of the best option purchasing opportunities in 1993.

On the option selling side, one of our most significant opportunities occurred in October 1993 in the bond market. Bonds had moved from the 105 area to 120 in the previous six months. Upon reaching 120 (the area of the old historical highs) treasury bonds had begun to run into resistance and had trouble working much higher. At that point, although we did not know where bonds were going, we felt confident that they would not work much higher than the 124 level. Therefore, we sold out-of-the-money 124 calls that contained only time value when the market was resting near 120. Although our timing was not perfect and the bonds did work their way up to 122, the out-of-the money 124 call option gained little during the bond rally as its time value was working against it. Subsequently, when bonds corrected, this option quickly lost almost all of its value. In this instance, the combination of time value decay and the resistance of the market provided strong benefits—our "trading edge."

The soybean market in July 1993 was an example of being able to use disparity in option premium. While soybeans moved from under $6 to $7.50 in one month, option volatility soared, particularly for the out-of-the-money options. The out-of-the-money options in soybeans at that time were trading at volatility levels of 50–100% higher than the at-the-money options. This allowed the initiation of ratio spreads (buying an at, or close-to-the-money and selling multiple out-of-the-money calls) that will provide the trader with a position that would have a huge profit range. For example, initiating the Ratio Option Position of long the $7.50 call and short two $9 calls at a credit would provide a position that would be profitable from 0–$10.50.

This is the type of trade that makes it easier to sleep at night.

What do we do if only one of the elements is present? For example, in December 1993 in the grain markets, we felt that these markets would continue higher as the technical pattern and fundamentals were quite favorable. However, there was no option strategy available that would provide us with a "trading edge" over these markets.

Therefore, we recommended no trading position until a pullback occurred. We prefer to wait until "special circumstances" occur that provide us with our best trading opportunities. This might mean that we are not always in the market or might miss some opportunities, but we still prefer to be very choosy and pick only the best opportunities. We find that these occur often enough to present a significant number of trading opportunities during the year.

In doing our actual market analysis and study, I find it easier to first study and analyze the technical patterns of all of the markets. Then when we find a market that has a reliable pattern or a pattern that provides strong evidence of the direction the market is heading (or where it is likely not to go) I next review the option volatility levels for that market. Option volatility levels are compared over the short term (the last 3 months); over the intermediate term (over the past year); and long term (over the option's history). This is to determine whether the option is relatively high or low priced. Finally, the volatility levels of each individual option of all active trading months are compared to determine whether there is disparity in premium that would allow the initiation of an option strategy, that can provide us with an additional "edge."

Just as in any other successful business, there is no easy way to do this work. No computer program yet has been programmed to be able to analyze all of these factors and determine the best strategy to use. To be a successful trader, you must not only find time to do all of this work on a regular basis (we do most of our analysis on the weekends so that we are prepared for the next trading week); but also must be knowledgeable on all types of option strategies and keep up to date with new material and research. There is no question that this is demanding work, but for the hard-working trader, the potential rewards are well worth it.

The amount of work necessary to be successful in trading is no less than that which is necessary to be successful in any other business or venture. Any successful business requires years of work, experience, and modification before successful results can be shown. I would recommend that a trader spend at least three to six months in reading and research before any trade is initiated. During that time you should begin to keep a record of your trades. Any time you initiate a trade, mark down the position taken, the reason for it, and the stop loss points and profit objectives. At the end of each month, evaluate the results and only if you can do this profitably two out of three months should actual trading begin.

For some reason, actual trading is always much tougher. While you should not hesitate to pull the trigger, you should also be very cautious in the number of positions you do. For example, if your account could afford two or three gold positions, when you begin, trade only one initially and wait for profits to accrue before adding an additional one on a pullback. The worst that can happen by trading smaller quantities at first is that your profits will be slightly smaller. However, where this can really save you is if a losing streak occurs before you can modify your trading plan, so you will still be able to "stay in the game."

Several other points are also very important to any trader. Every trader must have a trading plan. Without a trading plan even the most talented trader is doomed for failure. This has been proven over and over again and should be followed by all traders. Your trading plan should be specific; however, flexible enough to be modified if conditions change.

Trade with a Long-Term Perspective Only (Except for Neutral Option Positions).

The silver market in 1993 is a good example of why one must keep a long-term perspective. Since April, we had recommended long term bullish positions be initiated on any consolidation or pullback. From then on we saw silver move from $3.80 in April to $4.80 in mid-May; decline 50 cents over the next 30 days to $4.30 in June; then surge to $5.50 in July; followed by a gap lower several days later which caused losses of almost $1 in the next two weeks; followed by another 50 cent drop to close to the original breakout point, under $4 in September; then followed by several gap higher moves that brought silver to $4.60 in October followed by a decline of 40 cents at the end of the month; finally followed by a rally bringing silver over $5. Although in totality, silver rose over 30% ($5,000 per contract) since our initial recommendation, some traders lost money, as they were trading with too short-term of an objective and were unable to weather the normal market movements that occur. Trading with a long-term perspective allows one to use the natural market gyrations in your favor by hedging or turning positions into "free trades" on moves in your favor, and then use pullbacks to initiate new positions at favorable prices.

Also, it is much more difficult to determine short-term market movements, than the general long-term trend of the market. It is also much easier on a trader mentally not to be thrashed around by the short-term market gyrations, but to maintain a long-term perspective.

Neutral Option Positions Can Be Effective Using Short- to Intermediate-Term Trading Scenarios.

In Neutral Option Positions we are seeking to profit by collecting the "time decay" value from an option. This value accelerates as an option approaches expiration. This type of position is very effective in choppy or trading range markets. For example, in November treasury bonds moved from above 118 at the beginning of the month down to almost 114 midmonth before recovering back to close to 118 again. This choppy action caused the closer to expiration out-of-the-money options to lose most of their value during this time. As the "time value" of options increases in decay as the option approaches expiration, short-term positions are preferred.

GETTING A TRADING EDGE OVER THE MARKET

Without a plan and the discipline to follow it, even the best trader or system is destined to lose. This is the case in options trading, the same as it is in everyday business.

There have been many instances of successful companies failing because of their inability to make long-term plans. This is magnified to an even greater degree when trading the markets. This is because of both the leverage factor and the short time periods in which large moves may occur. This is, of course, one of the attractions of the market—that large profits and huge returns can be made quickly; but these same factors can work against the trader who does not have a plan.

I have devised several rules that are part of my general trading plan. Although the majority of my work is directed toward using disparity in option premium to my advantage, I found that I cannot trade in a vacuum. I must know what the trend of the market is, either neutral, bullish, or bearish, and must also be able to recognize chart patterns that have been reliable in the past to give me an indication of the most likely future course of the market.

My plan encompasses what I feel are the strongest points of mathematical probability, money management, system trading, and discipline. It includes the following:

1. Determination of the trend by simple trendline analysis;
2. Using technical formations that in the past have had a high degree of reliability;
3. Using strict principles of money management requiring option purchases only on pullbacks within a trend, and then to sell or hedge part of the position on significant rallies;
4. Trading on a long-term basis most of the time (where prices are more predictable);
5. Trading only in the direction of the trend;
6. Using disparities in option pricing to our advantage, as well as positions that are profitable over a wide range of prices;

7. Using Neutral Option Positions to trade flat or choppy markets.

This system provides flexibility to take advantage of many different types of market situations. In markets that have very high option premium and great disparity in option prices, I place greater weight on Principle number 6. In contrast, in markets with reliable chart patterns, I place the strongest emphasis on Principle number 2. (However, none of these items can be ignored when taking trades; all must be considered.)

Also important is the concept of risk/reward and probability of profit. Risk/reward can be determined absolutely by comparing the actual dollar risk with the profit objective. However, the probability of profit is more of an "art" and can only be estimated. In general I give all option purchases a 50% probability of profit; synthetic futures positions 50–80%; neutral option positions 75–90%; ratio and reverse-ratio spreads 65–80%. In all cases I have found as the probability of profit increases, the risk/reward ratio will decrease. For example, the risk/reward on free trades with a 50% probability of profit can be 30–1 or better; while the risk/reward of neutral positions normally is in the 4–1 range.

My guideline is that a trade should have at least a 75% probability of profit or a 10–1 risk/reward before I will consider initiating it.

ADJUSTING YOUR PLAN TO MARKET CONDITIONS

Most trading systems or technical indicators are designed with a limited number of variables by researching the action of past markets. This is because of traders' perceptions that the markets are likely to behave similar to the way they have in the past. Systems are then designed that would have been profitable in previous years, with the expectation that similar action in the future will also produce successful results.

Problems occur when markets begin to act either differently than they have in the past, or when the system is not designed for the types of markets that are presently occurring. For example, a system that was designed prior to 1987 would fail to take into account the large moves that occur now after the release of government reports, particularly the monthly trade deficit figures. Therefore, the moves caused by the release of these reports or by newly active European institutional traders could cause a good position to be "stopped out" by a short-term volatile move or, conversely, could cause large losses as the market flies by the traders' stop-loss points.

Similarly, a system designed to trade trending markets would have a difficult time trading a flat or choppy market. This is one of the biggest problems that many systems or technical indicators have. They are nonadjusting to different market conditions.

This is a benefit that you can acquire by using option strategies. You can constantly change your strategies to fit the market, since you have strategies that work with flat markets, choppy markets, trending markets, and volatile markets. There is no need to change your trading system, only the type of trade initiated.

Therefore, you can combine many strategies to fit the individual markets, not expecting one system or method to work each market. This is, of course, more logical—as how can one expect to have the same system work equally well in volatile and nonvolatile markets; and in flat or trending markets? This flexibility, being able to adjust strategies to the type of market, can provide the option strategist with a "trading edge."

HOW TO EVALUATE YOUR OWN TRADING SYSTEM

In *Market Wizards,* sixteen of the most successful traders in the world describe their trading methodology. Although the systems and methods used and markets traded were different for all of them, there was one thread in common for all of them. They all had a trading system or plan that they followed religiously. This theme is expressed in many other books, and in fact it has been said that even a bad plan is better than no plan at all. That is because without any plan you are then driven by the trader's worst enemies, fear and greed. Fear makes certain that you are taken out of a good trade prematurely, while greed gets you involved with the bad ones.

Most traders that I talk to are reluctant to discuss their trading plan. They might say, "Well, I look for a breakout and then follow it." However, this statement leaves many unanswered questions, such as: What do you consider a breakout? Do you require the breakout to be on a monthly chart or a five-minute tick chart? Can a breakout be valid opposite to the existing trend? How many contracts do you purchase for each commodity? What money management principles do you use? What type of stop-loss or trailing stop do you use? Do you have a provision for adding contracts or taking profits? Most of these questions I find that traders either do not answer or pick their answer by "the seat of their pants."

Studies have shown that 90% of traders do not have complete trading plans while almost 99% of traders do not have their trading plans in writing. (It's an interesting fact to find that most floor traders and professional traders do have trading plans, and these are the traders that are more often successful.)

Although most traders look at this as a painful exercise, there are easy ways to evaluate your own trading plan.

Write It Down

This is the first and most important step. A solid, concrete plan must be written down. If it is not, we find that it is easily modifiable to meet your current feelings during the day. You will find that any news article, or tip from a broker or friend can spur you to take emotional action without sufficient basis.

By writing your plan, you can actually determine whether you really do have a plan or merely fire out trades when you "feel like it." Once you have finalized your plans we recommend that you have at least two copies, one that is always on your desk, and another blown up on your wall.

Other important items to look at are whether your trading plan has provisions for taking profits as well as losses; and adding positions when the market moves in your favor. (We do this by the use of our "free trades" that allows us to add to our positions when the market moves in our favor, and also allows us to have enough capital ready to add new positions on pullbacks.)

Does Your Trading Plan Include Rules for Money Management?

These include risking no more than 10% of your capital on small accounts for any one position, and no more than 2% for larger accounts; as well as rules for hedging and increasing your positions as we discussed above.

Is Your Trading Plan Flexible to Allow for Changes in Market Conditions?

In the early eighties there seemed to be a direct relationship between markets such as stocks and bonds, which now often move in totally different directions. Similarly, options had much higher premium in 1982 through 1987, allowing for the successful initiation of option selling strategies. However, today's markets are fluid, and one must not be married to any particular strategy or method.

COMBINING TRENDLINE AND VOLATILITY IN YOUR PLAN

Probably the first item most traders have learned is use of the trendline. The trendline is a technical indicator that determines for the trader the long, intermediate, and short-term direction of the market. Simply stated, a trendline is a line drawn connecting the significant high or low points on a chart. A "long" position is taken as long as the prices are above the trendline and a "neutral" position on the break to the outside of the line and a short position when a new downtrend line forms. Drawing trendlines is more of an art than a science. Exhibit 5.1 shows charts of some selected markets with their trendlines as I would draw them.

How do we put these together for use in the trading plan? In my trading plan, I look at trends over a 10-year, two-and-one-half-year, six-month, and one-month period (Exhibit 5.2).

To initiate an option strategy, on the long side (converse reasoning will be used on a short side position), the one and six-month indicator should be up. If the two-and-one-half-year and 10-year trends are also in an uptrend I will take a stronger position.

I then examine volatility to determine whether the current volatility is at relatively low levels suggesting option buying strategies, or whether volatility is at a very high level in which case I would prefer ratio spreads or neutral option positions. I use these rules to initiate trades using option

Exhibit 5.1
Selected Market Trendlines

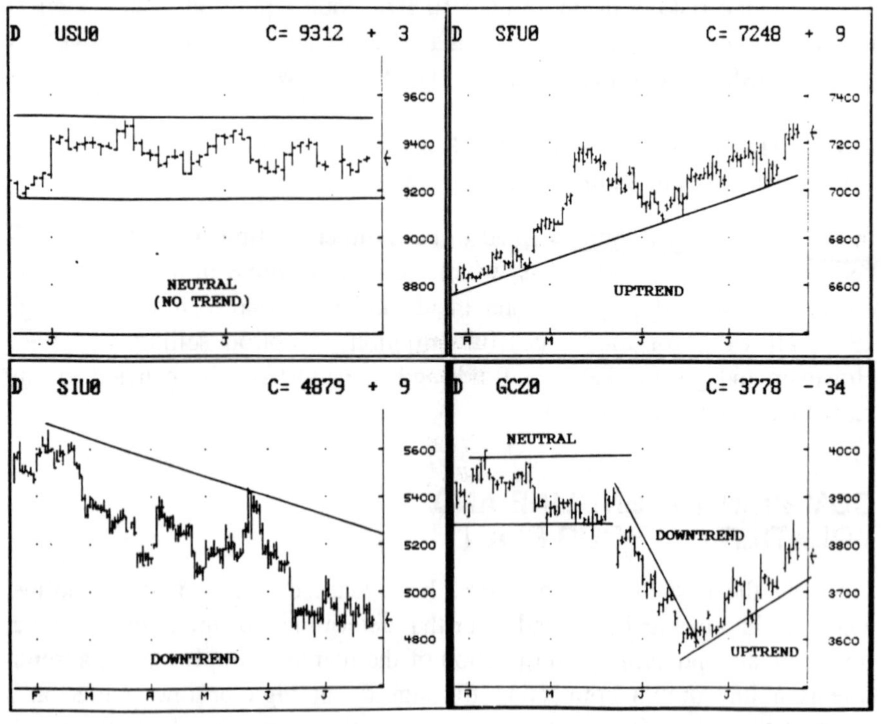

Exhibit 5.2
Gold Futures Charts of Trends

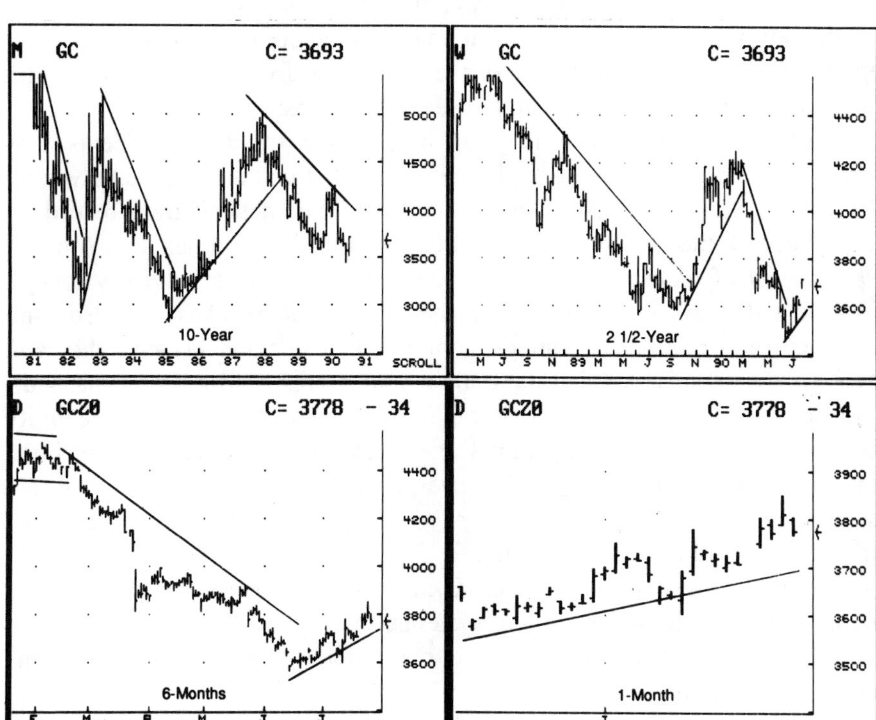

strategies that have the highest probability of profit by using both trendline and volatility analysis along with sound money management techniques.

USING TRADING SYSTEMS PROFITABLY

Most of us are familiar with the adage: "put an infinite number of monkeys at an infinite number of typewriters, with an infinite amount of time, and you can guarantee soon that all the great works of the world will be reproduced."

Unfortunately, from the traders' standpoint, this adage also applies to advisors, newsletter writers, and system development in the markets. We have an infinite number of them, making every imaginable prediction. The trader's question is whether he is following the right monkey. Time and time again, we have all heard claims that the "Holy Grail" (perfect system) has been developed. The basis of these systems ranges from main-frame computer based systems to the positioning of the moon and the planets. Unfortunately, they generally all have one thing in common . . . that is, once we begin trading them, the systems lose money for us. Although 95% of the advisory services claim their market predictions are correct 95% of the time, it still seems that 95% of the public that follow these services still lose money. Why is that? There are several reasons:

First of all, the system may just be no good, fraudulent or devised by "backtracking." For this reason, I recommend that you investigate very carefully any system, especially those with only a "hypothetical" track record.

Second, the system is modified by the user. Many times a person will spend a lot of money on a system, computer program, or advisory service and then decide to selectively use the trades that he likes, blended with another trading advisor's thoughts; or not take a trade because the *Wall Street Journal* indicates that the trade would probably lose. What that individual has done is produce an entirely new system, which in all probability will not be as good as the original one. Fred Gehm, in his excellent book on money management, states that even if one were to produce the perfect system and print it in the *Wall Street Journal*, it is unlikely that one out of ten traders would follow it exactly.

Although system misuse and lack of discipline as described above are major causes of losses in trading systems, the biggest cause for loss when an otherwise good system is used is poor money management. These include the following faults:

1. Systems that are developed only for entering and exiting positions, which may be excellent, but have not considered money management whatsoever.
2. Systems that are designed to trade on a short basis and fail to take into account slippage and commission charges, which can easily run 25% per year. This, on top of other costs such as charting, services, computers, and publications, can require the trader to produce a 30% return or more before he regains his initial capital each year.
3. Systems that have rules that make the trader uncomfortable can cause losses. For example, systems that require the trader to take large risks, take many consecutive losses, or trade contracts with which he is unfamiliar will eventually break down the individual's discipline and cause the trader to deviate from the system.

The final reason for system or advisor failure is not adjusting to changing market conditions. This causes a system that makes money in a trending market to lose it in a flat market; it causes many otherwise good systems to lose money in volatile markets because of their lack of recognition of these types of markets, and leads to otherwise good trades being terminated with "stops" that are too close, or cause large losses with stops that are too far away.

The following rules are designed for the better trading system:

1. **FOLLOW THE TRENDS**
2. **USE OPTION STRATEGIES THAT GIVE YOU A "TRADING EDGE"**
3. **TRADE ON A LONG-TERM BASIS!**

Research, statistics, and mathematical probability prove that long-term, well capitalized traders often make money, while short-term, under capitalized traders consistently lose money.

The reasoning behind this can be shown through mathematical probability. The bell shaped curves in Exhibit 5.3 provide you with the mathematical probability of gold prices during the next two years, one year, six months, and 30 days. As shown, the range of prices is greater the further out in time that you go; however, percentage-wise, it is far less than the increased holding period. For example, in 12 times the amount of time (from one month to one year) the 90% probable range of gold prices increases only three times.

This means that prices are much more volatile on a short-term basis, and less predictable. It is just this volatility coupled with the great leverage available in futures and options (sometimes exceeding 98%) that can cause a small or undercapitalized trader's loss.

Now, let's assume that you have found a system that meets all your requirements. What you do next to maximize your chances for success is:

1. Follow it exactly without exception, until it loses a predetermined amount of your capital (20%–50%);
2. If you lack the discipline, time, or ability to trade the system, find someone else who does to execute it for you; or
3. Have the advisor trade it for you (make sure that he also trades his own money and/or is compensated only by a percentage of profits).

The conclusion that we all want to hear, though, is—What is the bottomline? *Can you make money by boring long-term trading, "do-nothing" neutral option strategies, and the hard work involved in proper money management trading and planning?* No guarantees, of course! However, how can your trading not improve when you remove yourself from the class of traders who have been destined to lose 90% of the time because of

Exhibit 5.3

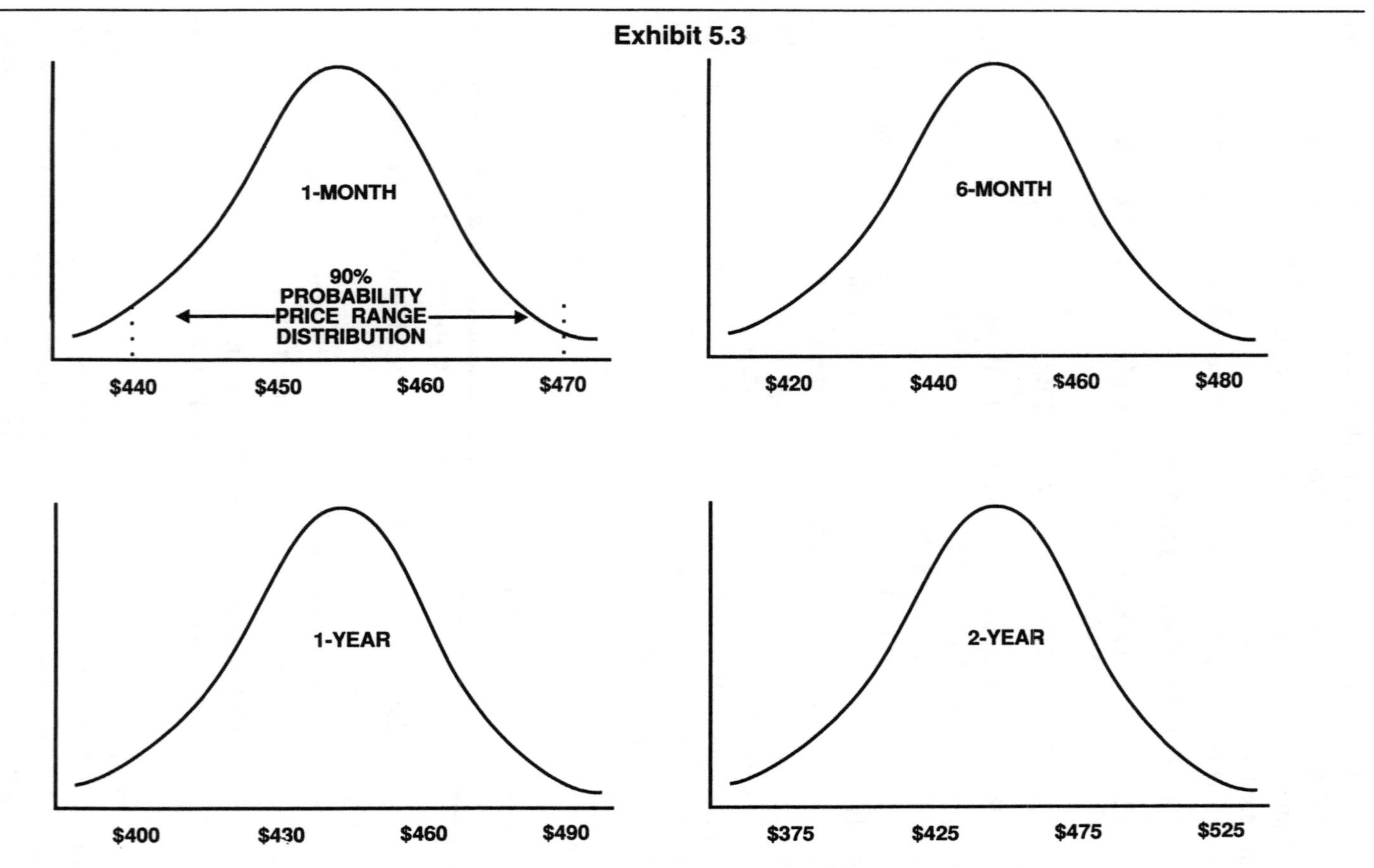
1-MONTH
90%
PROBABILITY
PRICE RANGE
DISTRIBUTION
$440
$450
$460
$470
6-MONTH
$420
$440
$460
$480
1-YEAR
$400
$430
$460
$490
2-YEAR
$375
$425
$475
$525

their requirement and necessity of everything going right for them; to the professional, long-term traders' arena, who use every available advantage to their benefit?

MONEY MANAGEMENT AND YOUR PLAN

Money management is another crucial, if not the most important, principle to obtaining a "trading edge."

Proper money management requires never risking more than 10% of your trading account's capital on any one position. (In fact, larger traders use even lower figures of between 2 and 5%. These figures may actually be better for strict money management principles; however, for smaller accounts and more aggressive traders, a 10% maximum would still be within reason on selected trades.)

Never vary from this principle. Does this mean that you can never build a large position, since you take so little risk initially? Absolutely not! You can still accumulate a large long-term position, and keep your risk within these manageable guidelines.

First, determine your risk level for every trade. Enter each trade with a certain set of principles. For example, recently I felt that bonds had broken out of a consolidation triangle and therefore recommended bullish option strategies. In determining the amount of potential loss, I have to determine what would change my mind from this reasoning. In bonds, I decided that a close under the area of the old lows would show a much weaker market than I expected when I entered into this position, and would violate my original reasons for initiating it.

Determine the options that you want to purchase by analysis of various options strategies and their benefits. In bonds, I noted that the close to expiration March options were 20% or more overvalued as compared to the June options, so calendar option spreads were constructed to take advantage of this disparity.

Next, determine what the loss level would be if the market "stopped us out." This makes it easy to determine how many positions you can afford to initiate. (I have a standard rule that I will not risk more than $500 per position, in any case, and occasionally, when I feel that there is not a great "stop-out" point, I limit my risk to either one-half of the premium of the option, or to some other arbitrary maximum amount, such as $300.)

All of these principles have one thing in common—the preservation of capital in times when positions are wrong. Limiting losses to 10% of your capital gives you at least nine more entry points into the markets. You would have to have a very bad string of luck to quickly lose your capital using this principle. In fact, this principle gives you even more than the 10 times it seems to challenge the markets.

Assume that in your $10,000 account you are stopped-out for the maximum 10% loss each time. The first time you would lose $1,000 and your account would be worth $9,000. The second time you would lose $900 and your account would be worth $8,100, etc. You would, in fact, have 20 chances at the market before your trading capital got down to $1,000.

Now let's look at the much more exciting time when your trading decision is right and the market begins to move in your favor. Are your profits limited because you entered into too small a position in the first place instead of using all of your capital as margin? Not at all. Although some initial profits may be missed, you are a long-term trader, and most markets in a long-term trend always pull back or consolidate many times on their way to give you many chances to enter.

One trader mentioned in the book *Market Wizards* did extremely well in silver's move in 1978–1980, when silver moved from under $3 to $50. He did not enter the majority of his position at $3 or $4 or $5, or even at $7 or $8 or $10. In fact, most of his position was entered into at $15 when the trend in silver was confirmed. Then was he lucky/intelligent enough to exit silver at the top near $50? No. He got out at $30 after the uptrend had been broken, and *only* made an average of $15 or $75,000 per contract! What he did was take the easy money out of the market looking for only 50% to 60% of the trend, out of the middle, without trying to pick tops or bottoms.

How do you apply this to your trading? After entering into your initial position you should always have a profit objective and look to hedge your trades, take some profits, or turn your positions into free trades after the market moves in your favor. When your initial capital is protected and more funds are available for new positions, then look to enter into new options positions on the next reaction.

This type of trading continues as long as the trend continues. It is entirely conceivable that over a period of a year that a single position could become a 10, 20 lot or more position, never having a risk exceeding your initial amount.

By keeping your losses small when the markets don't work, you are then in a position to hit the markets hard when you are correct! Using options to get a "trading edge," being disciplined to trade only at times when the best opportunities are present, and continually following your trading plan is the essence of good trading.

APPLYING OUR TRADING PLAN TO DIFFERENT TYPES OF MARKETS

We separate our trading into two distinct groups: our normal trading which includes option buying—"free trades," "ratio spreads," etc.; and our Neutral Option Account, in which we sell options only to collect premium. These two groups of trading have entirely different methods and objectives.

In our regular trading, we look for trending markets with reliable technical patterns, and either well-priced options or favorable spreads to initiate bullish or bearish positions to ride these trends.

We always go into these trades with a specific view of the market, and if it is violated we exit our positions. For example, if we purchase puts based on our view that there was a key reversal and significant change of trend, our views will be violated only if the market moved above previous highs. If our view of the market is violated, we would exit the position, and reevaluate. That is because the set of facts that we entered the trade upon would have then been violated, making our initial premise faulty. Therefore, it is our policy to reevaluate based on the new set of facts, and normally move to the sidelines. It would indicate that the potential reversal that we entered the market on was not valid, but only a correction in a continuing bull market.

However, subsequently, if the market were to fail again from that level, it would just add further strength to our argument that the market was bounded by that area as a top. In that case, we may reenter the market after closing out our original positions; however, it is now an entirely different situation with a new set of facts.

Once the market goes in our favor, then we have two objectives: protecting our profits and adding new positions.

We protect our profits by selling the most overvalued out-of-the-money options on extreme moves in our favor to turn our positions into "free trades." This, in effect, allows us to accomplish our second objective, since by turning our initial positions into "free trades", we minimize risk and free up capital to allow us to add new positions without substantially increasing our initial risk.

The final aspect of our trading plan is that we trade on a LONG-TERM BASIS ONLY. Shorter-term trading is both too stressful and costly. Additionally, my studies, and others', have shown that only floor traders, who are in a position to trade on a short term basis both because of their proximity to the trading floor, allowing for immediate executions, and ability to pick up the flow of the market, and with their extremely low execution costs, can consistently be successful with short-term trading. This makes it very difficult for even the most seasoned trader with instant quote equipment. We find that longer-term trading accomplishes several goals including keeping commission costs as low as possible, and allowing yourself to build a large position to move along with the trend of the market.

Also, you must be prepared to take many comparable small losses on trades that do not work as expected; while at the same time be prepared to hold on and add positions to hit the market as hard as possible on trades that move in your favor. We do this by only initiating trades that have at least a 10–1 risk/reward.

In our Neutral Option Positions our emphasis is somewhat different. Our objective here is to collect premium time decay by trying to determine where the market IS NOT going to go.

For example, in January 1994 when the S&P topped at 475 and began to decline it was our view that we were not going to see the market then move up over 475 by option expiration in one month. Therefore, we initiated our position of selling the 480 and 485 calls. This position provided us with several benefits.

First, if we were right in our market views, we would collect the entire premium on these options sold. Second, if the market remained within a trading range between 470 and 475 as it had been for the last month, we would collect all the premium on these calls since they were out-of-the-money calls and would be worthless at expiration. However, third, even in the case where we were somewhat wrong on our market direction, and the market slowly increased, but not above the price of the calls we sold, we will still collect the entire premium. (There are no other positions that I know of that allow you the luxury of not being correct in your market prediction and still coming out ahead.)

The objective of this method is shorter-term trades because of the significant premium decline of options as they approach expiration, while remaining as safely out-of-the-money as possible to prevent the market from hurting you with a move in either direction. These positions must be closely monitored and closed out or adjusted if the market moves towards the strike prices we have sold. Always adjust or close out your position if the market moves unexpectedly against one side or the other since the potential for large losses outweighs the profit potential of these positions.

We like to sell options that are in our view, as safely out-of-the-money as possible to prevent having to closely guess market direction. For example, in July 1992, we sold November soybean $8 and 850 calls with soybeans trading almost $2 lower. We could have, of course, done better by selling closer-to-the-money options, e.g., $6 or $6.50 calls; however, we did not want to be in the position of having to guess which way the market was going. We did not know that soybeans were going to decline immediately after we sold these calls. By initiating this position we were merely stating that we did not think that soybeans were going to go up to $8 prior to option expiration.

We find that these two types of trading strategies make a good mix with one another depending upon the technical pattern and option volatility of the particular market. Having these different opportunities available to us, also greatly enhances our flexibility and trading possibilities.

TRADING CHOPPY MARKETS

Is Your Cup Half Empty or Half Full?

When three traders look at the same chart we often get five different interpretations. Reasons for going long and short, stopout points, trends, etc., can all be justified in every direction. However, universally when a trader looks at a chart of a "choppy" market, we usually hear that there is no trading opportunity here. However, where other traders' cups are half empty, ours can be entirely full!

In past years it may not have been necessary to worry so much about using favorable situations. When I first became interested in trading, I was introduced to one of the most successful traders of that time, who was subsequently interviewed in the book *Market Wizards*. The "system" that he related to me for trading the soybean market in the 1970s was, "The trend of the market turned up. I came in the morning when soybeans were down and I bought some. Then in the afternoon the market was higher so I sold some of them. I hung on to a core position and let it ride during the trend of this market."

Well, that advice is great if you can take advantage of the grain markets during a drought, or other markets that occasionally exhibit these tendencies. However, the real world of trading usually requires more discrimination today than buying in the morning and selling in the afternoon, and traders that seek out and use special circumstances when they occur will be adding a serious weapon to their trading arsenal. (Interestingly though, I have modified the theory of this trader to be usable in our actual trading plan by buying on dips and selling part of the position or hedging it on extended rallies while following the trend. We discuss this further below.)

Why do we love choppy markets? How do we find that these choppy markets can in fact be some of our best trading opportunities? There are two ways we use choppy markets to our benefit. The first is to use pullbacks and periods of consolidation as "favorable situations" to allow us to initiate positions at excellent prices. We look for a market that has broken out or is trending, then once the market begins to pull back, we enter using the reaction low as our "stop out" point. Therefore, while many traders are being stopped out because of the short-term market gyrations, by using these techniques along with proper money management principles (not overtrading, etc.), you can avoid being a "weak hand" that has stopped out just as the natural market correction ends. Further, you can actually use this "difficult" market to obtain a better price on positions that you want to enter.

The second part of this plan is to use extended rallies to turn option positions into "free trades" or otherwise hedge positions. Selling or hedging part of a position on a rally allows us to use strong principles of money management to help protect our gains, while also allowing us to add to our position on pullbacks without substantially increasing our monetary risk. This also allows us to take advantage of the expanded volatility of options on extended rallies. Since we are selling out-of-the-money options which normally increase in premium to a much greater degree than the closer-to-the-money options that we purchased during "quieter" periods, this should provide another significant advantage and benefit to our trading.

The second method of using choppy markets to our advantage is in the use of Neutral Option Positions. There is nothing a Neutral Option Position loves more than a market that goes up a little one day, and down some the next. This inconsistent two-way action allows for erosion of the time value premium for the out-of-the-money options as they approach expiration. These are the options that we sell to collect time value premium. Choppy, neutral, inconsistent markets, that have no direction, which futures traders normally hate, are perfect for these option positions. Since I began trading, these have been some of my favorite option strategies, that allow us to trade without having to pick the precise direction of the market.

We cannot overstate the importance of these principles. We are now using these principles actively in our *NOPS* neural network trading program and in the continuing research and writing for our book *The Option Secret.* We will report to our clients and subscribers on our ongoing results in both the newsletter and hotline.

"THE BEST METHOD OF TRADING IS . . . "

The most important element in trading is not the direction of the market alone. For example, a trader may successfully predict the long-term direction of the market, but may be "stopped out" by short-term gyrations, only to then watch the market move in his favor. You must have a trading plan that fits your psychological makeup and risk level.

For example, some traders have no problem holding 100 coffee futures into a weekend that has potential weather problems; another trader with the same size account, might be nervous holding a single Eurodollar position overnight during a quiet trading period. A trading system that works for one trader may be incompatible with another trader's psychological makeup.

In reading the books that contain short autobiographies and discussions about the world's top traders (*Market Wizards, Market Masters,* etc.), one common thread that ran through all of the top traders' discussions was the necessity of not only a trading plan, but a plan that met their own risk parameters and personal psychology.

This is the reason that I began trading options. With futures I felt unable to both monitor risk on trades in volatile markets that I wanted to hold overnight, nor could I vary the size of the position as well as I could with options. Using options, I was able to initiate a position that would more closely approximate the directional bias I had on the market as well as allow me to take advantage of high and low option volatility and premium disparity. For example, in very bullish markets, where we were concerned with corrections, we were able to initiate "ratio spreads" at a credit that would be protected from loss if the market moved lower, while still being able to participate in profits on a further rally. These positions also allowed us to take advantage of selling the more overvalued out-of-the-money options.

In options, traders have many methods to take advantage of. This supports different methods including:

1. Traders whose objective is unlimited profit potential with limited risk (premiums, commissions, and fees) can purchase options;
2. Traders who like to use the mathematical probabilities to their advantage can initiate Neutral Option Positions to take advantage of the time decay and overpricing of out-of-the-money options;
3. Traders who seek to take advantage of the price disparity that exists in options at different times may use option spreads such as "ratio spreads," "calendar spreads," "free positions," etc.

All of these strategies have their benefits and detriments. What is important is that you pick the one that fits both your trading objectives and psychological makeup. A trader that is concerned with unlimited losses should never use Neutral Option Positions, just the same as a trader who hates seeing his options decay in value should not be an option purchaser. We prefer to use a combination of the best methods available at any time based on the technical action of the underlying market and the option premium levels that allow us to initiate positions to provide us with a "trading edge" over the markets.

USING FAVORABLE SITUATIONS TO TURN THE ODDS IN YOUR FAVOR

Thorp first noted in *Beat the Dealer,* that at certain times "favorable situations" arose that could turn the odds in the player's favor. In this book he also mentioned that the strategies could also be used in the stock market.

"The similarity between the casinos and the brokerage houses is striking . . . The stock exchanges and the ticker tape are the gambling devices . . . Stocks show the same mathematical characteristics . . . that are shown by the chance devices in the gaming houses. **With the advance in computer technology and mathematical theory, we can expect dramatic progress in predicting stock prices.** The winning strategies to be given in this book depend largely on the fact that if the composition of a deck changes during play (like the market does—ed.), the advantage in blackjack will shift back and forth between player and casino. **The advantage often reaches 10% for one side or the other and on occasion even reaches 100%.**"

This same theory used successfully by Thorp thirty years ago in Las Vegas is available in our option markets today. However, it is my opinion that more significant advantages exist in the option markets.

Option traders have a significant benefit in being able to take advantage of the disparity in option premium; high volatility in options that are approaching expiration, allowing us to take advantage of the time decay of option premium; and low volatility (premium cost) in option markets that are about to make a big move.

An additional significant advantage that applies particularly to option sellers who seek to take advantage of premium decay, is that traders do not have the same "limits" that casinos place on individual bettors. The reason that casinos use limits, is that they know that this is one of the most valuable tools of the gambler; i.e., if a bettor is able to continually raise his bet, the theory is that if he has enough money, eventually, he will be able to win. Because of this, casinos generally place limits on the amount of bets. However, although there are extreme limits in the markets that will be applicable to only the largest traders, these will not affect 99% of the traders (or even large traders who use proper money management principles).

One additional item of importance is that of PATIENCE. Be willing to wait for the best opportunities, and when they occur be ready to move quickly and take advantage of them. When they are not available, sit on the sidelines and use your time for the three R's—rest, recreation, and research.

"You Got to Know When to Hold Them; You Got to Know When to Fold Them"

This verse from *The Gambler* is one of the most important money management principles of the professional poker player. The professional knows that there is no odds in playing (trading) at the wrong time, and is content to be patient, sit back, and wait for when the cards (markets) turn favorable. The pro ends up playing only 10–20% of the time, but never loses sight of his goal, which is **making money**, and does whatever is necessary to accomplish it. He is not there to make friends or get a thrill from the "action." He is waiting for the right time when the probabilities turn in his favor, and then is ready to pour it on and ply his trade.

How different is this principle in trading? The U.S. markets are open 200 days a year ("our poker game") to allow us almost limitless action and opportunities. We have not just one poker hand to chose from, but over 40 as we can pick from any one of the markets that have the best opportunities, such as the Swiss franc, gold, sugar, etc.

The proper use of special circumstances and favorable situations, and only trading at the time when the best opportunities occur, can not only significantly increase your odds of success, but probably are the single most important item of any trading plan.

We have previously seen these theories mentioned in the gambling classic, *Beat the Dealer,* Edward Thorp's 1962 blackjack book. This theme is also a common topic in advanced textbooks for top professional poker players. HOWEVER, NOWHERE IN MY LIBRARY OF HUNDREDS OF FINANCIAL, COMMODITY, AND OPTION BOOKS HAVE I SEEN THIS PRINCIPLE EMPHASIZED!

We have used this principle without realizing it in the past; however, now that we know the extreme significance of it, we will even pay closer attention to it. To summarize: TRADE ONLY DURING THE MOST OPPORTUNE TIMES AND USE ONLY THE MARKETS THAT CAN PROVIDE YOU WITH A SPECIAL CIRCUMSTANCE OR OPPORTUNITY; USE OPTION STRATEGIES AVAILABLE TO ENHANCE YOUR "TRADING EDGE."

FLEXIBILITY AND MONEY MANAGEMENT—THE TWO MOST IMPORTANT, BUT OVERLOOKED RULES FOR SUCCESSFUL TRADING

With conditions in all markets constantly changing, successful trading requires flexibility; each market has its own individual characteristics requiring specific trading methods to be designed for it. Also methods must be different for markets that are bullish, bearish, or nontrending. If the system cannot take this into account, it will not be successful in the long term. Finally, money management principles must be built into the trading system. Without sufficient money management standards, even the best system will not stand up to scrutiny.

The need to have a flexible trading system that can not only adapt to the parameters of each individual market, including different methods for nontrending, bullish, or bearish phase is of paramount importance. Compare a Eurodollar chart of the past year with a chart of the coffee market, and you can see that a trading system devised for one of them would have extreme difficulty with the other. As you can see from these charts, while Eurodollars have had little volatility, moving about 2% during the year, coffee has been extremely volatile, moving almost 300% during 1994.

Secondly, a trading system that uses the same rules for bullish and bearish markets can also be destined to difficulty. Today's markets decline much quicker than they rise. For example, after a bullish year like 1993 in the S&P 500, where the contract gained 4,000 points, it then gave back almost the entire gain during six trading days in April, 1994. Also in October 1987, the S&P gave up almost all of four years of steady gains in two trading sessions.

Different rules should be used for the early, middle, or late stages of a trending market. For example, low risk entry points were available in 1993 when gold gave its first indication of breaking its steady two-year downtrend, and in September–October 1994, when the market broke out of its one-year consolidation, allowing positions to be aggressively entered; however, could a trader similarly take aggressively bullish positions after 10 years of bullish markets in the S&P 500? Even though the trend was of long-standing nature, this market could be subject to severe declines, causing large losses to a trader that would blindly follow the same methods for this market as the gold market in its initial bull stages.

We have a few basic money management rules that we follow in initiating positions:

1. Enter markets at the early stages of significant trend changes and on pullbacks; risk can more often be controlled by use of support and resistance levels.

2. Do not buy on rallies, especially in the late stages of a bull market. If you buy silver when the market is up 15 cents during the day, you begin to fight the laws of probability. 1993 was a bullish year for silver, which moved up over 30% during the year; however, the average price rise was approximately half a cent per trading day! If you buy silver on a day when it is up 15 cents that means mathematically it must decline on the average 30 days to maintain its mean price. Wouldn't you rather buy when the market was down 15 cents to provide yourself with the ability to use mathematics and probability in your favor?
3. The rule is different for bear markets. For example, we would not hesitate to take a bearish position in S&P 500 which began to decline, as this market is vulnerable to a collapse, and when the decline starts to occur, many traders are going to "jump ship." You must have flexibility in your trading and design your method or system to the market and times you are trading. And even when this design is complete, you must continue to use *flexibility* if conditions change.

Exhibit 5.4

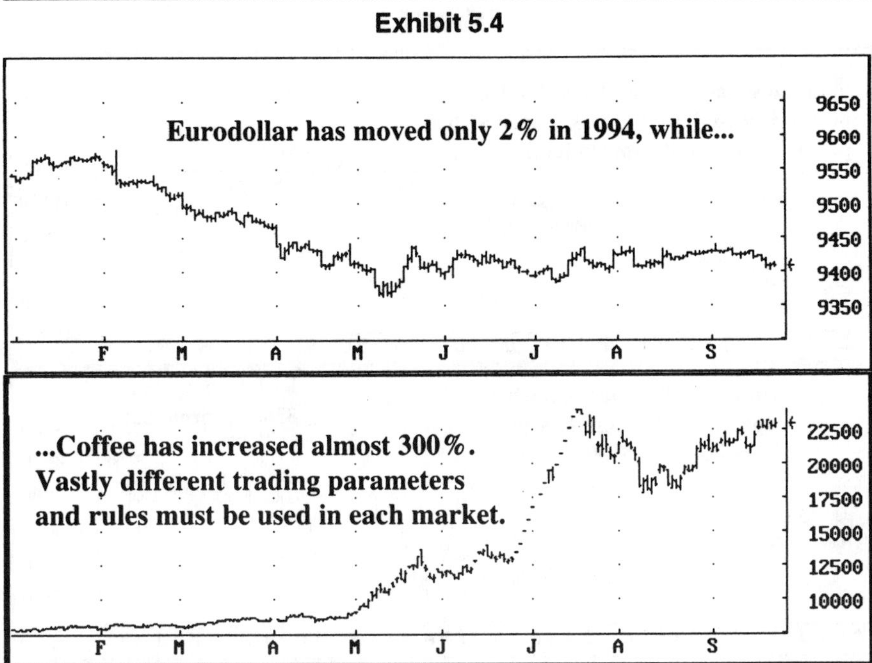

Exhibit 5.5

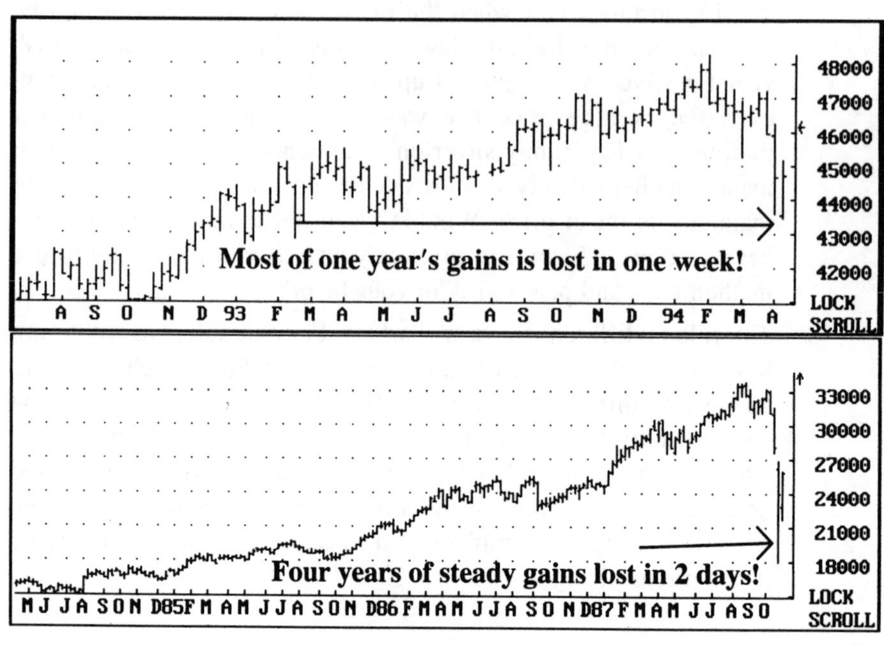
Most of one year's gains is lost in one week!
Four years of steady gains lost in 2 days!

Exhibit 5.6

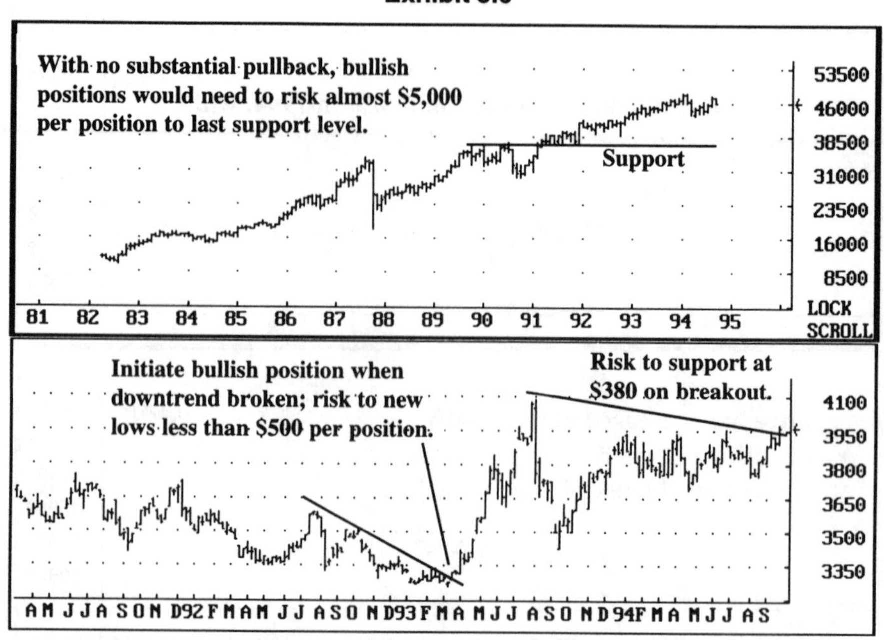
With no substantial pullback, bullish positions would need to risk almost $5,000 per position to last support level.
Support
Initiate bullish position when downtrend broken; risk to new lows less than $500 per position.
Risk to support at $380 on breakout.

CHAPTER 6

Other Important Option Trading Principles

Most traders look at options as a substitute for an outright position, where you merely buy a call when you are bullish, or a put if you are bearish. However, option strategies can be used to express a more exacting view on the market and can allow you to initiate types of positions that are otherwise unavailable.

If you trade only net positions in stocks or futures, you are limited to buying the market if you are bullish, or selling it if you are bearish. Of course, you may adjust the quantity of your position or stop/loss points based on your expectation of what the market might do; but this is the extent of your latitude.

What would you do if you felt you didn't know exactly where the market was going, but felt fairly certain that it was going to maintain a certain range of prices in the near future? Suppose you felt that a market had bottomed, but you missed buying at its best prices. How would you like to be able to buy this market at less than today's price or be absolutely guaranteed a profit? What if you were bullish on the market, however, you didn't want to lose if the market went slightly against you? And finally, what if you thought the market was going to slowly move up within a limited range and you wanted a position with a high probability of profit? Wouldn't it be advantageous to have a way to initiate these exact trades?

All of these positions are available to the knowledgeable option trader. These types of positions add another benefit to the list of advantages that can be found in options.

TRADING A BULLISH MARKET WITHOUT ANY RISK OF LOSS IF THE MARKET MOVES LOWER (AGAINST YOU)

In August of 1987, silver was trading at between $7.50 and $8 after having moved from $5.50 up to almost $10 over the previous several months. At that time I was bullish but, since silver had been in a long-term down trend, I felt a position in futures or options had too much risk. However, out-of-the-money silver calls had extremely high premiums (volatility), about twice that of closer to-the-money calls. To take advantage of this disparity, I initiated ratio option spreads (buying a call, selling two higher calls) by purchasing the December silver $9 calls and selling two December silver $11.25 calls for each call purchased. I was able to receive a premium of up to $1,000 per position more for the two calls I sold, than the one I purchased.

This position had no downside risk, since, if the silver options expired with the price of silver under $9, all of the options would be worthless. (In fact, I would profit by the amount of premium I had received.) If silver moved higher, I would make $50 for every one cent silver exceeded the strike price of the options I purchased (Exhibit 6.1).

In fact, these positions would be profitable through the $14 level of silver, a price that hadn't been realized since the early 1980s. The combination of these factors made this position an excellent one—no downside potential and profits available if the market continued to move up. The only risk at all in this position was if the strike price of the options sold were exceeded, since I was short two options for every one I had purchased. (I recommend closing out the entire position if this occurs.) However, since the closest to-the-money options would gain in value much quicker then the out-of-the-money options, and the out-of-the-money options would deteriorate in time value faster, this position would continue to work in my favor in most instances.

Buying a Market at Less Than Today's Price

In early 1991, when silver plunged to near $3.50 per ounce, some bullish investors thought it was an excellent time to purchase silver, while others wanted to wait until it was even lower. There was, in fact, a way that you

Exhibit 6.1
Profit/Loss of December Silver Ratio Spread

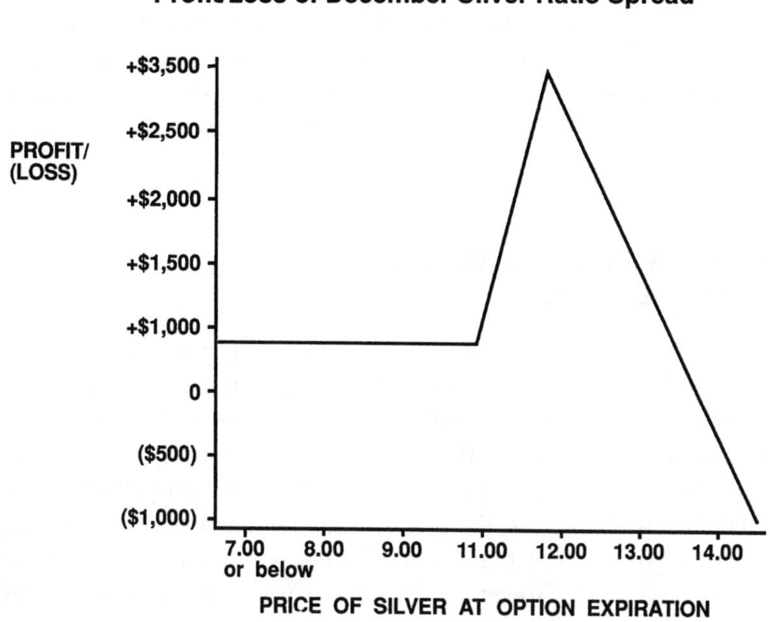

could satisfy both of these views by purchasing silver at $3.75 or receiving a return that would be over 50% annually.

You could sell a July $3.00 put option and receive a premium of $300. Since the maintenance margin required for this strategy was $1,000, this would produce a return of 30% (or 90% annually) if, when this option expired, the contract was above $3.00. This is because no purchaser of a $3.00 put would want to exercise this option, since they can sell silver at a higher price through the cash or futures market. Therefore, if silver expired above $3.00 this $300 premium was yours to keep when the silver option expired in four months, thereby producing a return of 90% per annum.

Once this put option expired, you could then proceed to the next active trading month, and again initiate this strategy. However, if silver fell to $3.00 or below and the purchaser of the $3.00 put option exercises the put, you would own silver at $3.00 per ounce less the $300 premium or 6 cents per ounce that you were paid for this put, an effective price of $2.94 per ounce for your silver. Since silver was trading at $3.50 per ounce when you initiated this strategy, you would be purchasing silver for 50 cents less than its previous price, a savings of more than 10%.

This strategy works similarly for any listed stock or commodity. However, this is for the long-term investor who has made a decision that he wants to purchase the stock or commodity at a lower price. This is because if the market continues to move lower, a trader will experience losses (in this case, below $2.94). And, although profits will be made if the market moves higher, you will not be "in the market" if a large move begins to occur. However, notwithstanding these two situations, it is an excellent strategy to lower your ownership costs or obtain a high return in almost any market.

MARKET VIEWS—TRADING RANGE TO SLIGHTLY BULLISH

At the end of September 1989, bonds were maintaining a wide range between the 94 and 98 area, after previously rallying to the 100 level early in the month. My market view was long-term bullish; however, it looked like an intermediate top was in place that could last for several months. Therefore, I recommended buying the March bond 100 call and selling the 90 put and 104 call. By doing this, the prices of the options I sold were paying for the call I purchased. The position would not lose money unless bonds went below the 90 level. However, since there was unlimited loss if this did occur, and it was my view in entering the trade that bonds would not go below the 94 level, I was using a close under 9400 as my signal to exit this trade. This would have produced a loss of approximately $300, depending on how quickly this occurred. (On the upside, my profit objective was $4,000, producing a position that had a risk/reward of 10 to 1 as shown in Exhibit 6.2.)

PROFITING FROM AN OPTION POSITION WHEN YOU DON'T KNOW WHERE THE MARKET IS GOING, BUT FEEL THAT YOU KNOW WHERE IT *ISN'T* GOING

There are two positions that can reflect your views on the market in these instances: the synthetic futures position and the neutral option strategy.

In late 1985, the S&P had been in a bull market for almost two years; however, it had been languishing at the 170 to 180 level most of the year. At that time, I wasn't certain that a large rally would occur (even though it subsequently did); however, I was confident that the 170 level would hold. Therefore, with the market trading at about 180, I was able to purchase a December S&P 195 call and sell the 170 put and receive a credit (*synthetic futures position*). This meant that as long as the market stayed above 170 (my view of the market), I would profit on the transaction. And, if the market did rally strongly, I would not only have a call that didn't cost me

Exhibit 6.2
Profit/Loss

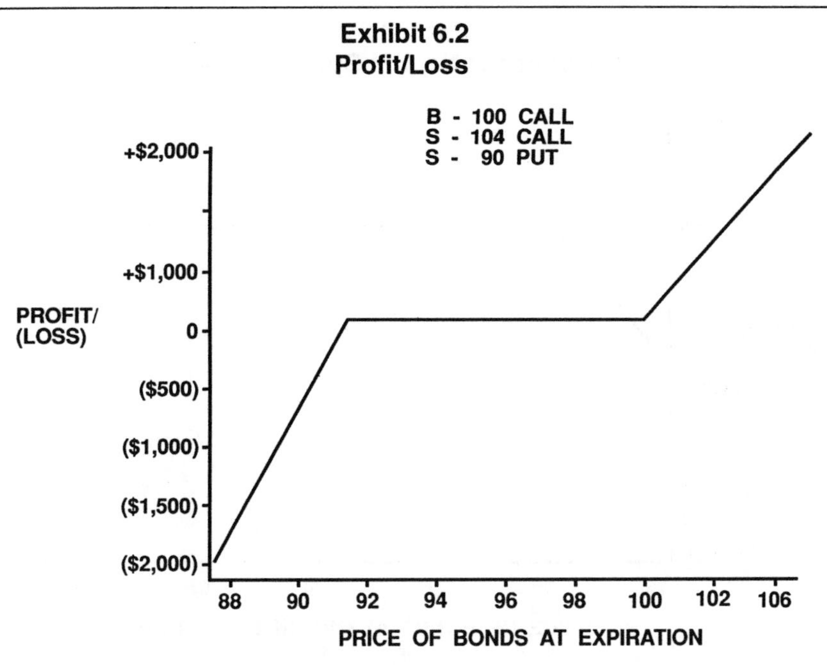

anything, but also had the potential for unlimited profits above the 195 level.

At the beginning of 1988, bonds were trading at the 90 level, and it was my view that I would see a range in the next several months between 80 and 100. Option premium was also at historically high levels at that time, allowing me to sell 80 puts and 100 calls (Neutral Option Position) for up to $1,000. Since these options would expire worthless in less than six months if bonds stayed within this large 20 point range, I would receive a return of almost 50% on margin (100% annualized) without having to predict market direction (Exhibit 6.3).

These examples show some of the circumstances that provide another benefit of option strategies—being able to profit by only knowing where the market *isn't* going.

ARE OPTION PUT AND CALL PRICES, RATIO, OR VOLUME PREDICTIVE OF MARKET DIRECTION?

Changes in Option Premium Levels

Option premium levels are determined by the volatility in the particular market. Quite simply, if a market is not making significant moves in either

Exhibit 6.3
Profit/Loss of Neutral Option Position

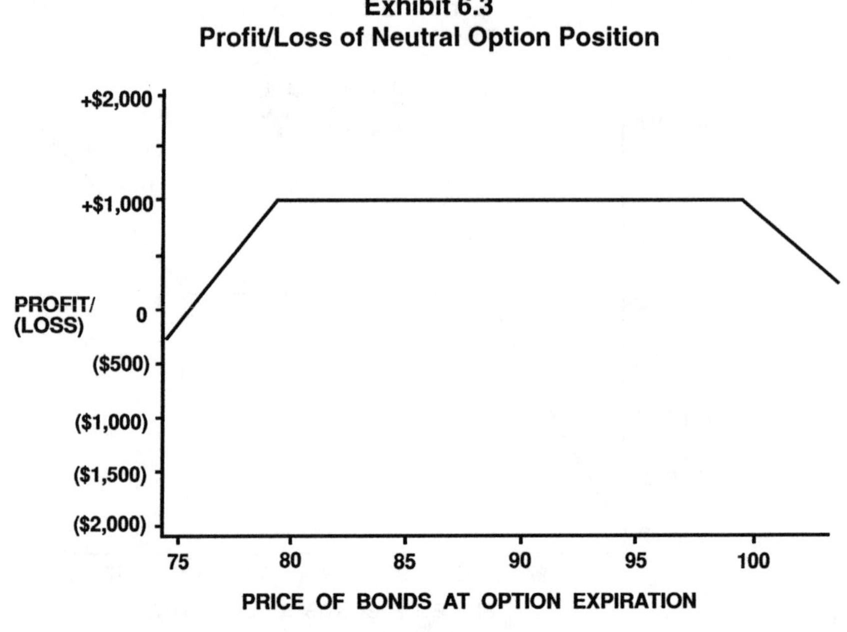

direction, option premium should be low, as buyers of options would not be willing to pay much for an option that has little expectation of value due to the inactive market. Option sellers would also feel more comfortable selling options in this type of market, and would be content with less premium than usual.

In a very active market, option sellers will refuse to sell options unless a high premium is received because of the unlimited risk of loss if the market moves against them. Also, option buyers would be willing to pay more for their purchases, which now have a higher probability of value.

The differences in option premium levels can be quite dramatic. For example, at the end of September 1989, with option premium near historical low levels in silver, I could purchase the March silver 575 call, the closest to-the-money option for $650. This option was only one strike price (25 cents) out-of-the-money and had almost five months before expiration. However, in 1987 when silver rallied quickly from $6 to $8 and volatility increased dramatically, I was able to sell $11.25 silver calls, options that were over 10 strike prices from the money ($3) for up to $2,000!

Most of the time, the change in option premium levels is not an advance indicator of what's likely to happen, but only mirrors the changes in the futures prices. Rarely are these changes in advance, providing any predictive value. And even when they do lead the market action, the changes are very subtle.

For example, prior to the 20 point break in bond prices from the 100 level in 1987, I noticed the premium on bond puts increasing around 20%, without any significant market action. Volatility was at that time close to historically low levels. This increase in volatility seemed to reflect the fact that large traders (professionals, hedgers, institutions) were entering the market, either speculatively, or to hedge their previously profitable positions. This increase in volatility was significant, because bond options are much more liquid than any other option contract, and the typical bond option trader is a more sophisticated investor. There are few incidents similar to this, and the changes are usually so subtle, that unless you have been watching the market closely, they will be missed by most traders.

CHANGES IN PUT AND CALL RATIOS OR VOLUME

After studying changes in put and call ratios and volume of options traded over the last several years in many different option contracts, I have been unable to find any correlation that would help to accurately predict future price action. The reason for this is that options are still in their infancy and are in the process of being "discovered" by many institutional traders. Many times the increase in volume in option contracts can be tied solely to the fact that more traders are now beginning to use options.

Another reason that this indicator can be inaccurate is that options can be used for many different purposes. A large trader who is bullish bonds may purchase 1,000 bond calls to profit from this expected move. However, another trader who is equally bullish bonds, but who may be long the futures or cash bonds may sell 1,000 bond options just to hedge this position and lock in a rate of return with which he is comfortable.

Therefore, with the many different types of trading objectives by those in the marketplace, there is usually no mathematical significance in the increase in volume or changes in put and call ratios.

HOW OPTION STRATEGIES CAN HELP OVERCOME THE HIDDEN FACTORS THAT CAUSE LOSSES IN TRADING

Making money is, of course, everyone's objective in trading. This is where you should place the emphasis of your time. Concentrate on the elements that can assist you in realizing this objective and, conversely, prevent and discard elements that interfere with your moneymaking objective.

Does buying these expensive, complicated systems, learning the intricacies of market behavior, and even option strategies, provide the basis for a profitable trading plan? More often than not, the answer to this question is no. This is because of several hidden factors that most traders overlook.

1. The Hidden Emotional Factors in Trading

Although fear, greed, and the lack of discipline are frequently discussed, two overlooked, often ignored subjects are "overtrading" (including failing to take breaks from trading for the necessary "rest and recreation" to "recharge one's batteries"), and only trading when situations present you with trades that have the highest probability of profit (either because of the market's technical pattern or disparity in option pricing).

Violation of these concepts is responsible for losses as much as any of the so-called important items such as trade timing, failure to pick market direction, and money management.

Traders are always very reluctant to be away from the markets; they do not want to miss any trading opportunities. However, with more than 30 markets that have options, each containing at least three months of option expirations and 10 or more strike prices, all in various configurations from bullish to bearish to neutral-choppy, flat, volatile, etc., enough opportunities for profitable trading will continue to occur, keeping even the most nimble trader very busy.

Traders are in battle every day with these markets, which can be very tiring and draining. After long stretches of trading, especially ones that have not been particularly rewarding, traders begin to act like "brainwashed" prisoners of war. They are ready to follow any system or pronouncement that promises profit and abandon all of their old trading methods. Instead of abandoning past work, it would be much more beneficial to take time out to examine previous errors and learn from them.

2. The Hidden Costs in Trading

We have all heard that:

1. Trading is a zero sum game.
2. For every winner there's a loser.
3. An average trader breaks even.

Unfortunately, these hypotheses are all wrong. As discussed in the introduction, this is because the trader, through commission, pays the salaries of all the brokers, brokerage firm personnel, all of the exchange personnel, from the floor runners to the receptionist, and all the regulatory agencies and their employees. On top of this, the trader must pay for chart services, publications, computer, phone, etc. These fees can total over 20% of an active trader's account. This means the trader must actually profit in his trading by that amount just to break even. Even Las Vegas casinos give their customers better odds!

What it really takes to make money trading is:

1. Making correct calls on the market (Market Prediction).
2. Having an appropriate plan that incorporates principles of money management (Trading Plan).
3. Preservation of capital during those times when trading becomes difficult and your calls become faulty (Money Management).

Protection from loss is one advantage of using option strategies. The reason for this is that many of the strategies are profitable over a wide range of futures prices, and some strategies allow you to break even or sometimes profit when you are incorrect with your market predictions.

How do you do this with option strategies? There are several positions that allow you these benefits and flexibility:

1. Synthetic Futures Positions (Option sold pays for option purchased).
2. Ratio Option Spreads (Profitable over a wide price range).
3. "Free Trades" (After completed, requires no margin and has no loss potential).
4. Neutral Option Strategies (Only positions that profit in flat or choppy markets).
5. Money Management Techniques with Options (Hedging futures or options positions).

Assuming that a market can move in five different ways:

1. Slowly lower,
2. Suddenly lower,
3. Neutral,
4. Slowly higher, or
5. Suddenly higher.

Most of the above strategies will be profitable if the market moves in any four out of five of the possible ways. This can be expressed as an 80% probability of profit.

Additionally, there are certain characteristics inherent in options that can provide the trader with valuable advantages including:

1. Buying undervalued options;
2. Selling overvalued options;
3. Combining the sale of overvalued with the purchase of undervalued options, allowing you to use the disparity of option pricing to get a "trading edge";
4. Using factors of option volatility in your favor;
5. Using the time decay of options in your favor;
6. Using the limited risk functions of options in your favor.

Remember, your objective is to make money; keeping it simple can perhaps be the biggest benefit and the most overlooked secret in trading.

USING OPTIONS PRIOR TO THE RELEASE OF SIGNIFICANT REPORTS OR EVENTS

As all traders are aware, the release of any major report, figures, governmental meeting, and potential raising or lowering of discount rate often cause large moves in the markets when the actual figure is different from the one expected.

Therefore, knowing the basic information regarding these reports is essential for all traders so that you can, at least, assess the potential for such a move. Additionally, when a report comes out significantly different than expected, you will want to observe the markets' reaction to the report. In fact, I feel that this is the most important indicator of the markets' strength or weakness. For example, when an unexpectedly favorable report fails to cause any significant move in the market, the market may be "tired" and you should be cautious about initiating new positions.

In 1984 and 1985, the markets eagerly awaited the money supply figures on Thursday evenings which would then significantly effect the metals markets and, to a lesser degree, the stock and financial markets. In 1987–88, the trade deficit figure resulted in major moves in the currencies, causing 300–400 point ranges in the Swiss Franc and Japanese Yen in a matter of minutes. The movement in the currency market then spilled over into other markets, thereby affecting their action also. Anticipated raising and lowering of the discount rate has also caused similar reactions in the financial and S&P 500 markets. Finally, the agricultural and livestock markets are greatly influenced by the release of government reports and figures.

Markets are also affected based on a government's or entity nonaction after a report. For example, in the last week of December 1987, the currency markets rose substantially when the foreign governments failed to support the dollar after a G-5 meeting. The traders took this to mean that they had decided not to support the dollar; this nonaction was interpreted bearishly for the U.S. dollar. However, the governments had actually agreed to support the dollar but decided to wait until after the first of the year based on either the holiday time period, or for whatever reasons that suited their purpose.

There is, however, a major difference between the actions of the futures and options markets, both before and after these events. Prior to the release of government reports, the futures markets become quite stagnant; then become most volatile right after the release of the report, stabilizing shortly thereafter. The option markets act quite differently. Instead of stabilizing in price before a report based on the nonaction in the futures market, option volatility and premium rise rapidly, peaking during the last hour of trading prior to the report. After the report is released, option pricing becomes random until the true market direction is shown, usually in the first hour after the report. However, due to the thinness of the markets and the tendency of option sellers to wait to determine the velocity of the move, it is difficult to buy options at a reasonable price until the market has stabilized (Exhibit 6.4).

Another difference between options and futures is that the out-of-the-money options increase greatly in value prior to the report. Then, after the report is issued, and it is determined that these options are still out-of-the-money, they lose their value even quicker.

An example of this is an April Swiss Franc neutral option position that initiated one day before the February 1990 trade deficit report. At that time, a premium of $1,000 was available for selling a far out-of-the-money put and call. After the report, although the Swiss Franc had moved 100 points lower, the put had gained only 5 points in value where the call had lost 27 points in value for a net gain of 22 points or $275.

This position was attractive because computer analysis showed that a move of 200 points in either direction on the day of the report would not have caused a loss in this position (Exhibit 6.5).

I used computer evaluations of option prices to determine which options had the greatest overvaluation. These trade sheets were compiled several days before the U.S. trade deficit report, which caused severe overvaluation of the Swiss Franc options. Based on this, with the contract at 7300, you could initiate neutral option positions in the April Swiss Franc 69 put and 78 call at a total premium of 80 points ($1,000). Its fair value was computed at 58 ($625). Our computer evaluation showed that this position would not lose money, if the futures moved 250 points in either direction. One week later, as volatility subsided and premiums dropped for

Exhibit 6.4
Relative Volatility Levels of Swiss Franc Options and Futures

(Before and after February 1988 Trade Deficit report. 0 = Lowest volatility level; 100 = Highest.)

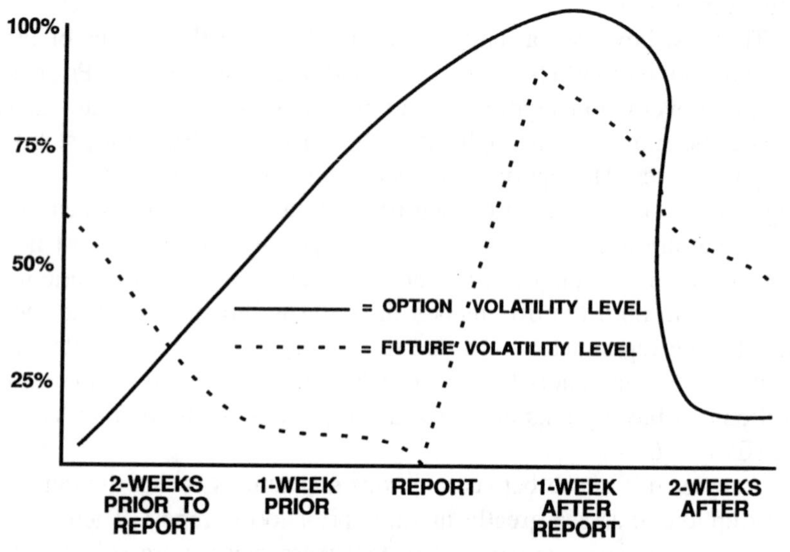

Exhibit 6.5
Computer Evaluation of Option Prices

SFJ - SWISS-FRANK - APR
VOLATILITY = 14.82% DAYS OUT = 53
INTEREST RATE = 6.50% 2-16-88

	*******CALLS********		
	76	77	78
70.00	.14	.08	.05
70.25	.16	.09	.06
70.50	.18	.11	.06
70.75	.20	.13	.08
71.00	.23	.14	.09
71.25	.26	.16	.10
71.50	.30	.19	.12
71.75	.34	.21	.13
72.00	.38	.24	.15
72.25	.42	.27	.17

	*******CALLS********		
	76	77	78
72.50	.47	.31	.20
72.75	.53	.35	.22
73.00	.58	.39	.25
73.25	.65	.44	.29
73.50	.72	.49	.32
73.75	.79	.54	.36
74.00	.87	.60	.41

SFJ - SWISS-FRANK - APR
VOLATILITY = 14.82% DAYS OUT = 53
INTEREST RATE = 6.50% 2-16-8

	********PUTS********		
	68	69	70
70.00	.75	1.10	1.56
70.25	.68	1.01	1.44
70.50	.61	.92	1.33
70.75	.55	.84	1.22
71.00	.50	.77	1.12
71.25	.45	.69	1.03
71.50	.40	.63	.94
71.75	.36	.57	.86
72.00	.32	.51	.78
72.25	.28	.46	.71

	********PUTS********		
	68	69	70
72.50	.25	.41	.65
72.75	.22	.37	.59
73.00	.20	.33	.53
73.25	.17	.30	.48
73.50	.15	.26	.43
73.75	.14	.23	.39
74.00	.12	.21	.35

Source: COM-TECH SOFTWARE, 141 W. Jackson Blvd., Suite 1531-A, Chicago, IL.

both puts and calls, this combination was trading at 36 points ($400) for a profit of $600.

While option traders had this 400 point "window" of profit, futures traders were having a much more difficult time. Shortly before the report was issued, the Swiss Franc moved up 100 points, potentially "stopping-out" many short future traders. Then the market plummeted 300 points immediately thereafter, then attacking those holding long futures positions.

This type of action also occurred before and after January's trade report. Out-of-the-money calls that became substantially overvalued the day before the report, were almost totally worthless the next day. Even the out-of-the-money puts gained very little in value, in spite of the fact that the market made a move of over 200 points lower that day.

Therefore, selling options in these instances can produce trades with high probabilities of profits. However, there are going to be times where you have a view of market direction, and want to consider buying options to profit from those expectations, so that it is not necessary to take the unlimited risk associated with future trades.

As seen in the examples above, purchasing out-of-the-money options close to reports can provide you with a trade that moves in the direction you predicted, and that may still only be slightly profitable, if at all. However, purchasing an option approximately one week prior to a report allows you to obtain a more fairly valued option. I would recommend purchasing an option at-the-money or no more than one strike price out-of-the-money, as these options are usually the most fairly valued, and responsive to a move in your favor.

The month that should be purchased is also of significance. If a longer-term trade is anticipated, I would recommend an option of between three and six months duration. If one is purchasing an option just to take advantage of the report, the closest to expiration option is recommended. This option will have the largest percentage move if the report is favorable to your position. (However, this will also lose the most premium if you have guessed wrong.) Traders caught between these two dilemmas would be advised to purchase an option between two and three months in duration to combine the effects of both of these circumstances.

There are several reports in addition to the Trade Deficit report that traders watch:

1. *The Gross National Product:* This report is a broad measure of the United States economic activity. A positive number causes commentators to indicate that economic growth is expanding and the economy is healthy. This may also indicate the potential for

inflation and may cause traders to perceive higher interest rates, metals prices, and potential for a weaker dollar.

2. *Unemployment Report:* This report by the Labor Department indicates whether industry is weak or strong by the number of jobs it is creating. A low number implies that there is a potential for inflation and strong economy as more people are employed and more money available in the economy.
3. *Consumer Price Index:* The Consumer Price Index is also issued by the Labor Department and reports prices for finished goods. A high CPI number indicates the potential for inflation; however, the number should be watched for seasonal variances and temporary aberrations that can cause faulty interpretation of otherwise reasonable figures.
4. *Producer Price Index:* This report is similar to the CPI; however, it measures only wholesale prices. It is important because it is released several days before the CPI and, therefore, gives a hint to the CPI's future direction.

Other reports whose names are self-descriptive of what they indicate and are interpreted similarly to the previous reports are the Index of Leading Economic Indicators, Consumer Spending, Factory Orders, Industrial Production, and Factory Capacity Utilization.

Exhibit 6.6, prepared by the Chicago Board of Trade, provides a concise summary of these reports and their possible effect on the markets.

PRICE ACTION AFTER AN IMPORTANT ECONOMIC REPORT

When I began trading in the early 1980s, I was told to "Buy the rumor, sell the fact." What this meant was before the news item was released it could be an important factor that would cause the market to move; however, after its release, it was "in the market" and already discounted.

I found that even a report that was favorable to a particular market would cause little movement, and often a setback would occur, as this information was already expected, and perhaps disappointing to traders who were hoping for a more bullish report. In fact, only if a report came out much better than expected was the market favorably affected.

The markets' reaction to major reports can vary so widely because of the emotion involved in making quick decisions, that traders should not attach major significance to that one day's reaction. Only when the report differs substantially from what is expected and the market fails to react, or

Exhibit 6.6
Reports That Effect on Markets

Consumer Price Index Rises	▼	Indicates rising inflation.
Durable Goods Orders Rise	▼	Pickup in business activity usually leads to increased credit demand.
Gross National Product Falls	▲	Reflects a slowing economy. Fed may loosen money supply, prompting a decline in interest rates.
Housing Starts Rise	▼	Shows growth in economy and increased credit demand. Fed less accommodating and may attempt tightening by allowing rates to rise.
Industrial Production Falls	▲	Indicates slowing economic growth. Fed may be more accommodating in allowing interest rates to fall to stimulate the economy.
Inventories Up	▲	Indicates a slowing economy since sales are not keeping up with production.
Leading Indicators Up	▼	Signals strength in the economy leading to greater credit demand.
Oil Prices Fall	▲	Reduces upward pressure on interest rates, thereby enhancing prices of debt securities.
Personal Income Rises	▼	The higher personal income, the more is consumed prompting increased demand and higher prices for consumer goods.
Precious Metals Prices Fall	▲	Reflects decreased inflation. Demand for inflation hedges abates.
Producer Price Index Rises	▼	Indicates rising inflation. Demand for goods rises as well as prices. Investors require higher rates of return, pushing rates up.
Retail Sales Rise	▼	Indicates stronger economic growth. Fed may have to tighten.
Unemployment Rises	▲	Indicates slow economic growth. Fed may ease credit, causing rates to drop.

if the market makes a significant reaction on an otherwise neutral report, should you become concerned. It is also my view, that these reports exaggerate the movement of the market by giving the traders an excuse to propel the market in the direction it was already headed.

Another difference is that, in the past, traders were more anxious to anticipate the information contained in the report. It seems that many times the large traders were correct about this information (either a good guess or advance knowledge). However, over the last few years, there seems to be less anticipation and more waiting for the actual report to be released. Then, the action begins to unfold.

RELATIONSHIPS BETWEEN THE MARKETS

In 1983, when I first began studying the possible importance of relationships between markets, the most widely watched relationships were between financial instruments and the foreign currencies. They were seemingly locked together; if United States interest rates were to rise, so would the dollar almost without fail. Another steady relationship at that time was between gold and silver, which were supposed to rise and fall on a 50–1 ratio.

Finally, the relationship between the currencies and the metals was also well established. The philosophy was that if the foreign currencies were rising it was because of inflation in this country and, therefore, a good reason for strength in the precious metals as well.

What most commentators failed to consider was that just because of mathematical probability with over 30 trading markets some of them will have similar patterns quite often. In fact, there can even seem to be correlations between unrelated markets that have no fundamental basis for the relationships. Probability shows that if you have 30 people in a room, the odds are better than 50% that two of them will have exactly the same birthday, seemingly a 12 to 1 shot. With over 30 futures markets, similar unrelated relationships will continually seem to be occurring. You must weed out these unrelated situations and determine whether any true relationships do exist, to the point that they can be relied on in your trading.

Let's look into the potential relationships between the most significant market groups to determine whether any basis occurs for their interrelation.

1. Interest Rates and Foreign Currencies

In 1983 this was one of the most relied-on relationships. And with good reason. As can be seen from the accompanying chart from 1983 through the middle of 1984, foreign currencies and bonds moved down in tandem.

When bonds reversed in 1984, the currencies failed to follow for about six months. However, commencing in early 1985 through the middle of 1986, they then proceeded to move up in tandem (Exhibit 6.7).

From this point on, divergence occurred. Although the foreign currencies continued to move higher through the end of 1988, bonds first consolidated during 1986 before plunging during the first nine months of 1987, only correcting after the crash in October of 1987. Then, while the foreign currencies continued to move lower for the last 18 months from the beginning of 1988, bonds first consolidated and then rallied in 1989.

Is there any substance to a relationship in these markets? There is very little. First, the basis for the original relationship was that if U.S. interest rates were rising the dollar should be safer and attract more foreign investors. This fails to take into account the potential for differences between U.S. and foreign interest rates, focusing only on the changes in our country or fundamental strengths or problems within the various countries.

My conclusion, therefore, is that while the strength of the dollar may be at times important in affecting the course of interest rates, and con-

Exhibit 6.7

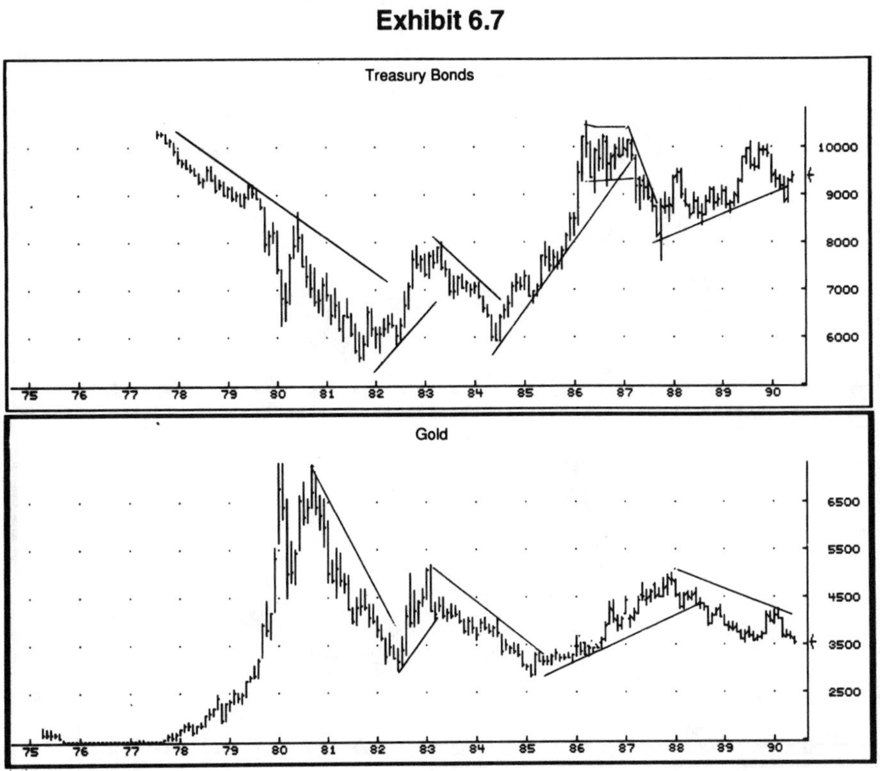

versely United States interest rates will always affect dollar foreign currencies exchange rates, one must not consider that the markets will have to move either opposite to or in tandem with each other.

2. Metals and the Foreign Currencies

Some correlation can be seen between the foreign currencies and gold. In the charts of gold and the Swiss Franc (Exhibit 6.8), we can see the markets rising in tandem in the late 1970s, falling together from 1980 to 1985, rising from 1985 through 1988, and then falling from that time until the beginning of 1989. From that time to the present, the markets have diverged with Swiss Franc moving higher and gold lower.

A fundamental basis exists for this relationship; as the dollar erodes in value, its purchasing power in terms of the international commodity of gold is lessened; and conversely as its value increases, more gold can be purchased for the same dollar.

However, there is currently no valid relationship between these markets. Not only are the major turning points of the markets different, as a

Exhibit 6.8

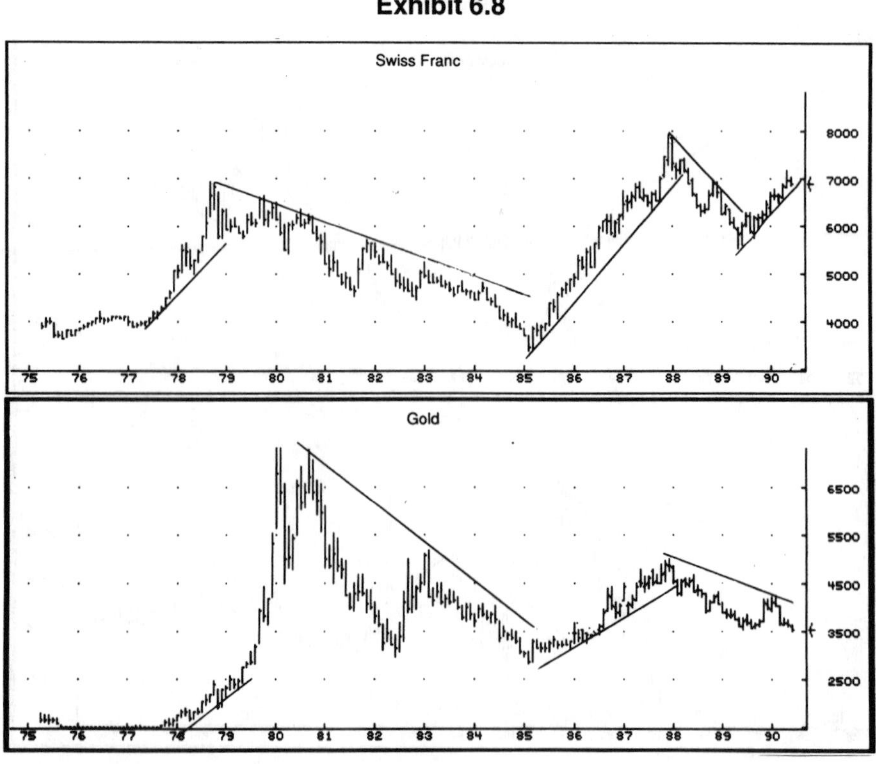

more emotional market can move substantially higher (or lower) and turn three to 18 months later, but there are also different forces at work in each market.

For example, in 1990 gold was being pushed lower partly because of cash needs by oil producing countries and the Soviet Union, which has no effect on the Swiss Franc.

3. Interest Rates and Metals

The common view that I often heard when I began trading was that higher interest rates would lead to higher precious metal prices. Higher interest rates are caused by an inflationary environment which also will cause the metals to rise; with lower interest rates there is little reason for people to invest in gold that has no return.

Currently, the view is that with the trend toward lower U.S. interest rates there is little reason for the metals to rise. However, the past history of the relationship between these markets provides little basis for these conclusions (Exhibit 6.9).

As can be seen from the charts, as bonds dropped from 1978 to 1982 (thereby denoting rising U.S. interest rates), gold prices alternately rose from 1978 to 1980, then dropped from 1980 to 1982. The markets did seemingly move in tandem from 1982 through 1986; however, this relationship began to diverge in the middle of 1986 with gold continuing to rise through the end of 1987. Then the reverse occurred; gold dropped and bonds rose.

These markets illustrate another rule. That is, it depends what set of economic principles is then governing them, as to what the relationship will be. Depending on the economic circumstances, gold and bonds can either rise and fall at the same time or act exactly opposite to each other. It is, of course, important to know which is occurring. Many times the true state of economic facts is not evident for a long time after the market turns. You certainly do not want to be operating under a faulty set of principles during this period.

4. Interest Rates and Stock Market

Today, one of the most followed relationships is that between the interest rates and the stock market. It is universally concluded that as interest rates continue to fall this will be supportive of the stock market. Conversely, higher rates would be damaging as people would move their money into interest rate sensitive instruments if rates increase and out of the stock market.

Exhibit 6.9
Interest Rates (Treasury Bonds, Gold)

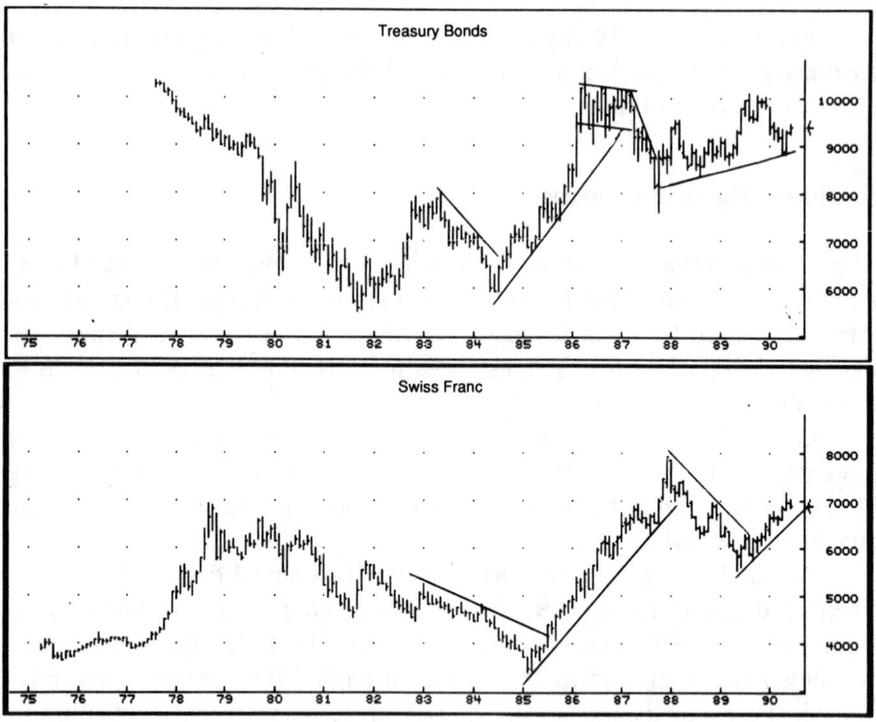

Treasury Bonds

10000
9000
8000
7000
6000

75 76 77 78 79 80 81 82 83 84 85 86 87 88 89 90

Swiss Franc

8000
7000
6000
5000
4000

75 76 77 78 79 80 81 82 83 84 85 86 87 88 89 90

Although this relationship has worked well from September 1990 to April 1991, and also from June 1984 to June 1986, when both markets moved in tandem, this has not always been the case. In fact from March of 1988 the reverse occurred, with interest rates moving higher along with the stock market. This also occurred in 1982 through 1985 when the S&P bottomed and then rose over 50% during this period while interest rates increased almost the same amount. This also occurred between July of 1986 and September 1987. During the stock market crash of 1987, rates dropped substantially as investors moved from the markets to bonds (Exhibit 6.10). Therefore, similar to the relationship between gold and interest rates, this one also depends on the current economic environment.

5. Other Markets

The agricultural markets seem to move in tandem only during severe drought or weather problem markets which affect all of the agricultural commodities

Exhibit 6.10
Interest Rates and the Stock Market (Treasury Bonds and S&P 500)

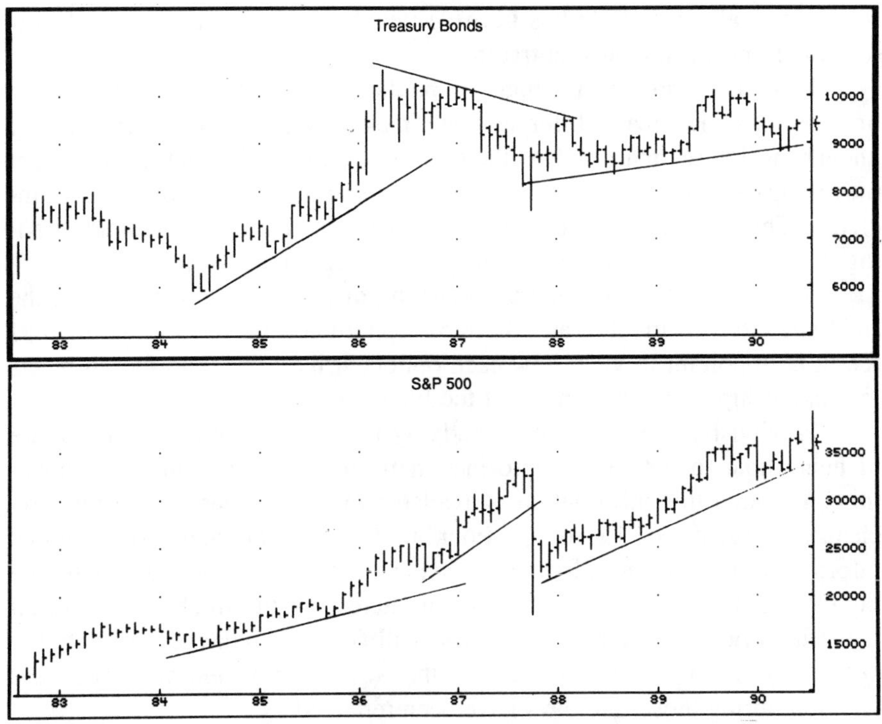

together. Also, strong evidence of inflation or recession has caused these markets to move together in the past. Otherwise, prices are determined by normal supply and demand factors for the individual markets.

Little relationship seems to occur in the soft commodities as could be seen in 1991 with sugar trading at seven-year highs while cocoa fell to 14-year lows at the same time.

In the livestock sector, little current relationship can be also seen between pork bellies and live hogs. Although in the past they have many times moved in the same direction, lately they have had little correlation.

Similar distinction can be made between live cattle and live hogs which have moved in opposite directions for the last three years and show no correlation previous to this time.

Currently our economy points to no positive correlation between any markets. However, as economic conditions change, underlying relationships can also change, so it is recommended that relationships between markets be constantly monitored.

INTERPRETING WEEKLY OPTION STATISTICS

Although many books have been written providing the mathematical basis for option valuation, little has been written on the practical nature of how to actually profit in real-time trading.

Further, I know of no book or publication that has been written on how options may react differently at times to various movements in the underlying futures market. It is the premise of all writers that if the market moves up—calls gain in value, and if the market moves down—puts increase. This simple premise, although usually correct during a single trading day, provides the basis for many losses in option trading.

Since I like to concentrate on finding disparity in option pricing, the right strategies to initiate, and the most opportune times to initiate them, I feel it is important to view how each option, strike price, and month reacts in relationship to the movement of the futures market.

Previously, one problem in studying this relationship was the failure of being able to obtain this information from a readily available publication. Although this information is available to floor traders on various exchanges, it is difficult for us "off-floor" traders to obtain and assimilate this information from each individual exchange. However, *Barron's* reports the high/low, net change, volume, and open interest for the week for almost all the strike prices of future/options. You will find it enlightening to note the net change of an option at the end of the week after all the movement and emotion during those five days have been removed.

For example, although treasury bonds moved up and down almost half a point a day during a week, the futures ended the week little changed. However, most of the out-of-the-money calls and puts lost value. This was because this directionless type of movement allows the natural time value decay of option premium to accelerate and causes premium to drop.

On the other hand, during the same week the upward movement in the currencies caused volatility to rise, with calls moving up in value and puts losing only little of their premium (Exhibit 6.11).

One final aspect to consider is the open interest for each individual option strike price. You may find that some of the options have a relatively small open interest. This does not concern me for several reasons. First of all, if I cannot close out a position because of either inadequate volume or too much slippage, I can always temporarily hedge with another strike price or month or even a futures contract. (However, I don't remember a time when this was ever necessary.)

Secondly, it is generally the far out-of-the-money options (that I have sold) that are the most illiquid. If these options remain out-of-the-money and stay illiquid, I have little concern, as I am profiting by the time value

Exhibit 6.11
Option Statistics (Swiss Franc and Treasury Bonds)

Swiss Franc

S-FRANC CALL

Month	Strike	Vol	Int	High	Low	Sett	Pt Chg	Future Sett
APR 88	71	25	172	—	—	3.04	+ 107	.7401
APR 88	72	143	885	2.15	1.05	2.09	+ 97	.7401
APR 88	73	428	788	1.36	.40	1.22	+ 70	.7401
APR 88	74	3020	2708	.65	.18	.56	+ 34	.7401
APR 88	75	295	718	.29	06	.22	+ 12	.7401
APR 88	76	113	188	.12	.07	09	+ 4	.7401
APR 88	77	5	163	.03	.02	.05	+ 2	.7401
APR 88	78	1	183	.02	—	.03	+ 1	.7401
APR 88	79		74	—	—	.01		.7401
APR 88	80		2	—	—	CAB	-1	.7401
APR 88	81		2	—	—	CAB	-1	.7401
MAY 88	72		313	2.45	—	2.40	+ 83	.7401
MAY 88	73	85	142	1.75	—	1.68	+ 67	.7401
MAY 88	74	190	456	1.17	.60	1.13	+ 52	.7401
MAY 88	75	145	155	.80	.35	.73	+ 38	.7401
MAY 88	76	22	50	.48	.22	.46	+ 26	.7401
MAY 88	77		1	.28	—	.28	+ 16	.7401
JUN 88	67		357	—	—	6.95	+ 108	.7401
JUN 88	68		126	—	—	6.01	+ 106	.7401
JUN 88	69		176	—	—	5.10	+ 103	.7401
JUN 88	70	7	66	4.20	3.25	4.23	+ 98	.7401
JUN 88	71	1	510	3.52	2.57	[illegible]	[illegible]	[illegible]
JUN 88	72	42	514	2.76	1.75	2.67	+ 78	.7401
JUN 88	73	612	2889	2.10	1.24	2.02	+ 66	7401
JUN 88	74	743	1398	1.60	.92	1.48	+ 53	.7401
JUN 88	75	173	779	1.18	.60	1.07	+ 42	.7401
JUN 88	76	282	914	.82	.44	.75	+ 32	7401
JUN 88	77	488	676	.60	.28	.52	+ 23	.7401
JUN 88	78	13	288	.42	.19	.36	+ 16	.7401
JUN 88	79	36	221	.27	.15	25	+ 10	.7401
JUN 88	80		360	.17	—	.17	+ 7	.7401
JUN 88	81		37	—	—	11	+ 4	.7401
JUN 88	82		72	—	—	.08	+ 3	.7401
JUN 88	83		38	.04	—	.05	+ 3	.7401
JUN 88	84		12	—	—	02	+ 1	7401
SEP 88	70		3	—	—	5.55	+ 89	.7494
SEP 88	71		150	—	—	4.79	+ 81	.7494
SEP 88	73		627	3.43	—	3.45	+ 68	.7494
SEP 88	74	260	738	2.90	—	2.87	+ 60	.7494
SEP 88	75		102	2.40	1.85	2.38	+ 53	.7494
SEP 88	76	4	21	2.09	1.51	1.97	+ 47	.7494
SEP 88	77	1	514	1.65	—	1.61	+ 41	.7494
SEP 88	78	22	340	1.35	—	1.31	+ 36	.7494
SEP 88	79	1	804	1.05	—	1.05	+ 30	.7494
SEP 88	80		153	.87	—	.84	+ 25	.7494
SEP 88	81	1	37	.67	—	.67	+ 21	.7494
SEP 88	82	21	55	.48	—	53	+ 17	7494
SEP 88	83	1	2	.38	—	.42	+ 14	.7494
SEP 88	84	1	32	.38	—	.32	+ 9	.7494
DEC 88	73		50	—	—	4.68	+ 85	.7593
DEC 88	74	125	75	4.05	—	4.07	+ 72	7593
DEC 88	75	150	300	3.55	—	3.54	+ 69	7593
DEC 88	76		1	3.05	2.20	3.08	+ 63	.7593
DEC 88	80	200	600	1.64	—	1.69	+ 41	.7593

S-FRANC PUT

Month	Strike	Vol	Int	High	Low	Sett	Pt Chg	Future Sett
APR 88	68		55	—	—	CAB	- 1	.7401
APR 88	69	1	327	01	—	CAB	- 2	.7401
APR 88	70	160	223	01	—	[illegible]	- 3	7401
APR 88	71	567	872	10	02	03	[illegible]	7401
APR 88	72	929	1422	.32	06	08	- 16	.7401
APR 88	73	714	843	.70	.17	.21	- 42	.7401
APR 88	74	208	273	.94	.50	55	- 77	.7401
APR 88	75		177	—	—	1.21	- 100	.7401
MAY 88	67		17	—	—	01	- 3	.7401
MAY 88	69	42	45	.15	—	.05	- 7	.7401
MAY 88	70	145	135	.26	—	.11	- 11	7401
MAY 88	71	84	156	.44	.23	.21	20	.7401
MAY 88	72	169	274	.73	40	.38	- 32	7401
MAY 88	73	23	154	1.16	67	65	- 47	7401
MAY 88	74	1	1	1.41	1.10	1.08	- 108	.7401
JUN 88	63		209	—	—	01	- 1	7401
JUN 88	64		221	.04	—	02	- 1	7401
JUN 88	65		261	03	—	.03	- 1	.7401
JUN 88	66		860	.06	—	.05		7401
JUN 88	67	1	660	.08	08	.08	- 1	.7401
JUN 88	68	29	350	.15	11	.12	- 3	.7401
JUN 88	69	59	492	.28	17	19	- 6	.7401
JUN 88	70	180	1029	.48	28	30	- 12	.7401
JUN 88	71	211	543	73	43	46	21	7401
JUN 88	72	116	2554	1.07	65	70	32	.7401
JUN 88	73	560	1594	1.52	.95	1.03	- 44	.7401
JUN 88	74	585	718	1.80	1.40	1.47	- 57	7401
JUN 88	75		275	2.30	—	2.04	- 68	7401
JUN 88	76	4	200	3.09	2.75	2.73	- 75	.7401
JUN 88	77		162	—	—	3.48	- 84	.7401
JUN 88	78		6	—	—	4.30	- 90	.7401
JUN 88	79		125	—	—	5.17	- 110	.7401
JUN 88	80		200	—	—	6.07	- 115	.7401
SEP 88	69	1	175	.72	—	.55	- 18	7494
SEP 88	70		110	.87	.78	.73	- 22	.7494
SEP 88	71	1	42	1.28	1.00	.96	- 29	.7494
SEP 88	72	4	3	1.63	1.21	1.24	- 35	7494
SEP 88	73		325	2.08	1.65	1.57	- 43	7494
SEP 88	74	261	735	2.57	1.96	1.97	- 51	.7494
SEP 88	75		16	2.70	2.50	2.45	- 59	7494
SEP 88	76		123	3.30	—	3.00	- 66	.7494
SEP 88	77		672	—	—	3.62	- 73	.7494
SEP 88	78		315	—	—	4.29	- 79	.7494
SEP 88	80		150	—	—	5.79	- 90	.7494
DEC 88	70	100	100	1.15	1.08	1.04	- 104	.7593
DEC 88	71		1	1.60	1.27	1.27	- 28	7593
DEC 88	74	125	75	2.70	2.24	2.25	- 43	.7593
DEC 88	75	150	300	3.20	2.70	2.65	- 50	7593

TOTAL	VOLUME	OPEN INT
CALL	7656	21037
PUT	5430	18595
COMBINED	13086	39632

Treasury Bonds

CALLS

Mth	Strike	Vol	Open Int	- - Week's High	Low	Last - -	Net Change	Futures Close
Jun 88	88	7248	4494	4 00	2 58	3 45	- 31	90 29
Jun 88	90	25745	23707	2 35	1 48	2 23	- 10	90 29
Jun 88	92	40116	36022	1 30	58	1 19	- 08	90 29
Jun 88	94	57324	47222	49	29	43	- 07	90 29
Jun 88	96	39537	33983	26	14	22	- 03	90 29
Jun 88	98	22084	24906	14	07	13	- 01	90 29
Jun 88	100	12640	21065	07	04	07	- 01	90 29
Jun 88	102	3240	8104	05	02	04		90 29
Sep 88	92	1161	3127	1 63	1 35	1 56	- 04	89 29
Sep 88	94	1201	10811	1 21	62	1 15	- 03	89 29
Sep 88	96	1830	6141	53	36	52	- 02	89 29
Sep 88	98	2501	3525	34	24	30	- 02	89 29
Sep 88	100	903	1376	22	14	20	- 02	89 29
Dec 88	94	783	934	1 42	1 28	1 38		88 30

PUTS

Mth	Strike	Vol	Open Int	- - Week's High	Low	Last - -	Net Change	Futures Close
Jun 88	82	6724	8863	18	11	11	- 03	90 29
Jun 88	84	13186	10997	30	18	19	- 02	90 29
Jun 88	86	40009	35020	51	31	32	- 04	90 29
Jun 88	88	57630	37445	1 20	53	56	- 07	90 29
Jun 88	90	71330	40710	2 03	1 23	1 29	- 07	90 29
Jun 88	92	35101	32671	3 11	2 15	[illegible]	- 03	90 29
Jun 88	94	4258	21033	4 44	3 35	3 50	- 34	90 29
Sep 88	82	3124	2482	1 00	50	50	- 02	89 29
Sep 88	84	1386	3038	1 30	1 10	1 10	- 05	89 29
Sep 88	86	2260	1805	1 63	1 34	1 38	- 06	89 29
Sep 88	88	942	1088	2 47	2 10	2 10	- 06	89 29
Sep 88	90	3653	3469	3 36	2 60	3 00	- 08	89 29
Sep 88	92	1168	2091	4 44	3 52	4 00	- 10	89 29

Call Volume 221,022; Open Int 245,626
Put Volume 242,142; Open Int 218,290
Volume Friday through Thu.
Open interest as of close Thu.
High and low Mon. thru Thu., close Fri.
Strikes with less than 500 contracts traded not shown.

decay and can merely choose to allow the option to expire as worthless. However, if the futures began to approach the strike price of the option sold, this option always becomes more liquid, and easier to liquidate, if necessary.

Studying these charts for one hour each weekend can provide a trader with invaluable information and insight.

INTEGRATING OPTIONS INTO YOUR FUTURES TRADING PLAN

If you are successful trader, I would not suggest that you abandon your current trading plan or methods and trade options only. But, by integrating options at opportune times with your trading, your probability of profit could be substantially increased.

However, if your trading has been only marginally successful or unprofitable, I would strongly suggest that you look either at trading options exclusively or at least integrating options trading into your plan.

The following methods can be most useful for integrating options into a futures trading plan:

1. Using an Option Instead of a Stop to Protect a Contract

Purchasing an option for protection will allow a trader to hold a contract with a greatly reduced risk. This is a significantly better way to protect a position instead of placing a stop in the market, which could be hit on a sudden reaction as the trader watches in horror as his stop is hit at close to the low of the entire move. In a situation such as this, the cost of this option is a very small price to pay for the protection given, considering the potential for profit on the futures contract.

2. Covered Option Writing

This strategy is initiated by selling an out-of-the-money call (put) option against a long (short) futures position. The best time to initiate this strategy is when a market is at a very oversold (put) or overbought (call) condition and the trader expects consolidation to occur. The trader receives premium (additional income) from the sale of the option in this situation. Many times the options sold can be profitable even if the market continues to move higher (calls sold), because the decay in their time value outweighs the move in the underlying future contract. It also requires no additional margin other than that already used for the futures position.

3. Protecting a Futures Position by Combining the Purchase of a Put with a Sale of a Call

This strategy is simply combining the above two strategies and is recommended any time a position is at a substantial profit. This position will allow a trader to have total downside protection, and the potential for additional profit, all at little or no premium cost. This is because the premium for purchasing the puts is paid for by selling the call. (The above three hedging positions are discussed in more detail in Chapter 4.)

4. Buy a Low-Priced Option when a Contract Is about to Expire

In the last several weeks prior to expiration, you can purchase options with little time value remaining.

For example, an at-the-money gold option with about two weeks to trade can be purchased for about $200. If your were to predict a gold move correctly, you would make only $200 less than you could have made with a futures contract. But at the same time you have limited your losses to $200 if the market moves against you.

5. Use Options in Volatile Markets

You may have strong feelings that a market is about to make an explosive move, but the risk involved in taking a net futures position is too great. You can still trade the market in such situations with limited risk by purchasing options or using option spreads.

6. Use Options to Profit from Trading Range Markets

More than 80% of the time markets are in a trading range. Net traders are often frustrated and frequently stopped out of positions. By using neutral option strategies, a trader can increase his trading opportunities and trade these markets. These kinds of markets, in fact, provide the option strategist opportunities that have some of the highest mathematical probability.

As the market moves up and down, the total position is affected little because as the underlying futures price begins toward an option sold, the loss will be compensated by a gain on the option on the other side. Both options lose time value each day. This continual loss of time value on both sides of the trade makes this strategy attractive anytime there is a neutral or nontrending market.

7. Use Options when You Need Lower Margin Requirements

Reduced margins for many option strategies allow you to develop a diversified portfolio with less capital. Many options strategies require no margin at all. You pay only a premium that is the maximum amount you can lose if the market moves adversely, which is also often less than a futures margin.

8. Higher Probability of Profit

By proper use of option premiums, positions can be constructed having a higher probability of profit than a futures position. For example, when volatility is high, ratio spreads, constructed by purchasing fairly valued close-to-the-money options and selling overvalued out-of-the-money options, have a very high probability of profit.

9. Increased Risk/Reward Ratio

By taking advantage of disparities in option premium by selling overvalued and/or buying undervalued options, trades can be initiated that have reduced risks, but still have significant profit potential.

10. Increased Trading Opportunities

There are circumstances in many markets that provide opportunities for the options strategist where it would be inadvisable for an outright position because of lack of trend or too much volatility. Additionally, the options strategist is the only trader that can trade flat, trendless markets profitably.

CHANGING CHARACTER OF OUR MARKETS; OUR TRADING METHODS MUST REFLECT THIS

Both the character of our markets and volatility have continued to increase in our current futures markets. There are several reasons for this new phenomena, including:

1. Larger traders involved in futures;
2. Increased government intervention in the markets;
3. Conflicting goals of our government leaders;
4. The effect of not having any person in our government who seems to have a grasp of the ultimate consequences of their actions.

There was no cohesive long-term economic plan in our government in mid-1994. The Clinton administration sought to balance the budget, while entering into costly programs (health care plans, etc.); and wanted to raise taxes without significantly impacting the stock or bond markets. Fed Chairman Greenspan focused on the potential of inflation and hiked rates to prevent any perception of inflation; while Secretary of the Treasury Bentsen felt that strengthening the dollar was the most important thing necessary for our economy.

These conflicting goals boiled into market turmoil in June 1994 with extreme volatility that caused the S&P 500 to lose two months of gains in one week in June; the Japanese yen to move to new highs; and the precious metals and bonds to alternate large daily moves in both directions.

There seems to be no "captain" of our economic ship. The markets are reflecting this fact as they move significantly in both directions but with no real trend. These moves seem to come after some form of Fed intervention through the comments of these administrative officials of what their latest idea is. Just like flying a plane without a flight plan, this type of "patchwork" economics is very dangerous. It also will continue to make trading very choppy, as fundamentals and market trends can be meaningless when someone in power can change his mind and cause significant short-term market moves.

Longer term, markets will eventually head where they were going anyway, as intervention can only affect short-term changes. However, intervention will exaggerate these shorter-term movements and volatility, which can cause much wider swings than the market would have had, if it could have moved in its own natural way.

Another factor causing increased volatility in our futures markets is the entry of institutional traders into the commodity markets. Hedge funds, derivative traders, and even mutual funds are now trading commodities, as many of these traders feel that the risk/reward of the stock market is poor, and they have now discovered the potential for significant new opportunities in futures. This has added a great deal of volatility to daily price action as many of these large traders look at similar factors, technical patterns, or breakout points and enter or exit the markets at the same time.

How can we as traders use all of this information? First of all, and most obvious, when the markets become extremely volatile and unpredictable, this presents excellent option purchasing opportunities. This particularly applies in markets where option volatility is still at low levels. For example, at the end of June 1994 in spite of the huge daily moves in the underlying markets, both the currencies still had relatively low option volatility. Any traders of cash or futures markets should consider purchasing options instead of futures in these markets.

On the other hand, out-of-the-money, grain, cattle, coffee and treasury bond options were priced extremely high. Traders would not only have a difficult time making money by purchasing these options; traders who either purchased futures positions or at-the-money options in these markets would have been well advised to sell out-of-the-money options in these markets to increase their probability of profit.

Increased volatility and change brings opportunity to the knowledgeable trader. However, you must always remain alert to be able to both recognize what has changed and then use it to your advantage to get your "trading edge."

WHAT IS NECESSARY TO SUCCEED IN TRADING

In writing the *Opportunities in Options* newsletter over the last nine years, we have not only analyzed the markets in each issue, but have presented and discussed the best new and old ideas; we find what works, and what doesn't; we've dissected and analyzed numerous trading methods, philosophies, and ideas. In this book, with a little help from *New Market Wizards* by Jack Schwager, Harper Collins Publishing, (hereafter referred to as *NMW*), we are going to put it all together.

VERY SIMPLY, THERE ARE COMMON IDEAS, PHILOSOPHIES AND METHODS USED NOT ONLY BY ALL OF THE TWENTY TRADERS IN *THE NEW MARKET WIZARDS,* BUT PROBABLY BY EVERY LONG-TERM SUCCESSFUL TRADER. (Of course, there are exceptions where traders have been "lucky." However, over the long term, the markets have a way of quickly unraveling any "lucky" traders.) There is nothing that can guarantee your success in trading; but, if you don't follow the rules these successful traders have used in the past, your chances will drop to well under 5%.

Let me say it again: IF YOU DO NOT FOLLOW THE RULES, YOU'RE DESTINED TO LOSE! In fact if you don't have the time, energy, or aspiration to read this 500-page book, you shouldn't be trading, However, there is a short cut that could work by reading "Closing Bell" (Part Seven of *NMW*). These 20 pages contain all of the important ideas discussed in the entire book. But, if you do only that, you'll be missing many fascinating stories about these traders, their successes and failures.

In fact one of the most fascinating aspects of the book is the humble stories by these extremely successful traders (most of whom measure their success in tens to hundreds of millions of dollars), how at times in their trading history, they either committed terrible mistakes causing them to lose large amounts of money; and other times when they were absolutely correct on the markets, and either did not profit or lost money on trades.

It shows that it takes more than just being right on the markets to succeed. At times, that can be only a small part of the success. I'm sure there are traders that have no plan, no discipline and no money management, and are able to be successful. I think these traders are very few, and probably even fewer actually kept these winnings over the long term. Although I must say there is not a single statement in the book that I don't agree with, I am going to single out the ones that have been the most influential to me in my trading career:

1. It Is Absolutely Necessary to Have an "Edge"

In our newsletters and books, we have discussed that every trade requires us to have some type of edge over the market either because of disparity in volatility, option pricing, etc. In our Neutral Option Positions, we obtain an "edge" by the overvaluation of out-of-the-money options and the probability that these options will be worthless at expirations; in our in-the-money debit spreads, we explore the "edge" of buying well-priced options and selling overpriced options that are likely to be valueless at expiration; in our ratio spreads, we have an "edge," at times of being successful even when the market moves in a direction other than we predicted. We never want to make a trade without some type of "edge."

"You can't win without an edge, even with the world's greatest discipline and money management skills. . . . If you don't have an edge, all that money management and discipline will do for you is guarantee that you will gradually bleed to death. Incidentally, if you don't know what your edge is, you don't have one." (*NMW,* page 463.)

"Make sure you have the edge. Know what your edge is. Have risk controls . . . When you get down to it, to make money you need to have an edge and employ good money management. Good money management alone is not going to increase your edge at all." (Monroe Trout in *NMW,* page 175.)

2. Trading Plan, Valid Methodology; Money Management; Risk Control; and Discipline

I am going to combine the above into one item because, we have discussed these many times in the past, and unless you are absolutely convinced that you need these to succeed, you don't have a chance. These items include: (a) a trading plan; (b) a tested, reliable trading method; (c) money management; (d) risk control (never risking more than 5% of your capital in any trade, having a predetermined exit point before you get into a trade, and having a cutoff point of 10–20% of your equity which will take you out of the market for a rest); and (e) discipline.

"Traders lose because they don't have a winning strategy. Second, even among those traders who do, many don't follow the strategy. Trading puts pressure on weaker human traits and seems to seek out each individual's Achilles heel. A good trader has a maverick mind. It is also important to have a blend between the artistic and scientific side. You need the artistic side to imagine, discover and create trading strategies. You need a scientific side to translate those ideas into firm trading rules and to execute those rules. Novice traders should follow the following rules:

"First, focus on trading vehicle strategies and time horizons that seek your personality. Second, identify nonrandom price behavior while recognizing that markets are random most of the time. Third, absolutely convince yourself that what you have found is statistically valid. Fourth, set up trading rules. Fifth, follow the rules. In a nutshell it all comes down to do your own thing (independence); and do the right thing (discipline)." (Gil Blake in *NMW*, pp. 247–8.)

"(1) Develop a competent analytical methodology. (2) Extract a reasonable trading plan from these methods. (3) Formulate rules for this plan that incorporate money management techniques. (4) Back test the plan over a long period. (5) Exercise self management so that you adhere to the plan. The best plan in the world won't work if you don't act on it. . . . No trading plan is the biggest cause of losses. It causes lack of self-confidence, fear of loss and poor execution." (Robert Krausz in *NMW*, pp. 455 and 457.)

3. Relationship of Trading to Techniques of Successful Poker and Blackjack Players

Several of the top traders in *NMW* were experienced blackjack or poker players. They compared their success in gambling to their success in trading (this is one of the main themes in our new book, *The Option Secret*).

"He came to trading by way of blackjack because there are strong parallels between the two activities. Consistent winning in both is a matter of strategy and discipline, not luck. Luck plays a role only over the short term, where its potential adverse impact must be neutralized by money management controls. Thorpe's book *Beat the Dealer* was responsible for Blair Hull becoming involved in the markets. It taught him the methods of blackjack and how to get an edge in both trading and gambling. Successful blackjack, chess and bridge players are usually likely to be good traders." (The author of *NMW* discussing a top trader's success on page 363.)

4. Varying Your Bet (Position) Size

Varying the size of your trading is similar to how a professional gambler varies his bet size. Playing blackjack or poker, you change the size of your wager in accordance to the probability you feel is likely for a successful result based on the cards already played, your hand, your knowledge of the other players, etc. This principle is so important that virtually every successful trader follows it. In fact, one trader says that he varies his position size by as much as 100 to 1.

"Vic Sperandeo became a trader by first becoming a poker enthusiast. In poker, if you only play the hands in which the odds were in your favor and folded when they were not, you would end up winning more times than you lost. I memorized the odds of every important card combination and was very successful with the game. I think successful trading or poker playing for that matter, involves speculating rather than gambling. Successful speculation implies taking risks when the odds are in your favor. Just like poker, when you have to know which hands to bet on, in trading you have to know when the odds are in your favor." (*NMW,* pp. 254–5, 275.)

5. Use a Trading Method That You Are Comfortable With

While I am extremely comfortable holding large complicated Neutral Option Positions with short options that scare most traders, I am nervous holding a small position in the agricultural markets into a crop report. The approach you use must be right for you; it must be comfortable. The importance of this can not be overemphasized—virtually every successful trader ultimately ended up with a trading style suited to his personality.

6. Trade Small

"Once you have a method you still need money management to prevent an adverse streak from taking you out of the game. It is critical to take in mind that even if you have the edge, you can still lose all of your money. Therefore, the bet or trade side must be small enough to keep the probability of such an event very low." (*NMW,* page 388.)

7. Listen to the Markets

"It is my firm belief that the markets wisdom is far greater than mine. In my opinion the markets price of an item is the best measure of its value. The general principle is that if you give up your ego and listen to what the markets are telling you, you can have a huge source of information." (Jeff Yass in *NMW,* page 407.)

There are at least 30 other important ideas in *The New Market Wizards*, including whether becoming a good trader can be learned; understanding that you are responsible for your own results; the need for independence; being able to withstand losses; how to overcome lack of confidence; other's advice; patience; staying with trades that are working; discovering low risk trading ideas; scaling in and out of trades; you can't win if you have to; etc.

Fortunately, these ideas are very easy to understand; unfortunately, they are harder to put into practice. And as is stated succinctly in the book, "The market is a stern master. You need to do almost everything right to win. If parts of you are pulling in opposite directions, the game is lost before you start."

I encourage all traders of stocks, futures, and options to read this book before putting on another position. If you already have this book and you've read it, read it again before you put on another position.

CHAPTER 7

Using a Computer When Trading Options

Many traders have avoided options because of the complexities involved—such as premium evaluations, hedge ratios, betas, deltas, volatility, time value decay, etc. Option traders who do not have a working knowledge of these factors can be at a disadvantage. Computer programmers have attempted to make traders' decisions easier.

The programs developed for both personal computers and large mainframes are similar in several aspects, including the fact that they all use pricing models and formulas to determine the theoretical value of options.

Factors used to determine these values also are fairly similar in that the variables considered include the option's strike price, price of the underlying instrument, time left until expiration, interest rates, and the calculated volatility of the option. These programs figure theoretical premium values, risk/reward ratios, and hedge and conversion factors.

However, traders who rely on computer-generated figures only are at a disadvantage in trading options. This is because the state of development in computer software in options has not yet progressed enough to be able to factor in all the variables on which an experienced trader would rely.

An option program that properly fits the trader's needs, however, can be a great aid in trade selection and monitoring market strategies. The computer can also be a great time saver in calculating actual volatility, hedge ratios, and other data.

Just as there are many computer services available to evaluate options and option strategies, there is also a wide range of other kinds of analysis services available. Some specialize in graphics capability and some scan option premiums for the best to use in certain strategies. Others specialize in arbitrage opportunities and position risk evaluations.

OPTIONS PREMIUM VALUATIONS

What kind of analysis do you need? How much does it cost? Before you can answer these questions, you must examine the basics of premium valuation.

Options premium valuations are calculated from these four variables, three of which are determined easily at any point in time:

1. Number of trading days left until the option expires.
2. Amount the option is in-the-money or out-of-the-money (relationship of the option strike price to the underlying instrument value).
3. Risk-free rate of return (usually the current T-bill or bank rate).
4. Volatility of the option premium (a measure of the swings in the option premium over a period of time).

Option Volatility

Option volatility is the hardest factor to quantify. This last input to the Black-Scholes, Parkinson, or other valuation model that an option pricing program uses to evaluate puts and calls causes the greatest headache for option traders.

Volatility measurements are historical, by definition, and are determined by putting the date into the option valuation model "backwards." That is, settlement price, trading days until expiration, risk-free interest rate, and in-the-money or out-of-the-money amounts are used to find one missing variable: the volatility.

This calculated volatility from the value the market is placing on the option is known as "floor volatility" or "Market Implied Volatility" (MIV). That changes from day to day and even from moment to moment. Because option valuation services use some form of MIV to calculate theoretical option prices for the present and future, it really depends on what form the MIV enters the model.

Typically, an option valuation service will use a weighted moving average of MIVs over a period of time. Differences in theoretical valuations result from the weighting (if any) and the period used in the MIV averaging calculation.

Heavier weighting to recent MIVs and a shorter period will result in theoretical pricings that change more quickly and usually will be slower to a day's settlement price. A longer period with no weighting can result in theoretical price consistently too high or too low.

These differences can result in two option programs coming to greatly different theoretical values, which can severely affect the results of an option strategy. The solution to the dilemma is to look at volatility and option premium valuations over a period of time in each market. Daily MIVs are compared with historical data to determine if options in that market can be used with various options strategies effectively. For example, in a period when options are relatively inexpensive historically, you might consider strategies involving buying options. In periods of high volatility, you may want to initiate ratio spreads.

Hedge Ratio

The second important calculation, a by-product of the option valuation model, is the hedge ratio or delta—the amount an option premium will change with a small change in the underlying instrument. A hedge ratio of 0.50 means that if the underlying instrument moves up $1, the option premium will move up 50 cents.

A rule of thumb is that if any underlying instrument is right at the strike price of an option, the option will have a hedge ratio of 0.50. Naturally, hedge ratios change as the in-the-money amount changes, so an option's hedge ratio is always changing.

Hedge ratios must also be considered when formulating option strategies. For example, if you expect the price of gold to increase by $10 an ounce and the hedge ratio of the option you purchase is 0.20, the option will increase by only $2. This may barely cover commissions on the trade. On the other hand, if you write options, you generally want the hedge ratio to be low so that a large fluctuation in the underlying instrument will not severely affect your profit on a position.

Hedge ratios of related options can be combined to provide a spread hedge ratio. In a vertical call bull spread, for example, the hedge ratio of the short call of the higher strike price is subtracted from the hedge ratio of the long call at the lower strike price to provide the spread hedge ratio. This figure will estimate the response of the spread as a whole to change in the underlying futures price. You can determine hedge ratios for other option combinations in the same manner.

A "delta neutral" spread is often used because of its unique characteristics. Delta neutral means that the combined option hedge ratios add up to zero. (Hedge ratios of long puts and short calls are considered negative numbers.) This will make the spread unresponsive to small changes in the underlying futures and is useful for strategies that capitalize on option premium decay.

The underlying futures hedge ratio, of course, is equal to 1 on a long position and –1 on a short position. Delta neutral strategies sometimes may require frequent adjustment, so careful monitoring is important.

Another statistic that a few programs will generate is the responsiveness of option premiums to volatility changes. This calculation can be especially useful for delta neutral strategies to determine at what volatility levels their strategies acquire undesirable characteristics.

Computer data can be obtained either "off-line" or "on-line." Off-line data are data that are obtained through various vendors after market hours. On-line data refers to real time price quotes and analysis as the markets actually trade.

Many traders assume that expensive on-line equipment is necessary. That is not always the case; there are successful traders who only use weekly chart books. On-line option evaluation software is not a guarantee of making profits. In fact, if used improperly or without a good trading plan, it will only increase your losses by the cost of the equipment.

OFF-LINE OPTION ANALYSIS

Over twenty different firms provide various forms of option analysis software. The costs vary from $99 to $1,000+. Although most provide the basic services described above, they differ mainly in the extent of their analysis and their "user friendliness." Any software should be sampled before purchase, through either a demo or a trial period. Most manufacturers of software provide this for potential users.

There is one program that, in my option, stands in a category by itself. *OptionVue IV* (OptionVue Systems, Inc., 175 East Hawthorn Parkway, Ste. 180, Vernon Hills, IL 60061, 708-816-6610), is perhaps the most sophisticated and user friendly of any off-line systems that I have tried. It is a "comprehensive decision support system" for option trading. Its purpose is to assist the trader in selecting the best option strategy in any given situation. It has "what-if" capability and will project profit-loss scenarios. It will generate buy and sell signals based on your price forecast and risk level, as well as determine the best strategy to use. It also tracks, and tracks volatility, expirations, and margins.

I asked the analysts at OptionVue to provide commentary and studies on several different trade selections that were being considered. The following is their analysis and commentary.

1. Best Short Strangle, Any Market

We used *OptionVue IV's* database survey function to discover a market whose current implied volatility was high compared to recent historical levels. Wheat was selected by the program because I.V. (implied volatility) was at a historically high level of 23%, also significantly higher than S.V. (statistical volatility) (16%) (Exhibit 7.1). (Note: Exhibits 7.1 through 7.19 can be found at the end of this chapter.)

We asked *OptionVue IV* to find the most attractive strangle to sell, based on the idea that wheat would continue to be priced around 287½ and continue to exhibit a volatility of 16% or so. *OptionVue IV* recommended the following strangle: sell two Jul310 calls and sell two Jul280 puts (Exhibit 7.2).

Looking at this strategy in the matrix (Exhibit 7.3), the program recommended selling the Jul310 calls because the I.V. on these calls was 26.0%, a good deal higher than the I.V. of other calls at that time. However, the sale of two out-of-the-money calls along with two near-the-money puts results in a delta imbalance. If delta neutrality is desired, we might consider increasing the number of calls sold to four. Referring to the illustration, this brings the total position delta down to +7.69, which is near zero.

The next illustration is a profit/loss graph of this 4 × 2 strangle (Exhibit 7.4). This position yields a profit across a wide range of underlying prices. The dark shaded area represents the first standard deviation of underlying wheat prices (presuming a 16% volatility), while the lighter shading encompasses the second standard deviation of underlying wheat prices.

2. Best Long Straddle in Gold

The historical volatility chart for gold shows that 1991 levels were currently at an extreme low, hence the recommendation by the program to purchase a straddle (Exhibit 7.5). Anticipating a "spike" back to the 20% level or so, sometime during the next couple of months, we asked *OptionVue IV* to recommend the best straddle (or strangle) to purchase (Exhibit 7.6).

It recommended the following: Buy two Oct390 calls and buy two Oct350 puts (Exhibit 7.7). The next two illustrations show what this position looks like in the matrix, and how it would perform based on a profit/loss graph (Exhibit 7.8). Again, this graph displays the first and second standard deviations of probable prices for the underlying, using dark and light shading (Exhibit 7.9).

3. Best Bullish Strategy in U.S. Bonds

If we project bonds to go up to 102 in the next three months, *OptionVue IV* recommends a simple call purchase (Exhibit 7.10). (As you can see from the illustration, the top three recommendations are call purchases.) Graphing these, you can see that their performances are very similar, especially around the target price of 102, depicted on the graph as a vertical line (Exhibit 7.11).

The historical volatility chart and a snapshot of the matrix are included for reference (Exhibit 7.12).

4. Hedging a Short Position in Swiss Franc Futures, with Swiss Francs Currently at 6800 and Expecting Them to Go Lower

The historical volatility chart shows volatilities to be at a high level (Exhibit 7.13). This suggests selling puts as a hedge rather than purchasing calls. Looking at the matrix, you can see that there are several puts available and trading in the June expiration. Which one you pick depends largely on how much room you want to leave the Franc to go down further (Exhibit 7.14). The illustration shows you shorting the 67's. However, the profit/loss graph shows the results of shorting these (solid line) *or* the 68's (dashed line). Obviously, if you short the 67's, you make more money if the Franc falls below 67.5 or so. In the graph, the shaded area encompasses a hypothetical projected trading range between 65 and 68 (Exhibit 7.15).

Although *OptionVue's* price is much higher ($900–$1400) than most other off-line software packages, its capabilities are also greater than any other software I have seen. It is my opinion that if you are going to use computer software, and risk substantial money in trading, that only the best should be considered.

ON-LINE SYSTEMS FOR EVALUATING OPTIONS

The three most powerful on-line systems that I have identified are *OptionVue, Optionomics*, and *FutureSource.* The differences between them have to do with the type of trading you are doing rather than inherent weaknesses or strengths within each system.

OptionVue on-line is exactly the same as we have described for the off-line system above except that instead of manual input, prices, graphs and scenarios are updated real time. This requires an additional $500 package from *OptionVue* along with a monthly fee from a quote vendor of $500+.

Optionomics (3191 South Valley Street, Suite 155, Salt Lake City, UT 84109, 800-255-3374), provides on-line option evaluation, similar to *OptionVue,* but in a somewhat more advanced package, with extra "bells and whistles." *Optionomics* sophisticated option evaluations may be lost on the average off-floor trader. We feel that it is better suited for the professional option trader or floor trader who is able to take advantage of its advanced functions. Exhibits 7.16 and 7.17 are examples of information generated from *Optionomics.*

FutureSource (955 Parkview Blvd., Lombard, IL 60148, 800-621-2628), is an on-line system combining futures and options charts and option evaluation. It allows you to use your own computer and access all of these services in one easy to use machine. I find it convenient and time saving, particularly in being able to switch back and forth at a single key stroke from current prices to charts of up to 15 years, and then in being able to switch quickly to evaluation of option strategies. Although missing a few features from specialized option software, its speed, convenience, and reasonable price for on-line data make it a very practical choice. Exhibits 7.18 and 7.19 are *FutureSource's* computer generated trade sheets analyzing the value of the December bond 94 call for market prices between 90 and 100 at three dates I selected in the future.

I keep my uses of a computer very simple in my trading.

1. I calculate option volatility to determine whether it is high or low (I have monthly calculations for at least five years in all options);
2. I calculate the "fair value" of all of the option strike prices and monitor based on the current implied volatility;
3. I have a "spread sheet" of what my gain or loss will be if the market moves up or down in the future; and
4. I have the computer scan for the best strategies in the selected markets.

Remember, your computer can be a valuable aid; but you must still act as the trader and make the final decision on all trades.

Exhibit 7.1
Short Strangle

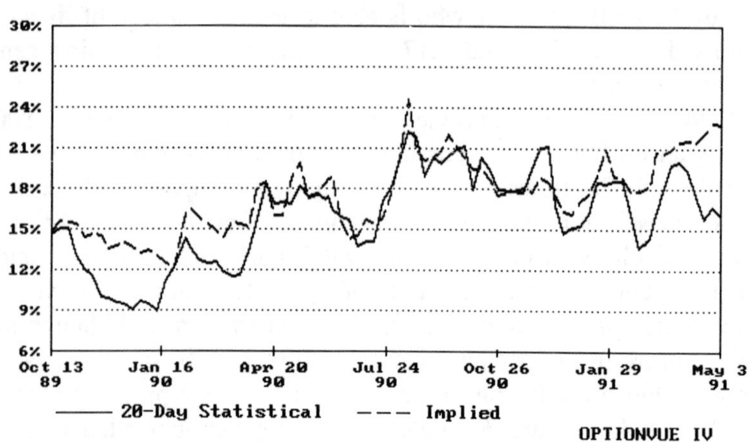

Exhibit 7.2
Attractive Strangle to Sell

* * * OPTIONVUE IV SELECTIONS * * *

SYMBOL: WN1 TODAY'S DATE: MAY 08 1991 VALUATION DATE: JUN 15 1991
CAPITAL: $4,000 PRICE: 287 1/2 CALL VLTY: 21.9 21.9 21.9
STRATEGY: Sell Naked Straddles PUT VLTY: 21.9 21.9 21.9
TG.PRICE: Bell curve centered around 287 1/2 INTRST: 7.9%
RANKING BASIS: 50% Exp.Ret. / 50% 1st St.Dev.Downside Exp.Ret.

	Recommended Trade								Exp.Ret.	St.Dev.
1.	S	2	Jul310c	@2 1/2,	S	2	Jul280p	@4 5/8	+347	-521
2.	S	2	Jul300c	@3 3/4,	S	2	Jul280p	@4 5/8	+339	-599
3.	S	3	Sep320c	@5 7/8,	S	3	Sep280p	@5 7/8	+209	-376
4.	S	2	Jul290c	@6 3/4,	S	2	Jul290p	@9 3/8	+373	-849
5.	S	3	Sep330c	@4 1/8,	S	3	Sep280p	@5 7/8	+215	-399
6.	S	2	Jul300c	@3 3/4,	S	2	Jul290p	@9 3/8	+382	-869
7.	S	3	Sep310c	@8 5/8,	S	3	Sep280p	@5 7/8	+223	-461
8.	S	2	Jul310c	@2 1/2,	S	2	Jul290p	@9 3/8	+389	-894
9.	S	2	Jul290c	@6 3/4,	S	2	Jul280p	@4 5/8	+330	-791
10.	S	2	Jul320c	@1 1/4,	S	2	Jul280p	@4 5/8	+252	-529
11.	S	2	Sep310c	@8 5/8,	S	2	Sep300p	@14 1/4	+155	-383
12.	S	2	Jul280c	@11 3/4,	S	2	Jul290p	@9 3/8	+307	-789

[END OF REPORT. Press any key...]

Exhibit 7.3
Strangle to Sell Matrix

```
OPTIONVUE IV              MATRIX             Wheat (CBT)*              WED MAY 8 1991
/FUTURES=====================================================================\
| |=======JUL=(54)========| |-------SEP-(118)-------| |-------DEC-(208)-------||
|  287 1/2           11:13   296 3/4 296 3/4    11:13   309 1/2 309 1/2   11:13 |
|OPTIONS==========================================================================|
|!       |------JUL-(38)-------| |------SEP-(101)------| |------DEC-(192)------||
|CALLS     2 1/2    15.0      -4     8 3/4     36.6 ______     18         50.6 ______ |
|310       26.0%   WYN31   2 1/2     22.9%    WYU31              19.1%    WYZ31        |
|CALLS     3 3/4    28.3 ______     12 1/2     47.5 ______     23 1/4     58.4 ______ |
|300       22.8%   WYN30             21.2%    WYU30              21.6%    WYZ30        |
|CALLS>    6 3/4    46.1 ______     17 1/2     58.9 ______     29 1/2     66.0 ______ |
|290       21.5%   WYN29             21.4%    WYU29              21.9%    WYZ29        |
|^       ---------------------------------------------------------------------------|
|PUTS     15 1/2   -70.9 ______     14 1/2    -50.4 ______     13 3/4    -37.6 ______ |
|300       20.7%   WZN30             20.9%    WZU30              21.3%    WZZ30        |
|PUTS>     9 1/2   -53.0 ______      9 1/4    -39.0 ______     10        -30.0 ______ |
|290       22.2%   WZN29             20.4%    WZU29              20.7%    WZZ29        |
|PUTS      4 1/2   -33.8      -2     6        -28.1 ______      6 1/2    -22.9 ______ |
|280       21.5%   WZN28   4 5/8     21.2%    WZU28              20.8%    WZZ28        |
|                                                                                    |
|SUMMARY=============================================================================|
| Orig.Reqmt:     $2,025   Commis:    $150.00    Delta:     +7.69    AvgMIV: 21.8% |
|Maint.Reqmt:     $3,444                         Gamma:     -8.16     Calls: 22.1% |
|   Cash Flow:      +$812    Theta:  +$22.07/day  Vega:     -78.2      Puts: 21.2% |
\- [F1]=Help ---------------------------------------------------------- 22K ----/
```

Exhibit 7.4
Profit/Loss of Strangle to Sell

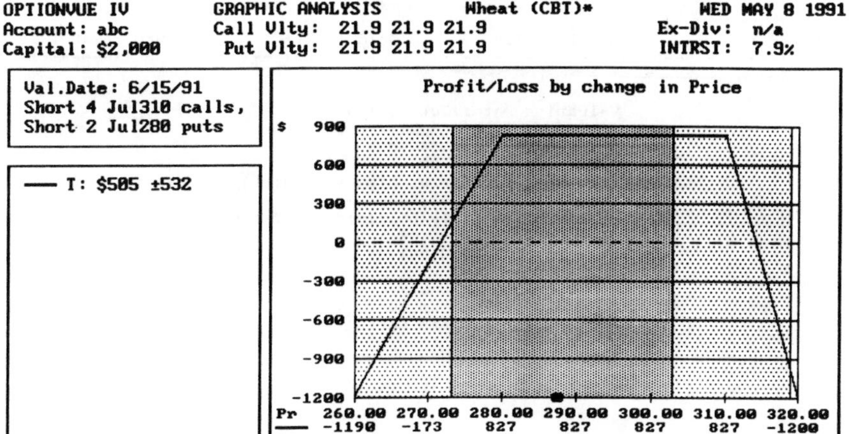

Exhibit 7.5
Long Straddle

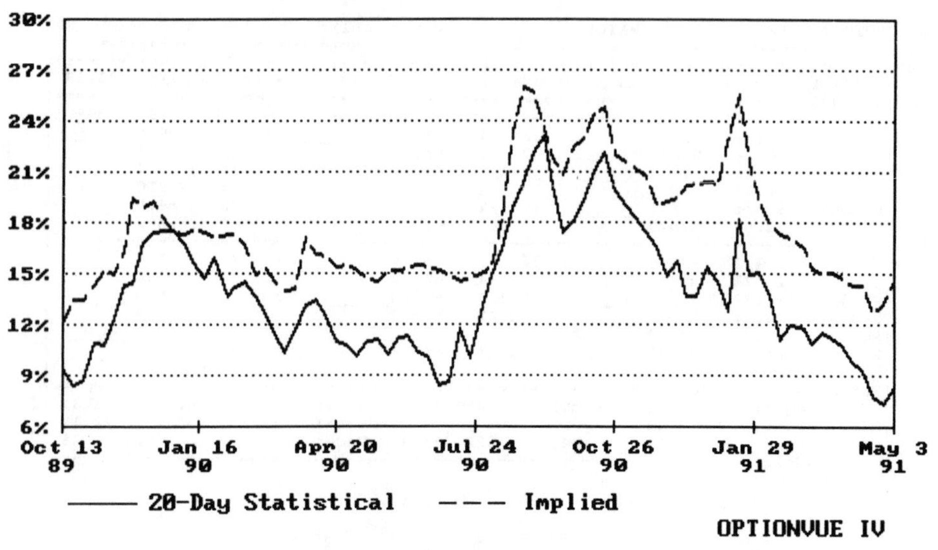

Exhibit 7.6
Straddle to Purchase

```
OPTIONVUE IV          DEF. SELECTION          Gold (CEC)*          WED MAY 8 1991
--------------------------------------------------------------------------------

                  Valuation Date: JUL 13 1991
                     Target Type: [Bell]/Price/Range
                    Center Price: 358.70
                      Volatility:  20.0%
                        Strategy: [Purchase straddles]/...
                Capital Provided: $2,500
                Comparison Basis: [P/L]/Yield/Ann.Yield
               Volatility Change: +5.0%
                 Int.Rate Change: 0.00%

                           RANKING BASIS
                     Proportion Exp.Ret:   1
            Proportion Downside Exp.Ret:   1


-- [F1]=Help -------------------------------------------------------- 77K -----
```

Exhibit 7.7
Long Straddle Recommendations

```
                   * * *  OPTIONVUE IV SELECTIONS  * * *
--------------------------------------------------------------------------
  SYMBOL: GCM1        TODAY'S DATE: MAY 08 1991    VALUATION DATE: JUL 13 1991
 CAPITAL: $2,500              PRICE: 358.70           CALL VLTY:  19.7 19.7 19.7
STRATEGY: Buy Straddles                                PUT VLTY:  19.7 19.7 19.7
TG.PRICE: Bell curve centered around 358.70              INTRST:  7.9%
  RANKING BASIS:  50% Exp.Ret. / 50% 1st St.Dev.Downside Exp.Ret.
--------------------------------------------------------------------------
     Recommended Trade                                      Exp.Ret.    St.Dev.
     -----------------                                      -------     ------
 1.  B   2 Oct390c  @4.50,      B  2 Oct350p  @6.40          +1,141     ~1,865
 2.  B   2 Oct380c  @6.70,      B  2 Oct340p  @4.00          +1,150     ~2,060
 3.  B   2 Oct390c  @4.50,      B  2 Oct340p  @4.00            +985     ~1,756
 4.  B   1 Oct370c  @9.60,      B  1 Oct360p  @10.30           +773     ~1,088
 5.  B   1 Oct360c  @14.20,     B  1 Oct360p  @10.30           +780     ~1,182
 6.  B   1 Oct370c  @9.60,      B  1 Oct350p  @6.40            +758     ~1,137
 7.  B   1 Oct360c  @14.20,     B  1 Oct350p  @6.40            +765     ~1,300
 8.  B   1 Oct380c  @6.70,      B  1 Oct360p  @10.30           +684     ~1,041
 9.  B   1 Oct380c  @6.70,      B  1 Oct350p  @6.40            +669     ~1,010
10.  B   1 Oct370c  @9.60,      B  1 Oct340p  @4.00            +678     ~1,221
11.  B   1 Oct360c  @14.20,     B  1 Oct340p  @4.00            +685     ~1,434
12.  B   1 Oct390c  @4.50,      B  1 Oct360p  @10.30           +601     ~1,044

                   [ END OF REPORT.  Press any key... ]
```

Exhibit 7.8
Long Straddle Performance Based on Profit/Loss

```
OPTIONVUE IV            MATRIX            Gold (CEC)*              WED MAY 8 1991
/FUTURES=====================================================================\
| |=======JUN=(26)========| |-------AUG-(85)--------| |-------OCT-(146)-------||
|  358.70            11:39   361.30  361.60    11:39   364.70  364.50    11:39 |
|OPTIONS=====================================================================|
|v        |-------JUN-(3)-------| |------AUG-(66)-------| |------OCT-(129)------||
|CALLS     ....    0.00 ______       1.40   11.4  ______       4.40   22.7      +2 |
|390             OGM390             15.3%  OGQ390             15.2%  OGV390    4.50|
|CALLS     0.10    0.00 ______       2.50   21.5  ______       6.60   32.5  ______ |
|380             OGM380             14.3%  OGQ380             14.8%  OGV380        |
|CALLS     0.10    0.99 ______       4.80   35.8  ______       9.50   43..9 ______ |
|370             OGM370             13.8%  OGQ370             14.1%  OGV370        |
|!     ----------------------------------------------------------------------- |
|PUTS     11.50   -98.9 ______      14.10  -62.8  ______      15.70  -53.4  ______ |
|370             OGI370             15.0%  OGO370             15.3%  OGR370        |
|PUTS>     2.50   -60.4 ______       7.50  -45.8  ______      10.20  -41.2  ______ |
|360      13.7%  OGI360             13.5%  OGO360             14.7%  OGR360        |
|PUTS      0.20   -3.17 ______       3.80  -29.0  ______       6.30  -29.5      +2 |
|350             OGI350             13.8%  OGO350             14.7%  OGR350    6.40|
|                                                                              |
|SUMMARY=====================================================================|
| Orig.Reqmt:      $2,280   Commis:    $100.00      Delta:   -13.46   AvgMIV: 14.2% |
|Maint.Reqmt:      $2,280                           Gamma:   +4.02     Calls: 14.3% |
|  Cash Flow:     -$2,280    Theta:  -$15.33/day   Vega:     +281      Puts: 13.9% |
\- [F1]=Help ----------------------------------------------------------- 22K ----/
```

Exhibit 7.9
First and Second Standard Deviations of Probable Prices

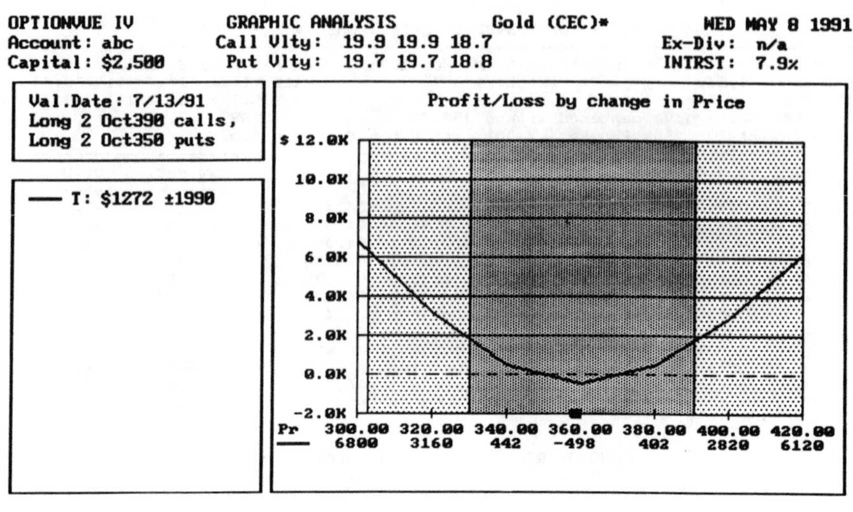

Exhibit 7.10
Call Purchase (U.S. Treasury Bonds)

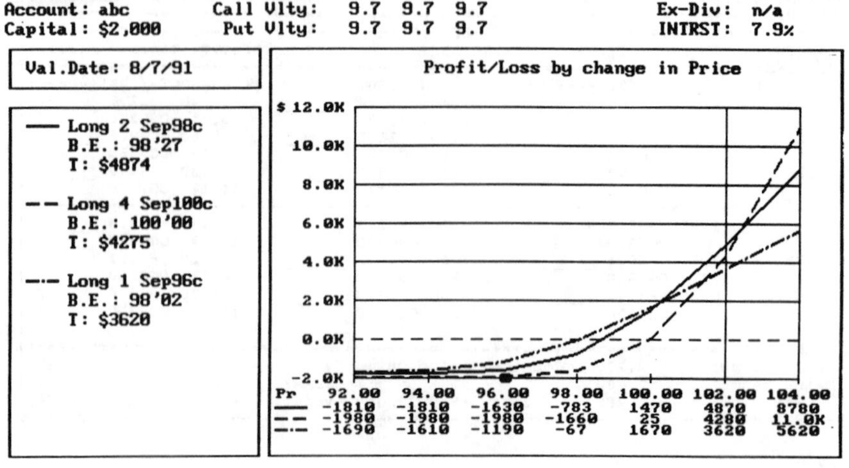

Exhibit 7.11
Call Purchase (U.S. Treasury)

```
OPTIONVUE IV         MATRIX        U.S. Treas Bonds (CBT)*         WED MAY 8 1991
/FUTURES=====================================================================\
| |=======JUN=(26)========| |-------SEP-(118)-------| |-------DEC-(208)-------||
|  96'02              14:26  95'09  95'13      14:26  94'20  94'26       14:26 |
|OPTIONS=====================================================================|
|        |------JUN-(10)-------| |------SEP-(108)------| |------DEC-(192)------||
|100c     ....                ______    0'27     9.2% ______    ....           ______ |
|98c      0'07     10.6%      ______    0'55     9.3% ______    1'17     9.6%  ______ |
|96c>     0'39      9.1%      ______    1'39     9.6% ______    1'56     9.4%  ______ |
|94c      2'11     11.7%      ______    2'45    10.0% ______    2'48     9.3%  ______ |
|92c      4'02                ______    4'00    10.0% ______    4'00     9.7%  ______ |
|90c      6'02                ______    5'37     9.7% ______    4'50     6.2%  ______ |
|        ---------------------------------------------------------------------|
|100p     ....                ______    ....          ______    ....           ______ |
|98p      1'62                ______    3'34     9.3% ______    4'34     9.7%  ______ |
|96p>     0'36      9.4%      ______    2'18     9.4% ______    3'17     9.7%  ______ |
|94p      0'06     10.8%      ______    1'26     9.8% ______    ....           ______ |
|92p      ....                ______    0'50    10.0% ______    ....           ______ |
|90p      ....                ______    0'28    10.5% ______    ....           ______ |
|          Last       MIV    Trade                                            |
|SUMMARY=====================================================================|
| Orig.Reqmt:          $0   Commis:      $0.00    Delta:    0.00   AvgMIV:  9.9% |
|Maint.Reqmt:          $0                         Gamma:    0.00    Calls:  9.9% |
|  Cash Flow:          $0    Theta:  $0.00/day    Vega:     0.00     Puts:  9.9% |
\- [F1]=Help ------------------------------------------------------- 22K ----/
```

Exhibit 7.12
Historical Volatility Chart (U.S. Treasury Bonds)

U.S. Treas Bonds (CBT) Volatilities

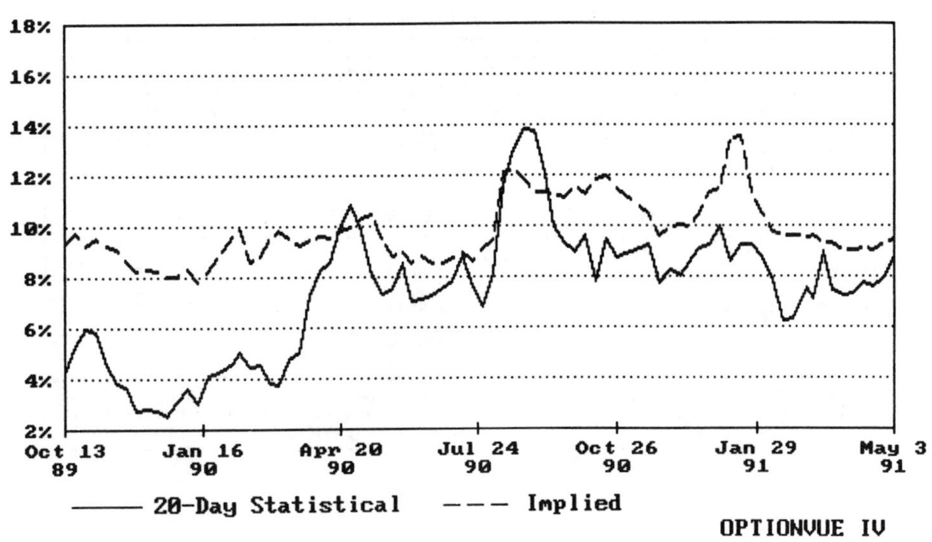

Exhibit 7.13
Historical Volatility Chart (Swiss Franc)

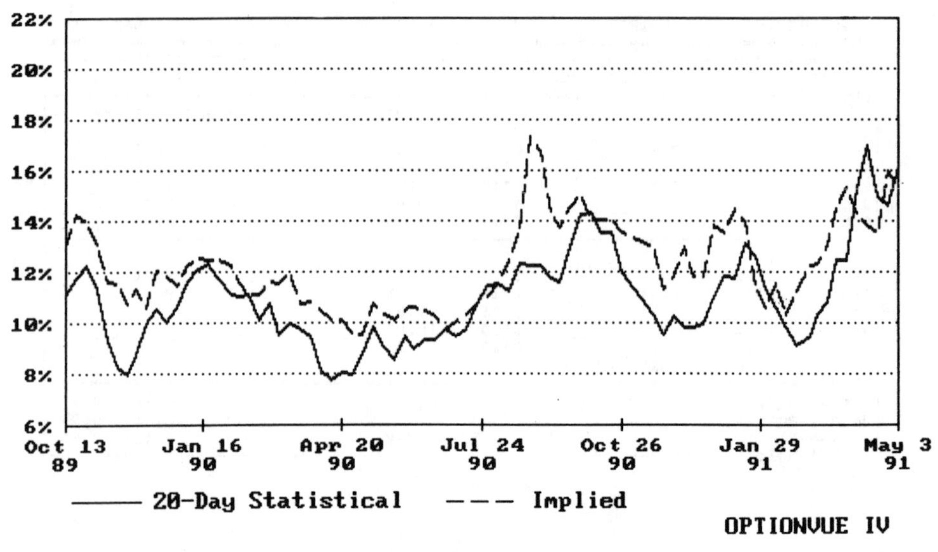

Exhibit 7.14
Profit/Loss Matrix

```
OPTIONVUE IV          MATRIX          Swiss Franc (IMM)*          WED MAY 8 1991
/FUTURES===========================================================================\
|  |=======JUN=(42)=========|  |--------SEP-(133)--------|  |--------DEC-(224)--------||
|     68.17        -2   14:20      67.78 _______      14:20      67.53 _______      14:20 |
|OPTIONS===========================================================================|
|v         |------JUN-(31)--------|  |------JUL-(59)--------|  |------AUG-(94)--------||
|CALLS        .....    .....  ______       .....    .....  ______       .....    .....  ______ |
|68.50        13.9%   CFM685                        CFN685                        CFQ685         |
|CALLS>       .....    .....  ______       .....    .....  ______       .....    .....  ______ |
|68.00                CFM680                        CFN680                        CFQ680         |
|CALLS        .....    .....  ______       .....    .....  ______       .....    .....  ______ |
|67.50                CFM675                        CFN675                        CFQ675         |
|!         ------------------------------------------------------------------------ |
|PUTS>         0.97     1.00______       .....    .....  ______       .....    .....  ______ |
|68.00        13.6%   PFM680                        PFN680                        PFQ680         |
|PUTS          0.78     0.82______       .....    .....  ______       .....    .....  ______ |
|67.50        14.1%   PFM675                        PFN675                        PFQ675         |
|PUTS          0.57     0.61     -2      .....    .....  ______       .....    .....  ______ |
|67.00        13.8%   PFM670    0.57    13.4%   PFN670                        PFQ670         |
|                                                                                   |
|SUMMARY===========================================================================|
| Orig.Reqmt:      $4,600    Commis:      $50.00     Delta:   -135.1    AvgMIV: 13.9% |
|Maint.Reqmt:      $11,008                           Gamma:    -26.0     Calls: 13.9% |
|  Cash Flow:      +$1,375    Theta:  +$39.79/day   Vega:      -179      Puts: 13.7% |
\- [F1]=Help ------------------------------------------------------------ 22K ----/
```

Exhibit 7.15
Projected Trading Range

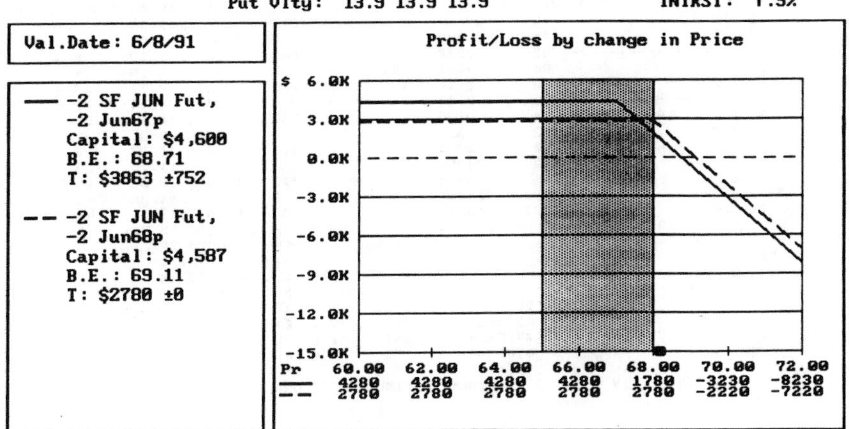
OPTIONVUE IV
Account: abc
GRAPHIC ANALYSIS
Call Vlty: 13.9 13.9 13.9
Put Vlty: 13.9 13.9 13.9
Swiss Franc (IMM)*
WED MAY 8 1991
Ex-Div: n/a
INTRST: 7.9%
Val.Date: 6/8/91
-2 SF JUN Fut,
-2 Jun67p
Capital: $4,600
B.E.: 68.71
T: $3863 ±752
-2 SF JUN Fut,
-2 Jun68p
Capital: $4,587
B.E.: 69.11
T: $2780 ±0
Profit/Loss by change in Price
$ 6.0K
3.0K
0.0K
-3.0K
-6.0K
-9.0K
-12.0K
-15.0K
Pr 60.00 62.00 64.00 66.00 68.00 70.00 72.00
4280 4280 4280 4280 1780 -3230 -8230
2780 2780 2780 2780 2780 -2220 -7220

Exhibit 7.16
"Optionomics" On-Line Option Evaluation

```
APR-26-91 FRI    9:15 OPTIONOMICS CORP.                      P.02

            LCM1     PREM VAL. 06/07/91             MP   76.13 AIV  10.50 DAYS  43
  82 1.C                 86     -28880                  82C    .03  11.16     2.7
     2.P                 84     -20880                    P   5.88   9.58    98.8
---------------------- 82     -12880                  80C    .10  10.29     8.3
  80 3.C                 80      -4880 ALPHA=  1.10       P   3.93   9.16    94.1
     4.P                 78       3120 UPS    78.33   78C    .35   9.71    23.8
---------------------- 76       3120 DWS    73.95     P   2.20   9.46    76.8
  78 5.C -  10      .35  74       3120                  76C   1.15  10.40    52.6
     6.P                 72      -4880                    P   1.03  10.50    47.4
---------------------- 70     -12880                  74C   2.53  11.37    77.2
  76 7.C                 68     -20880                    P    .43  11.75    23.5
     8.P                 66     -28880                  72C   4.30  13.06    89.7
---------------------- NET UPSIDE=   -10                 P    .23  14.28    12.2
  74 9.C                 NET DNSIDE=    10                70C   6.18  13.66    96.5
    10.P -  10      .43     BASIS SPREAD =      .00      P    .10  15.68     5.6
-----------------------             To be delta     F3. CHG FUTURES PRICE:
  72 11.C                             neutral       F4. +/- VOLATILITY:
    12.P                            YOU NEED TO:    F5. CHG DAYS TO EXP:
-----------------------             BUY          .03    NET PREM.=          3120.0
  70 13.C                    $DELTA=       -12     -.0  TOT COMM =            0
    14.P                     $GAMMA=      -892    -2.2  CASH P/L =           .00
-----------------------      $VEGA =      -644    -1.6  FUTRS P/L=           .00
 LF/SF                       $THETA=       572     1.4  EQUITY   =            .0
 LC/SC                       Theta Days =  7            ACC VALUE=            .0
F1=Opt Val IV=Chg IV & GVT F6=%ChgMkt F8=SIMULATE F9=GRAPHS F10=UPDT         OK

                 ***** TODAY'S DATE = 04/25/91 *****
LCM1  MKT PRICE =   76.13 DAYS TO EXP =   43 AIV =  10.50

    INTRINSIC VALUE                      ALPHA=  1.10   NET PREM.=          3120.0
      86      -28880                     UPS    78.33
      84      -20880                     DWS    73.95
      82      -12880
      80       -4880
      78        3120
      76        3120
      74        3120
      72       -4880
      70      -12880
      68      -20880
      66      -28880                AVE OF TOTAL =      -11425.4545
-------------------------------------------------------------------------------
 UPS ALPHA PRICE =    78.33  NET UPS =    -10 BK EVEN UPS =    78.78
                    ALPHA UPS BK EVEN DIF =      .45
                    ALPHA DWS BK EVEN DIF =      .73
 DWS ALPHA PRICE =    73.95  NET DWS =     10 BK  EVEN DWS =    73.22
    MARGIN =       5600  AVE. PROFIT =      3120.0000  SCORE = 470.85%
-------------------------------------------------------------------------------

              PRESS ANY KEY TO RETURN TO DISPLAY PAGE
```

Exhibit 7.17
"Optionomics" On-Line Option Evaluation

```
    Opt Price USM2    +/-       %     % of Mkt Chg  MP  107.00 AIV    9.20 DAYS 296
  118 Call     .01    .34   34.00      .04   C*       118C    .35    9.20 *  12.7
                                                         P 11.35    9.20 *  87.3
  118 Put    24.39 -13.04    -.53     -.96   P*       116C    .52    9.20 *  17.5
---------------------------------------------------     P   9.52    9.20 *  82.5
  116 Call     .03    .49   16.33      .06            114C   1.11    9.20 *  23.5
                                                         P   8.11    9.20 *  76.5
  116 Put    22.40 -12.52    -.57     -.94            112C   1.42    9.20 *  30.5
---------------------------------------------------     P   6.42    9.20 *  69.5
  114 Call     .04   1.07   17.75      .08            110C   2.18    9.20    38.5
                                                         P   5.18    9.20 *  61.5
  114 Put    20.42 -12.31    -.60     -.92          F3. CHG FUTURES PRICE:
---------------------------------------------------  F4. +/- VOLATILITY:
  112 Call     .06   1.36   16.67      .11          F5. CHG DAYS TO EXP:
                                                    F6. CHG COMM RATE :
  112 Put    18.44 -12.02    -.64     -.89
---------------------------------------------------  SET FOR BUYING OF OPTIONS
  110 Call     .10   2.08   13.60      .16           C /  P    COST    +/-     %
                                                   118/ 110  16.49-10.60  -.65
  110 Put    16.48 -11.30    -.68     -.84         116/ 112  18.47-11.17  -.60
---------------------------------------------------  114/ 114  20.46-11.24  -.55
Orig. Mkt Price  =  93.13  Mkt Chg   =  13.19      114/ 112  18.48-10.59  -.58
Orig. Volatility =   9.20  VOLAT CHG =    .00      116/ 110  16.51-10.45  -.64
Orig. Days to Exp= 386     DAYS CHG  =  -90
F1=OPT VALUE,F2=SET TRADES,F8=CHG MKT PRC %,F10= HELP          OK
```

Exhibit 7.18
"FutureSource" Trade Sheet

Option: US	Valuation Date: 7/27/90	Interest: 0.07	Div/For: 0.00

	Theoretical Market Value		
Futures	Time: 8/01/90	9/15/90	11/15/90
9000	30	15	0
9020	39	21	0
9100	50	29	0
9120	62	39	2
9216	112	52	5
9304	128	103	12
9324	147	121	26
9412	203	141	47
9500	226	201	111
9520	251	227	144
9608	314	255	218
9628	342	321	256
9716	409	354	332
9804	440	424	408
9824	510	459	448
9912	544	532	524
10000	615	606	600

Futures Prices				
Sim	U	MY	Spread	Value
	Y	U0		9325
*	Y	Z0	-9	9316
	Y	H1	-12	9304
	Y	M1	-6	9230
	Y	U1	-11	9219
	Y	Z1	-8	9211
	Y	H2		
	Y	M2		

Range: FUTURES
From: 9000
To: 10000

Contour: TIME
- - - : 8/01/90
— — : 9/15/90
——— : 11/15/90

Exhibit 7.19
"FutureSource" Trade Sheet

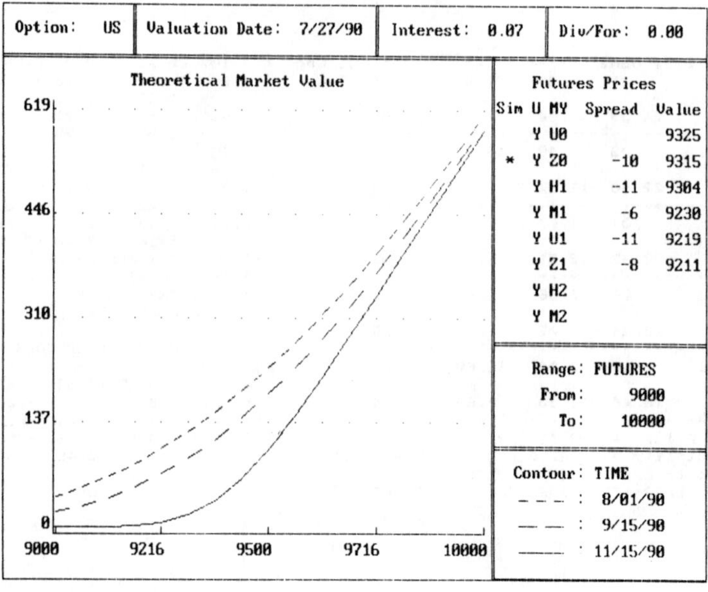

Appendix

VOLATILITY CHARTS 1992–1995

The charts on the following pages are of implied volatility from 1992 through February 1995 of some of the most popular markets. (These charts are courtesy of OptionVue, 1117 S. Milwaukee Ave. # C-10, Libertyville, IL 60048, 800-733-6610.)

These charts can give you an idea of the approximate ranges in volatility that these markets have had in the past. You can then determine whether current implied volatility is relatively high, low, or mediocre. This is, of course, important in determining the best strategy to use when initiating a position in that market.

Chart 1

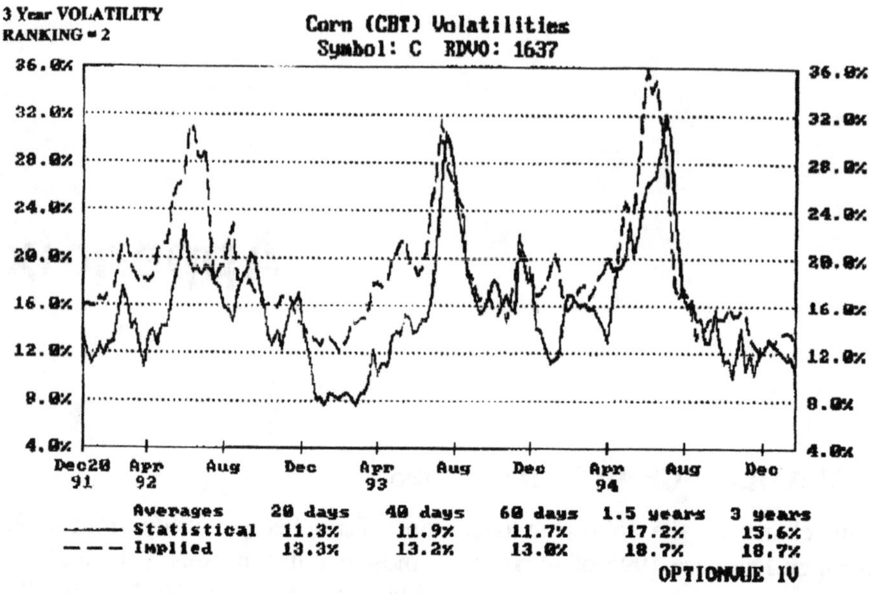
3 Year VOLATILITY
RANKING = 2
Corn (CBT) Volatilities
Symbol: C RDVO: 1637
36.0%
32.0%
28.0%
24.0%
20.0%
16.0%
12.0%
8.0%
4.0%
Dec20 91
Apr 92
Aug
Dec
Apr 93
Aug
Dec
Apr 94
Aug
Dec
Averages 20 days 40 days 60 days 1.5 years 3 years
Statistical 11.3% 11.9% 11.7% 17.2% 15.6%
Implied 13.3% 13.2% 13.0% 18.7% 18.7%
OPTIONVUE IV

Chart 2

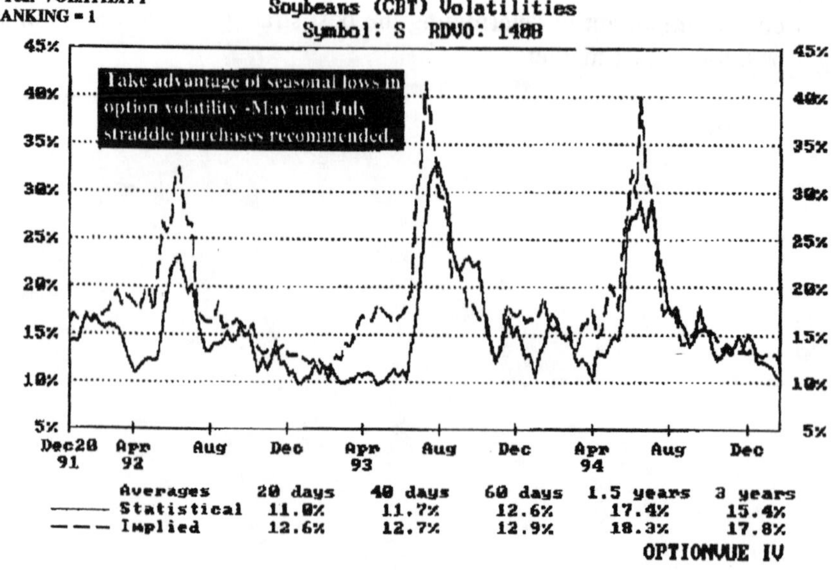
3 Year VOLATILITY
RANKING = 1
Soybeans (CBT) Volatilities
Symbol: S RDVO: 1408
Take advantage of seasonal lows in option volatility -May and July straddle purchases recommended.
45%
40%
35%
30%
25%
20%
15%
10%
5%
Dec20 91
Apr 92
Aug
Dec
Apr 93
Aug
Dec
Apr 94
Aug
Dec
Averages 20 days 40 days 60 days 1.5 years 3 years
Statistical 11.0% 11.7% 12.6% 17.4% 15.4%
Implied 12.6% 12.7% 12.9% 18.3% 17.8%
OPTIONVUE IV

Chart 3

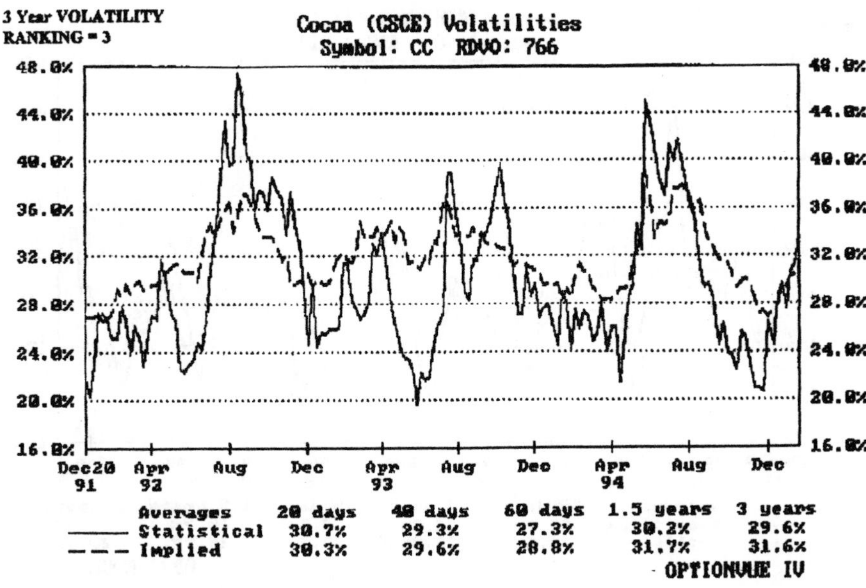

Chart 4

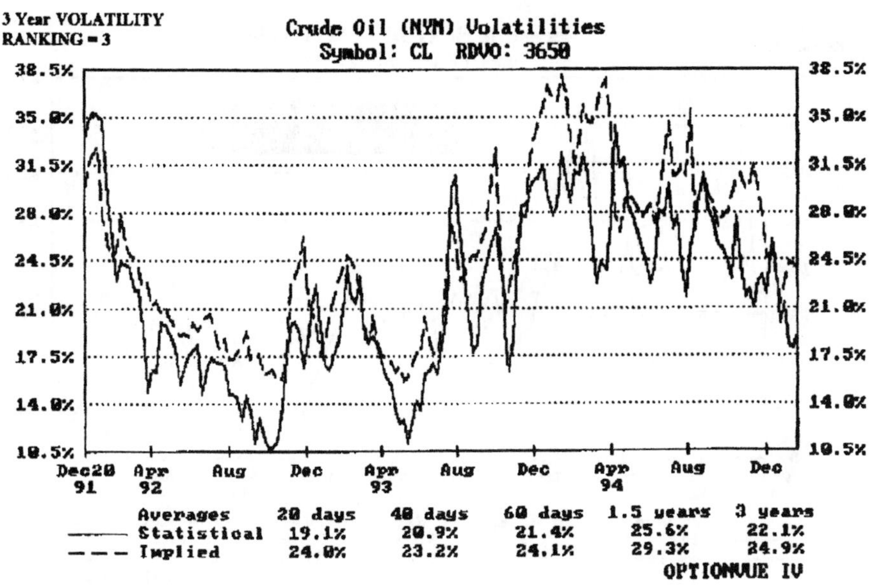

Chart 5

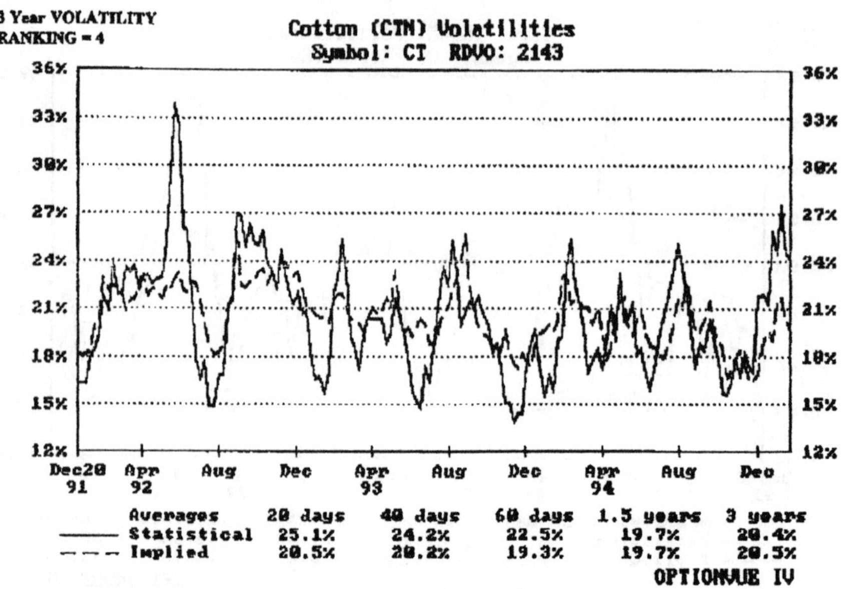

Chart 6

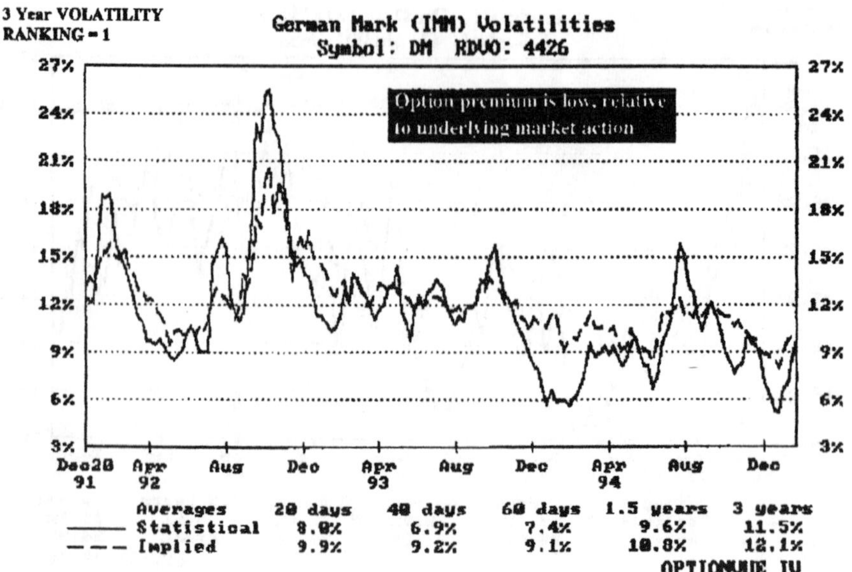

Chart 7

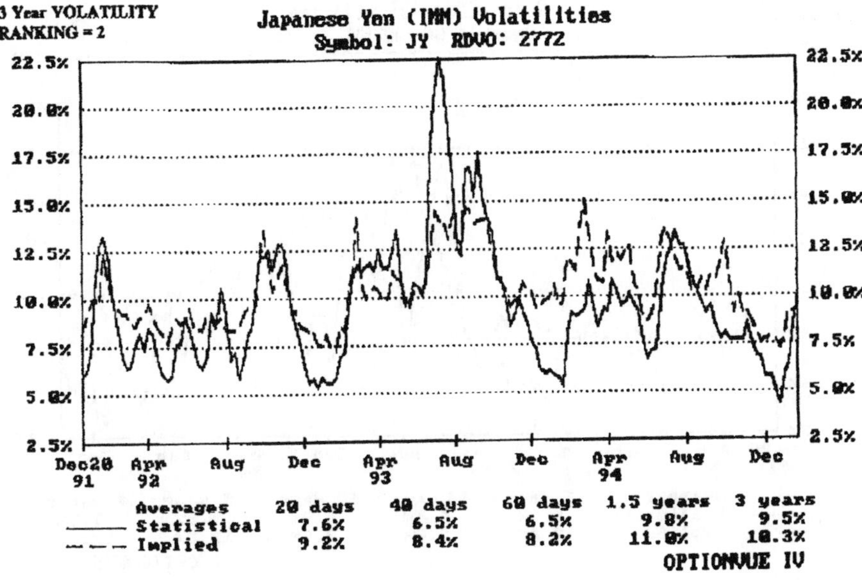

Chart 8

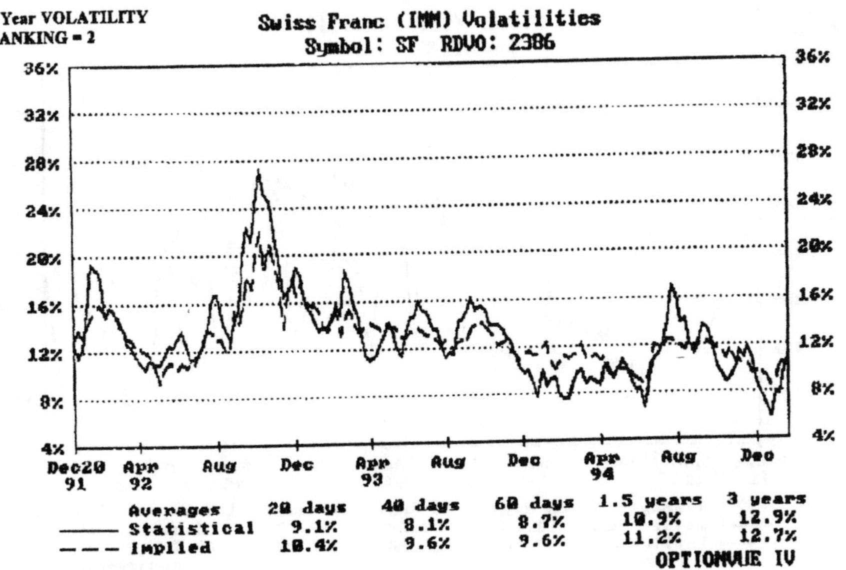

Chart 9

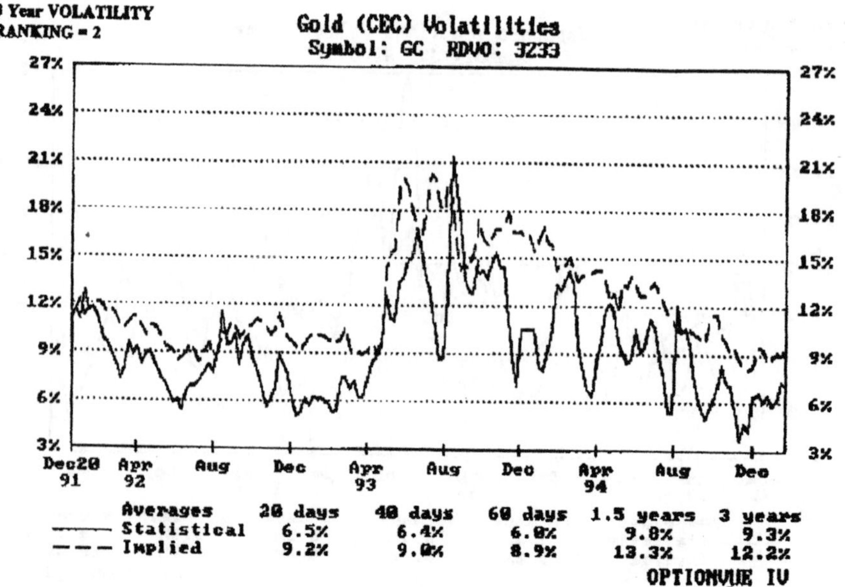

Chart 10

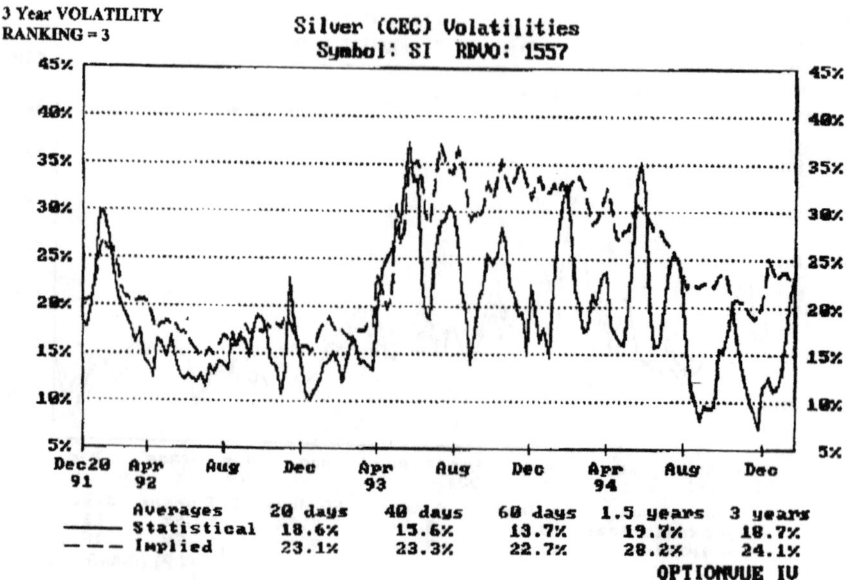

Chart 11

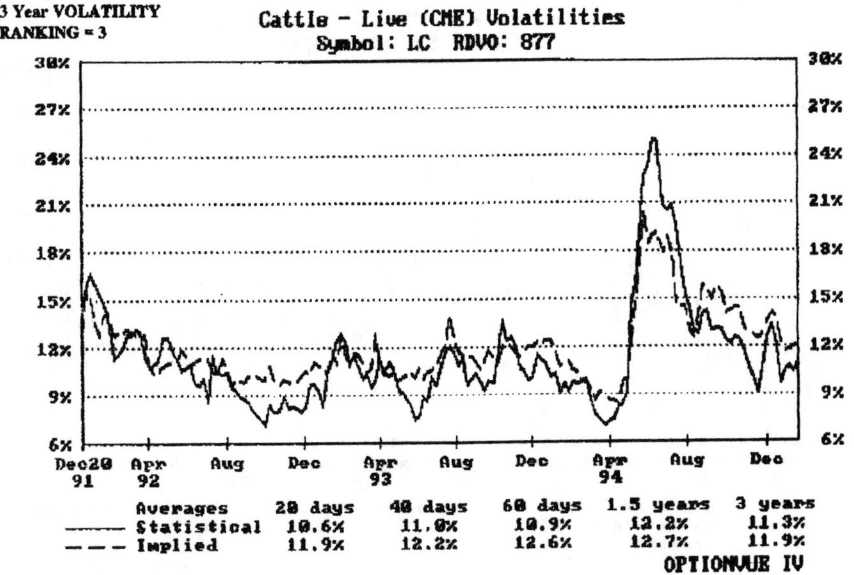
3 Year VOLATILITY
RANKING = 3
Cattle - Live (CME) Volatilities
Symbol: LC RDVO: 877
30%
27%
24%
21%
18%
15%
12%
9%
6%
Dec20 91
Apr 92
Aug
Dec
Apr 93
Aug
Dec
Apr 94
Aug
Dec
Averages 20 days 40 days 60 days 1.5 years 3 years
Statistical 10.6% 11.0% 10.9% 12.2% 11.3%
Implied 11.9% 12.2% 12.6% 12.7% 11.9%
OPTIONVUE IV

Chart 12

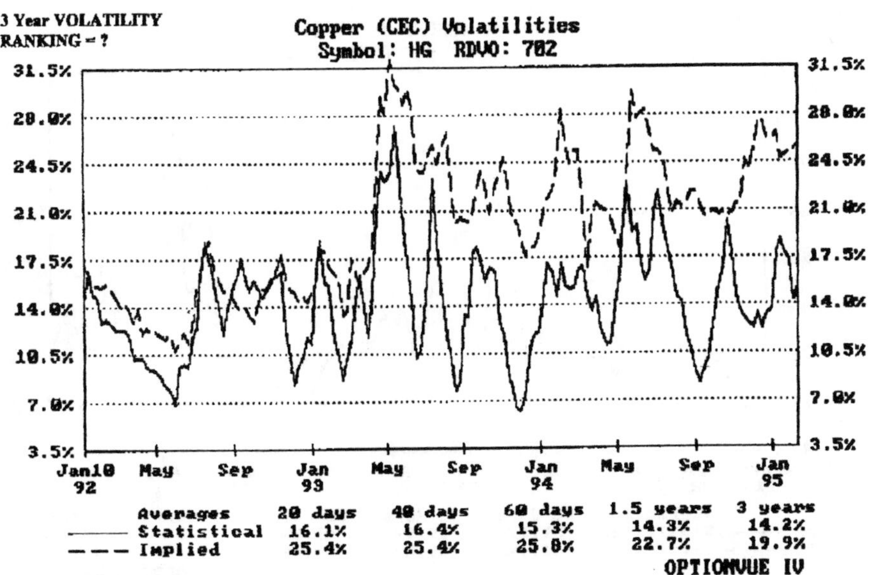
3 Year VOLATILITY
RANKING = ?
Copper (CEC) Volatilities
Symbol: HG RDVO: 702
31.5%
28.0%
24.5%
21.0%
17.5%
14.0%
10.5%
7.0%
3.5%
Jan10 92
May
Sep
Jan 93
May
Sep
Jan 94
May
Sep
Jan 95
Averages 20 days 40 days 60 days 1.5 years 3 years
Statistical 16.1% 16.4% 15.3% 14.3% 14.2%
Implied 25.4% 25.4% 25.0% 22.7% 19.9%
OPTIONVUE IV

Chart 13

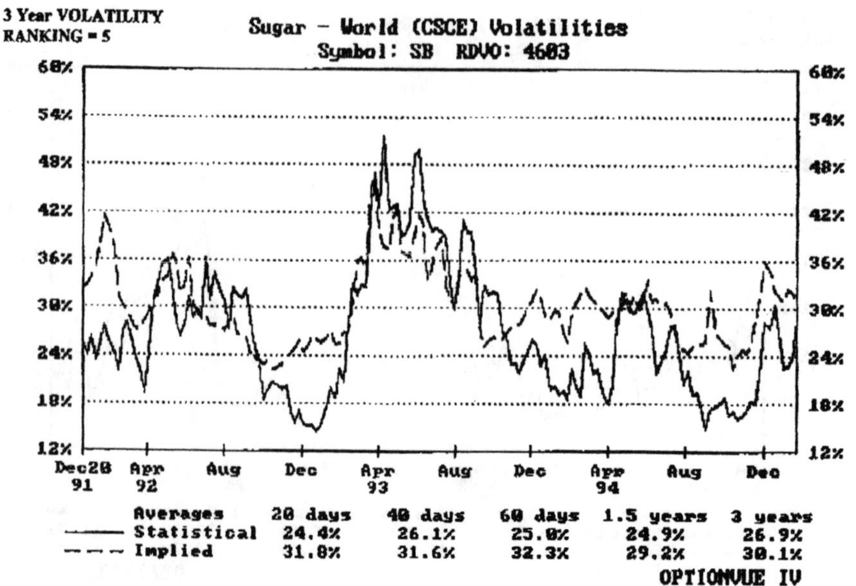
3 Year VOLATILITY
RANKING = 5
Sugar - World (CSCE) Volatilities
Symbol: SB RDVO: 4603
60%
54%
48%
42%
36%
30%
24%
18%
12%
Dec20 91
Apr 92
Aug
Dec
Apr 93
Aug
Dec
Apr 94
Aug
Dec
Averages 20 days 40 days 60 days 1.5 years 3 years
Statistical 24.4% 26.1% 25.0% 24.9% 26.9%
Implied 31.8% 31.6% 32.3% 29.2% 30.1%
OPTIONVUE IV

Chart 14

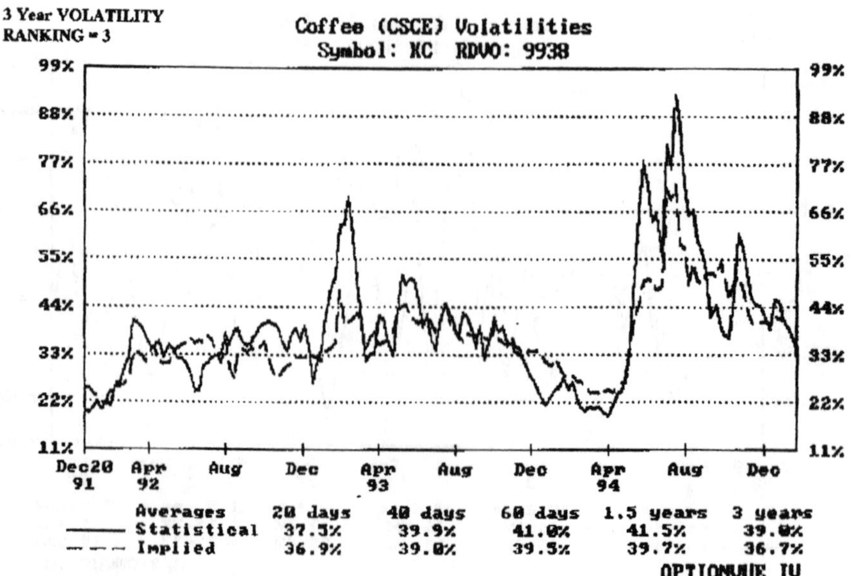
3 Year VOLATILITY
RANKING = 3
Coffee (CSCE) Volatilities
Symbol: KC RDVO: 9938
99%
88%
77%
66%
55%
44%
33%
22%
11%
Dec20 91
Apr 92
Aug
Dec
Apr 93
Aug
Dec
Apr 94
Aug
Dec
Averages 20 days 40 days 60 days 1.5 years 3 years
Statistical 37.3% 39.9% 41.0% 41.5% 39.0%
Implied 36.9% 39.0% 39.5% 39.7% 36.7%
OPTIONVUE IV

Chart 15

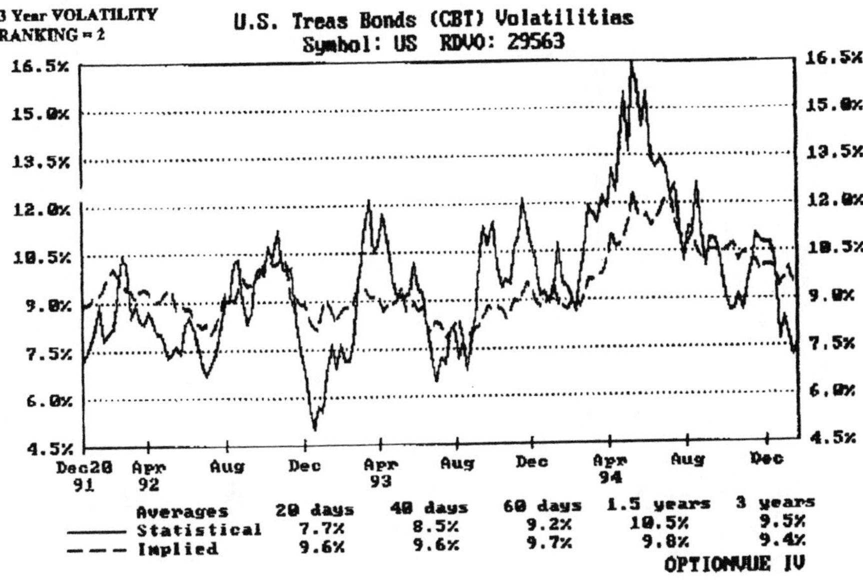

Chart 16

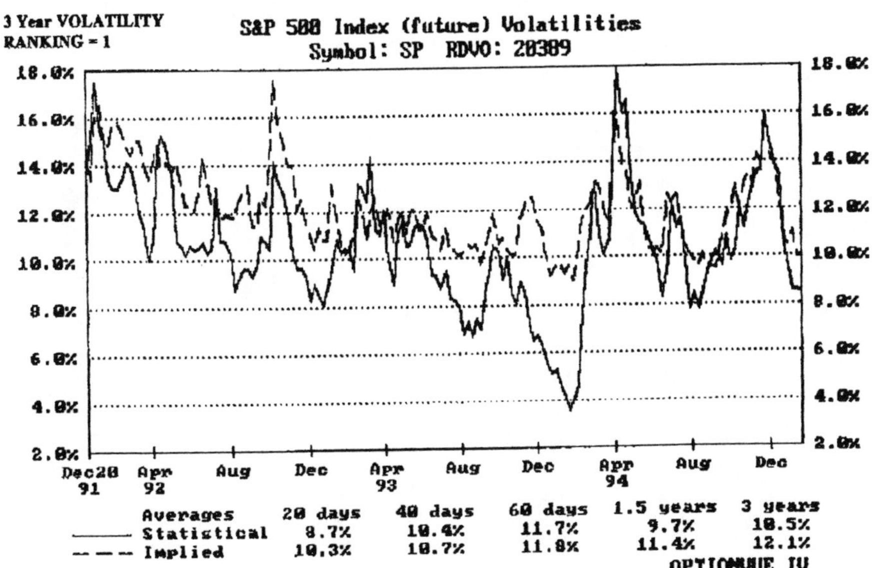

Glossary

Arbitrage The simultaneous buying and selling of the same, or equivalent, option in different markets.

Assignment A notice to an option writer that the option has been exercised by the option holder.

At-the-Money An option whose strike price is equal to the market value of the underlying futures contract.

Beta Measure of how the options market correlates to the movement of the underlying futures market.

Call Option An option which gives the option buyer the right to buy the underlying contract at a specified price within a certain time; and the the seller's obligation to sell the contract for the premium received before the expiration time of the option.

Covered Option An option written against an opposite in the futures or cash market.

Credit Money received from the sale of options.

Debit Money paid for the purchase of options.

Delta The amount by which an options price will change for a unit change in the underlying future's price.

Exercising Options Over 98% of option positions are closed out prior to the expiration of the option period. This is accomplished by the reverse of the initial transaction. For example, an option buyer will sell his position at the current market price for a profit or loss to close out his position; and the option seller will buy back his position to do the same.

However, the option buyer has an additional right to "exercise" his option prior to the expiration. In doing this, the buyer of a call option would give notice to his broker to turn the option into a long futures position; and the purchaser of a put would do the same to turn his option into a short futures contract.

Expiration Every option must have a specific time during which the option can be traded or exercised. After that time, the option is deemed to have expired and has no value.

Free Trade An option spread initiated by purchasing a close-to-the-money put or call and later completed by selling a further out-of-the-money put or call of the same expiration period at the same premium. When completed, it requires no margin or capital and has no loss potential.

Hedge The buying and/or selling of offsetting positions in order to provide protection against an adverse change in price of the contract.

In-the-Money A term describing any option whose strike price is lower than the future's price for calls and higher than the future's price for puts.

Intrinsic Value The amount of money that could be realized if the option were to be exercised immediately (out-of-the-money options have no intrinsic value).

Margin The sum of money which must be deposited and maintained by the seller of option positions.

Naked Writing Writing an option on a futures contract on which the writer has no cash or futures position.

Neutral Option Position An option spread initiated by selling an out-of-the-money put and call of the same expiration period to collect premium in a flat or choppy market.

Option An option is a contract between two parties to purchase or sell a commodity futures contract at a predetermined price within a specific time period. Every option transaction has an option buyer and an option seller.

Option Buyer A buyer of a put or call option always has the right (not obligation) to purchase (call) or sell (put) the commodities futures contract. For this right the buyer pays a premium, which is the most he can lose even if the market goes drastically against his predicted direction. However, if the market goes in his favor his potential profits are unlimited.

Option Seller The option seller receives a premium from the option buyer at the time of the option transaction. The option seller has the obligation to sell to the option buyer (call) or purchase for the option buyer (put) a commodities futures contract. For undertaking this obligation, the option seller receives a premium at the time of the opening of the option transaction. This premium is his to keep if the option is not exercised or sold. This option premium is the maximum amount of profit that the option seller can make, and the option seller always has unlimited risk if the market moves against his position.

Out-of-the-Money An option which has no intrinsic value—a call option whose strike price is higher than the market and a put option whose strike price is lower than the market.

Premium The premium is the amount of money paid by the option buyer to the option seller to open an option transaction. The option premium represents the maximum amount of money that the option buyer has at risk, while the option seller's maximum profit is restricted to the amount of this option premium.

The amount of premium is determined on the exchange trading floors by negotiation between option buyers and sellers depending on market conditions.

Put Option An option which gives the buyer the right to sell the futures contract and the seller the obligation to deliver the futures contract at the strike price on or before the expiration date.

Spread A position consisting of two or more options.

Strike Price The strike price is the set amount at which a buyer of a call can purchase the underlying futures contract or at which the buyer of a put can sell his contract. Every option transaction must contain this specified price.

Theoretical Value The price of an option as computed by a mathematical model.

Time Value The amount by which an option premium exceeds the option's intrinsic value.

Volatility A measure of the change of an option's premium over a period of time.

Index

N

O

T

U–V

W–Y–Z